The Politics of Economic Reform in the Middle East

Also by Henri J. Barkey

The State and the Industrialization Crisis in Turkey

The Politics of Economic Reform in the Middle East

Edited by
Henri J. Barkey

St. Martin's Press
New York

First published in the United States of America in 1992

Printed in the United States of America

ISBN 0-312-05276-6

Library of Congress Cataloging-in-Publication Data

The politics of economic reform in the Middle East / edited by Henri J. Barkey.
p. cm.
Includes index.
ISBN 0-312-05276-6
1. Middle East—Economic policy. 2. Economic stabilization—Middle East.
I. Barkey, Henri J.
HC415.15.P66 1992
338.956—dc20 92-10698
CIP

TABLE OF CONTENTS

Part III
Economic Reform and the Politics of Regime Transformation

Part IV
Conclusion

CONTRIBUTORS

Henri J. Barkey, Associate Professor, Department of International Relations, Lehigh University, Bethlehem, PA.

Daniel Brumberg, Assistant Professor, Department of Political Science, Emory University, Atlanta, GA.

Patrick Clawson, Director of Research at the Middle East Council of the Foreign Policy Research Institute and editor of *Orbis,* Philadelphia, PA.

Mahir Fisunoğlu, Professor, Department of Economics, and Assistant Dean of Administrative Sciences, Çukurova University, Adana, Turkey.

Steven Heydemann, Staff Associate, Social Science Research Council, New York, NY.

Karen Pfeifer, Associate Professor, Department of Economics, Smith College, Northampton, MA, and a contributing editor to *Middle East Report.*

Robert Satloff, Assistant Director, The Washington Institute for Near East Policy, Washington, DC.

Dirk Vandewalle, Assistant Professor, Department of Politics, Dartmouth College, Dartmouth, NH.

Birol A. Yeşilada, Associate Professor, Department of Political Science, University of Missouri, Columbia, MO.

LIST OF TABLES AND FIGURES

Tables

Israel

Tunisia

Algeria

Turkey

Conclusion

Figures

Israel

Turkey

Conclusion

1

Introduction: Economic Reform in the Middle East

Henri J. Barkey

The diversity of the Middle East has always made it a difficult region for scholars to define and treat politically. This is no less true from a political-economy angle. It is a region in which the political has dominated the economic and where the interests of the state have often eclipsed those of society. It is a region in which states and governments, preoccupied with war and peace, with survival, with nascent democratic currents and constant challenges to their authority, have often relegated economic issues to the bottom of their lists of priorities.

But economic matters matter. What this book tries to demonstrate is how the interplay of economics and politics has affected the states in the Middle East. The seven countries chosen, Algeria, Egypt, Israel, Jordan, Syria, Tunisia, and Turkey, are unquestionably dissimilar in many respects, including levels of development, workings of the market, integration with the world economy, and systems of governance and legitimation. However, they all have had to confront the difficult choices involved in readjusting an economy that showed signs of serious deterioration and stagnation. In part this was because, sheltered for many years by either the winds of the Cold War or the flow of petrodollars into the region, they allowed their economic structures to atrophy. The ensuing crises, manifested by foreign exchange shortages, high inflation rates, low or no growth, and even riots, galvanized the respective governments into action, often with mixed results.

Understandably, given their diversity, the methods used by these states to confront the challenge of economic deterioration through stabilization measures have varied greatly. Nevertheless, since economic reform and stabilization measures are never easy to devise or implement, a common thread can be found in the difficulties encountered by each of the state leaderships or regimes. Typically, these programs, whether influenced by International Monetary Fund (IMF) prescriptions or not, have involved the restructuring of foreign trade regimes and the domestic fiscal and monetary policies. Since the contractionary nature of these programs generates popular discomfort and discontent, their shaping, timing, and implementation require great political skill and often help from abroad.

Economic reform programs are first and foremost attempts at rationalizing economic structures that have diverged from the more efficient core country counterparts. Invariably, they target the most inefficient aspects of an economy. Because we are moving increasingly toward a world economy, a society's economic well-being and survival depends on its international competitiveness. To become more competitive, Third World societies have found that their choices are increasingly being limited by the dynamism of not only their industrialized and developed counterparts but also by their more successful newly industrializing peers, such as South Korea and Taiwan. Another factor in favor of greater competitiveness is the increasingly free trade-oriented international trade regime institutionalized through the General Agreement on Trade and Tariffs (GATT) and other agreements.

Economic reform programs are not one-shot deals. To be successful the changes they introduce must be followed up. They can and should be viewed as stage-by-stage processes. To distinguish between the different phases it is useful to refer to the early stage as stabilization and the latter one as structural adjustment.[1] In the stabilization phase, the focus is on remedying the most obvious of the immediate imbalances: balance-of-payments and/or budget deficits and high inflation rates. Currency devaluations, which seek to redress the overvalued exchange rate, usually give an immediate boost to the rate of inflation by increasing the prices of imported goods and, indirectly, of domestic products that contain foreign inputs. Simultaneously a devaluation will increase the competitiveness of exports, thus attacking the trade imbalance. Since government budget deficits accentuate inflationary pressures and distort domestic prices and savings rates, cutting this deficit by generally reducing expenditures and subsidies and eliminating services is a necessary component of all stabilization programs.

The second and more difficult stage of any economic reform program is sustaining it and institutionalizing the changes introduced during the first phase. Maintaining a competitive exchange rate, resisting pressures to inflate an economy propelled into a recession by cuts and further reducing government expenditures by privatizing state-owned enterprises, which usually serve as conduits for employment or indirect subsidization of the private sector and consumption, requires considerable resilience on the part of the state authorities. Additionally, reform of the foreign-trade sector, reducing impediments to international trade, and of the financial markets, freeing interest rates and offering greater opportunities for raising capital, are also necessary to the long-term viability of stabilization measures. It is often during the second stage that governments fail; budget deficits creep up, privatization efforts, if attempted, are not pursued with vigor, and trade and other reforms are not undertaken.

The fear that stabilization measures are (or can be) harmful to the tenure of regimes or well-being of states is the primary reason for the delay in instituting these economic programs. Yet, despite this perception of danger and the delays caused by the desire to postpone the unpleasant and the difficult until the very last possible moment, states and regimes, in the final analysis, do initiate such policies. They do so because the longer an economic crisis endures the greater is the potential for political upheaval. In developing nations, the threat of political instability affects authoritarian and democratic regimes equally. And when governments implement stabilization measures, they invariably find that these delays have significantly complicated their tasks. The problems needing attention have deepened, the sacrifices required of the population have increased, and the time necessary for the reforms to take hold has become longer. Thus the longer the delay, the more severe the new measures are likely to be and the less likely they are to succeed.

On the other hand, when successful, economic reform measures often result in the strengthening of existing regimes. Herein lies a paradox: If well-conceived and implemented early, a stabilization program offers the best chance of achieving positive economic and political results. Why then do regimes and governments do their utmost to avoid the inevitable? Some governments will simply postpone all action hoping that the future may bring better tidings in the form of improved global economic conditions, increased infusions of aid, and so on. More realistically, delays have to be viewed in the context of civil society's awareness of an existing or impending economic crisis. In the early or impending stages of a crisis, demand for action is at its lowest. Hence, opposition to early moves by the government is at its highest. In other words, when the chances of success of economic reform measures are greatest so is the civil society's opposition to them. Consequently, under such conditions, governments faced with this matrix prove reluctant to impose measures which are deemed premature. As a result, the short-term political gains achieved by sacrificing long-term considerations prepare the ground work for the ultimate radical surgery.

Considering the fact that next to war, stabilization measures are possibly some of the most difficult sets of policies a government has to institute, how a state or regime fares in such an endeavor reveals a great deal about its inner workings. How a state stabilizes selectively, as in the case of Syria, or in a dramatic fashion, as in the cases of Israel and Turkey, is only part of the story. Successful measures are not one shot deals, but rather part and parcel of a long-term process. Hence, endurance is as important as the method used in their initiation. For many of the countries examined here, their stabilization plans represent only the first steps; they will, in the near future, undoubtedly retrace these steps to learn from their mistakes and successes.

The aim of this book is twofold. One the one hand, given the diversity of the countries and of their political economies, we have the opportunity to analyze and compare the politics and methods of economic reform measures. This book offers a panoply of such measures implemented under varying conditions—political and economic—and shows how these affected the course of stabilization and liberalization. On the other hand, the book does not rest with the story of the stabilization and/or structural adjustment measures but also hopes to provide the reader with a deeper understanding of the political economy of these countries and of their inner workings. Each chapter explores the difficult political questions involved in putting forward and maintaining such stabilization measures and the complex relationships that exist between state and society and between political power and the different groups on the economic ladder. Independent of the measures' successes and failures, the study of economic reform in the Middle East can provide an understanding of the fragility and resiliency of regimes and of political systems in this part of the world. In this sense the book's aim is not to be current.

Aside from the delicate balancing act involved in marrying the economic reform measures to the political system, another question raised by the chapters in this book is that of success. How do we define success? Understandably, in every case studied in this book compromises had to be devised and, as a result, the final outcomes may have proven less than satisfactory to purists. But is it the purist's perspective that needs to be adopted? In many instances, the relative improvements achieved by the stabilization programs were far more significant than anything else undertaken in the past. Hence, this very difference may justify the claim that these countries were on the right track. From another perspective, the question often asked—as in many of the contributions to this volume—is whether the social cost of obtaining even the smallest improvements is worth it.

In assessing their political orchestration, success, and costs, we can observe that the Middle Eastern stabilization attempts proved to be a mixed bag. The book starts with Steven Heydemann's chapter, which demonstrates how Syria's "selective" stabilization program was first and foremost a political operation designed to strengthen the authoritarian regime's foundations. Its program was just sufficiently "rational" to carefully invigorate certain segments of the economy and produce the extra revenues needed by the state without upsetting the delicate balance between the state-sponsored and state-supported large public sector and its dependencies on the one hand and the smaller private sector on the other. Yet, such meticulous arrangements can only be temporarily sustained, especially in the absence of political changes, and hence the regime's stability will ultimately depend on how often and how successfully it can resort to such policies.

The Israeli heterodox program, by contrast, provided dramatic short-run results, especially considering the heights the inflationary spiral had reached. But as I demonstrate, the state capacities marshalled to implement the program fell short of achieving long-term remedies to some of the chronic deficiencies of the economy primarily in the public sector. While inflation has not risen again, the Israeli case is significant because it shows the limits to state power. Never had an Israeli government achieved the kind of success it had with the heterodox plan, yet it proved incapable of transforming these gains into permanent reforms. In the final analysis, the exigencies of a competitive political system tilted the scales in favor of immobility.

Daniel Brumberg's depiction of the Egyptian state's struggle to stabilize as a "strategy of survival" illustrates the dilemma faced by authoritarian regimes in their delicate and piecemeal approach to economic reform. Nasser's legacy was a "populist authoritarian" state replete with patron-client arrangements between the state and the social groups that constituted its backbone. Sadat's attempted "reforms" proved to be insufficient to create a new coalition of interests that would benefit from their institution, primarily because he was not ready to allow for the accompanying and necessary democratization of the political process. Mubarak, by contrast, tried to experiment with political pluralism. But when this process threatened the state, he was quick to reverse course and abandon political reform. Yet forced by external economic changes, such as reductions in foreign exchange earnings from workers and the Suez Canal, the Egyptian government continued to institute macro reforms.

Just as in Jordan, Tunisia's experiment with economic liberalization is deeply enmeshed with a political opening. Dirk Vandewalle suggests that the coming to power of President Ben Ali, who pushed aside Habib Bourguiba, was supposed to usher in a new era of political change designed to reduce societal tensions arising from a state-fundamentalist conflict. In effect, economic liberalization can be viewed as the state elites' desire to broaden their base of support, especially since the state itself has been unable to resume its traditional role of the engine of growth. How has Tunisia fared? The inclusionary nature of the Tunisian state is giving way to a more exclusionary one as it increasingly finds itself challenged politically despite the modest improvements in the economy.

It is in Jordan that the turbulence of the Middle East is felt most strongly. Despite the economic team's adherence to the IMF-sponsored stabilization plan, Robert Satloff argues that the combination of weak political leadership and radical changes in the country's external political environment served to undermine the potential economic gains. The unexpected results of King Hussein's attempts at experimentation with political reform following a stabilization program ultimately undermined confidence in Jordan and its political economy.

For Algeria, according to Karen Pfeifer, the decision to institute a stabilization plan à la IMF without the IMF has not produced an outcome significantly different than if this organization had been invited in from the outset. But it was the debt service burden that forced the Algerian government to finally seek IMF help. This help, which came in exchange for promises to continue the reform, demonstrates the weakening of one of the seemingly strongest states of the Third World.

Birol Yeşilada and Mahir Fisunoğlu show that in Turkey, despite what is outwardly considered the most successful of all the stabilization attempts, this country paid a relatively high price for its post-1980 accomplishments—most notably for the explosion in its export revenues. Indebtedness since then has dramatically increased, along with unemployment, while real wages have declined commensurably. The achievements are due to both the consistency of the economic leadership and the initial repression which followed the September 1980 military coup d'état. The end result was a significant redistribution of national income away from the poor and lower middle classes. The Turkish case exemplifies the importance of time gained. Of all the stabilization experiments in the Middle East, Turkey's was the longest in duration. Did the coup of 1980 and the subsequent constitutional changes introduced buy sufficient time for the stabilization program to effect a long-term transformation of the Turkish political economy? While the answer is not apparent at this point in time, with the change in government following the October 1991 elections, this is the closest Turkey has gotten to testing the durability of these changes.

In the final chapter, Patrick Clawson asks whether or not stabilization is worth the price. Stabilization measures, according to him, have helped more than hindered the movement toward democracy in the region, irrespective of the pace or the fits and starts exhibited.

Underlying the cases of Algeria, Egypt, Jordan, and Tunisia is a great deal of societal unease that is waiting to surface. Algeria and Jordan attempted to open up the system as they stabilized. However, much to the disappointment of state leaders, the opening benefitted their opponents.[2] Egypt and Tunisia have had to resort increasingly to exclusionary means to push through their economic reforms. These states have yet to devise methods of reforming moribund economic structures that will slowly integrate societal discourse; this may be impossible. The state in each of these countries is now faced with the prospect of dealing with situations that it must take responsibility for creating. Can these states succeed and yet remain basically as they exist today?

Somewhat ironically, it is in Israel and Syria that the political systems did not show any significant signs of change. If in Israel this was to be expected, given the well-accepted rules of participation, it is the resiliency of the Assad regime (as opposed to an Assad state) that is noteworthy. It has weathered some of the most difficult economic and political times of its existence to emerge intact. In Israel, however, the solution to hyperinflation also points to the need to strengthen some of the state institutions that have been battered by years of neglect and sense of permanent crisis conditions.

Only in Turkey has there been a major regime change. Two to be precise: the regime first transformed itself into an authoritarian one only to revert back to civilian rule—admittedly under stringent rules of democratic participation. The Turkish case cannot serve as an example simply because the return to authoritarianism, which is credited with instituting a new way of thinking, is not an available option to regimes that are already authoritarian and have been "colonized" by state-spawned interest groups. However, what Turkey does provide is an example of a country where, given enough time, mind-sets—especially those regarding the international market—can be changed.

During the course of this book's preparation two major events, the Gulf War and the dissolution of the Soviet Union, shook the region to its core. These events underscored the vulnerability of all states in the region to the vagaries of their not-so-distant environment. All, including Israel, were affected by these momentous changes, which in the long run strengthen the need to continue with reforms—political and economic—while at the same time efface some of the precious steps taken forward.

NOTES

1. Joan M. Nelson, "Introduction: The Politics of Economic Adjustment in Developing Nations," in *Economic Crisis and Policy Choice: The Politics of Adjustment in the Third World,* ed. Joan M. Nelson (Princeton: Princeton University Press, 1990), 3-4.
2. Events in Algeria would show that the regime was ultimately unable to manage the limited political opening it had initiated. The Algerian article was written before the military crackdown of 1992. By contrast, in Jordan the King's stand during the Gulf War may have helped him to defuse some of the opposition to his rule. The writing of the article on Jordan preceded this development.

Part I

Economic Reform and Political Continuity

2

The Political Logic of Economic Rationality: Selective Stabilization in Syria[1]

Steven Heydemann

How do authoritarian regimes cope with economic crisis? How do they respond to the political challenges of economic reform? With the collapse of authoritarian regimes in Eastern Europe and the reemergence of democratic regimes across Latin America—events caused in large part by the failure of economic policies pursued by authoritarian elites—the answers to these questions seem at once clearer and more complicated than they were a decade ago. In contrast to earlier assumptions, authoritarian systems of rule do not inevitably enhance the ability of state elites either to achieve economic development or to manage painful economic reforms.[2] Economic stabilization programs have proven as politically *destabilizing* to authoritarian regimes as they have to newly democratic regimes in the Third World.[3] Recent experiences indicate that authoritarian regimes face significant political and social constraints in meeting the requirements of stabilization and/or structural adjustment programs.[4] These experiences challenge assumptions about the positive relationship between authoritarianism and successful management of economic crises, and about the effects of stabilization programs in promoting either the breakdown of democracy, or the rise and consolidation of authoritarian regimes.[5]

Current research on the political economy of stabilization and adjustment has underscored the flaws in these assumptions.[6] It has focused on the structural, institutional, political, and ideological factors that influence prospects for successful stabilization under democratic and authoritarian rule.[7] Moreover, it has made significant advances in articulating the constraints that hobble the capacities of some authoritarian regimes, erode the autonomy of seemingly "strong" states, and undermine the use of coercion as a tool in economic policy-making. Through the application of a broadly comparative approach to the study of stabilization and adjustment in the Third World, this research has produced theoretically sophisticated and empirically fine-grained typologies of authoritarian and democratic responses to economic crisis.

Several of these studies have now tested the relationship between regime type and differences in state responses to adjustment and stabilization. By exploring a range of domestic and external variables—variations in the severity of economic crises, state administrative capacity, the nature of political institutions, political leadership, and the organization of social coalitions—the political and social forces shaping state responses to economic crisis have been reasonably well specified across a wide range of cases. Perhaps the most striking result of this research is the conclusion that regime type may be a relatively unimportant variable in explaining differences in state management of economic reform programs.[8]

Almost inevitably, however, the typological character of large-scale comparative case studies raises questions about the fit of certain cases, and the categorization of others. This observation would be of limited interest if it merely implied that country *A* belongs in category *Y* instead of category *X*. It is more important if the typology misspecifies the relationship between regime type and stabilization experience, and thus fails adequately to explain economic policy-making and the response to economic crisis in a particular kind of regime. This chapter will focus on one such example, examining some prevailing explanations for the failure of stabilization and adjustment in patronage-based and weakly institutionalized authoritarian regimes, and drawing on the example of Syria during the 1980s to develop an alternative explanation of how this type of regime manages economic crisis and economic reform.

THE LOGIC OF POLITICS VERSUS THE LOGIC OF ECONOMIC RATIONALITY

The problem can be illustrated by reference to the work of Stephan Haggard and Thomas Callaghy.[9] In brief, both Haggard and Callaghy argue that successful stabilization and adjustment programs require that the short-term political interests of ruling elites and powerful social interests be subordinate to, or insulated from, a technocratic process of economic policy-making. Decisions regarding the economy must be governed not by the logic of politics but by the logic of economic "rationality." If the logic of politics governs decision-making, the fate of economic stabilization is jeopardized by the high social costs and the high political risks it engenders.[10] This is the core dilemma associated with the introduction of stabilization programs for governments that are accountable to their electorates and subject to the pressures of competitive politics: how to make and then implement politically difficult but economically "necessary" decisions. It was the presumed incapacity of democratic governments to implement such decisions in Latin America that underscored earlier pessimism about prospects for the consolidation of democracy in that region and led to a generation of theorizing that is now rapidly being revised.[11]

Callaghy and Haggard agree, however, that this is not solely the dilemma of democratic regimes. Authoritarian regimes also face constraints in their management of stabilization programs. These are greatest, Haggard argues, in authoritarian regimes where "governments are weakly institutionalized or where societies are ethnically divided"—a category in which he places Zaire, Guyana, and Haiti, and in which I place Syria.[12] Callaghy, on the other hand, locates these constraints primarily in the "crony capitalist" character of African regimes. Drawing on the work of Douglass C. North to define the postcolonial "syndrome" of African political development, Callaghy argues that Africa has experienced the rise of highly predatory regimes that maximize the flow of revenues to regime elites despite the cost to society as a whole.

> As political rather than economic logics prevailed, the dominant form of political economy became a crony statism consisting of three interrelated characteristics: (1) clientalist networks used to build support through the extraction and distribution of rents, (2) expansion of state size, including the creation of an extensive parastatal sector, and (3) purchase of primarily urban support via state welfare services and subsidies. . . . Most African states were transformed into highly personalistic authoritarian, but weak, administrative states—lame Leviathans—in which crony statism and a subordinate crony capitalism prevailed.[13]

In these cases, constraints on economic rationality stem primarily from the opposition of favored constituencies whose privileges are threatened by economic "rationalization." For highly personalistic and clientalist authoritarian governments, the opposition of such constituencies to economic reform makes the adoption of stabilization and adjustment packages highly "irrational," indeed potentially fatal, from a political point of view. In such regimes, Callaghy and Haggard suggest, economic and political logics are virtually incompatible, and the advance of the former can only be achieved at the expense of the latter. Both the capacity and the will of regime elites to make such a zero-sum trade-off is low.

This argument is an important revision of the view that authoritarian regimes are better adapted than democracies to meet the demands of economic stabilization. It represents a useful effort to desegregate various forms of authoritarianism and explain variations in economic policy-making among them. However, while recognizing the need for a more regime-sensitive approach to the analysis of economic stabilization, the specific explanation that Haggard, Callaghy, and others advance for the "failure" of economic reform in patronage-based authoritarian regimes is itself not sufficiently sensitive to the variety of responses such regimes have exhibited in the face of economic crisis.

Specifically, this chapter challenges the notion of a structural conflict between political survival and the implementation of economic stabilization policies in weakly institutionalized and highly clientalistic authoritarian regimes. My intent is not to revive the view that authoritarian regimes in general are institutionally more capable than democracies of successfully stabilizing their economies. It is my intent, however, to show that even the kind of authoritarian regime that Haggard and Callaghy identify as least able to manage economic stabilization can under some circumstances successfully implement a set of rationalizing economic reforms, and to explain the structural incentives that lead such regimes to pursue rationalization as an economic strategy.

THE POLITICAL LOGIC OF ECONOMIC RATIONALITY

In contrast to the assumptions of Haggard and Callaghy, a range of conditions can be specified in which the political logic of clientalist authoritarianism is not only compatible with the economic logic of stabilization and adjustment, but dependent on it: authoritarian elites can never be fully insulated from their economic failures. In general, such conditions arise when an economic crisis threatens the continued flow of resources needed to satisfy either the regime's own rapacity or the demands of its clients. These circumstances seem unlikely to arise without serious strains in, if not the breakdown of, the regime's capacity to satisfy its fiscal commitments to the general population in terms of subsidized food, welfare programs, health care schemes, and so on, suggesting that the political fallout from economic crises can not easily be localized within patronage networks. Though resilient and flexible in many respects, systems of rule in which legitimacy is purchased and compliance bartered in exchange for employment, privileged access to goods, or welfare benefits, appear singularly vulnerable to shifts in economic performance.

Interventionist economic and political strategies common to crony-capitalist or patronage-based authoritarian regimes—protecting inefficient state-owned industries and overstaffed bureaucracies; restricting the investment activity of private sectors; controlling domestic marketing channels, foreign trade, commodity prices, supplies of essential goods, and access to foreign exchange—themselves become potentially destabilizing when their consequences begin to affect the economic standing of the regime's core constituencies. Heavy-handed intervention promotes capital flight and the transfer of resources to less regulated sectors and the informal economy, further shrinking the state's extractive base. External forces—declining prices for agricultural and mineral exports; rising prices of essential manufacturing inputs, oil, and food; a growing debt burden—create additional strains and force a maladaptive economy over the threshold of crisis. Combined with deeply embedded and politically driven domestic sources of inefficiency and with bruising levels of military spending, these forces can push local economies into a cycle of negative economic growth and rising political pressure on regime elites from clients whose positions and benefits look increasingly insecure.

Predatory regimes, in other words, often find they have eaten the goose. Even under relatively benign external economic conditions they have a tendency to exhaust the extractive capacity of the local economy. Once this occurs, economic reform no longer represents the leading political threat. Increasingly, the continued erosion of domestic production, of capital accumulation, and thus of prospects for extraction, undermine the regime's ability to reproduce its system of rule. Under these conditions, the logic of politics becomes, in some measure, the logic of economic reform. The alternatives—increased repression, more coercive efforts to enhance the collection of revenues, abandoning or pruning clientalist networks—are few, politically unattractive, and unlikely to produce the desired economic results.[14]

Within the context of this overarching process are other factors that can add to the pressure for economic restructuring and help shape the response to economic crises. These include the ideological, military-strategic, and economic-structural settings within which crises take place. Even patronage-based authoritarian regimes rely on ruling formulas in their search for legitimacy and accord their ideological principles more than rhetorical attention. When, as in Syria's case, this formula is of a transformational nature and is built around a set of radically populist and redistributive norms, economic crisis becomes a serious ideological issue. The capacity of the regime to fulfill its populist commitments is an important measure of its legitimacy. When the state is entangled in (multiple) open-ended military conflicts, as Syria has been, burdens itself with crippling levels of military spending, and employs an ideology of national security and mass military mobilization as elements of its ruling formula, its ability to balance military and domestic political commitments during a period of economic decline is severely diminished. Issues of "guns or butter," or perhaps "guns or cadres," become concerns that threaten not just the political fortunes of one set of elites, but the structure of the political system as a whole.[15]

Not all of these factors must be present to force patronage-based authoritarian regimes in the direction of economic stabilization and/or liberalization. Regime ideology may be relatively unimportant. Military-strategic conditions may not impose additional pressure in support of economic reform. What is required, however, is that the extractive requirements needed to satisfy the patronage networks of the regime exceed the extractive capacity of its inefficient and politically driven economic institutions. Once this threshold has been passed, the stability of existing patronage arrangements can no longer be guaranteed. Economic restructuring becomes a crucial component of the logic of political survival, even while political imperatives determine the scope of reforms, the target of reforms, and, to an extent, the timing of reforms. Locating this threshold, moreover, is exceptionally difficult. When does it become apparent that political arrangements are economically irrational? What kind of analysis can be done to establish the marginal cost of adding one additional client to a patronage network? How much support is enough? Authoritarian elites confront these questions all the time in the context of coalition management. Yet the impossibility of answering this question with any precision drives the expansion of patronage-based authoritarian regimes across the threshold of economic crisis, and into the position where they must rationalize or risk the collapse of their political enterprises.

SELECTIVE STABILIZATION AND THE POLITICS OF ECONOMIC REFORM

Together with another Middle Eastern case discussed in this volume—that of Algeria—Syria represents a clientalist, weakly institutionalized, ethnically divided authoritarian regime that has implemented an "implicit" stabilization package. That is, Syrian leaders have independently implemented a set of measures that look much like an International Monetary Fund (IMF) stabilization program, without entering into a relationship with the IMF.[16] These include loosening restrictions on foreign trade and on access to foreign exchange, devaluing the Syrian pound, promoting export-oriented industries, and imposing austerity measures on the local population.[17] In the case of Algeria, implicit stabilization eventually led to the negotiation of a formal, explicit stabilization package and to wide-ranging political reforms that have substantively transformed Algerian politics. In Syria, stabilization measures remain implicit, and the prospects that economic restructuring will spill over into the political arena remain highly limited.

There are, no doubt, distinctions between regimes confronting severe economic stress that have turned to the IMF for economic relief and those that have not. Authoritarian regimes that accept IMF-sponsored loans and conditions typically face resource constraints, political pressures, and social risks far greater than those present in cases of implicit stabilization, where the decision to stabilize is taken domestically, and not as an unpalatable concession to Western-dominated international lending agencies (although the availability of the IMF as an external bully and scapegoat can be an important resource in regime bargaining with domestic constituencies). By avoiding IMF conditionality, Syria's leaders have been able selectively to tailor reforms to take political considerations into account. They have not been compelled to accept the IMF's indivisible package of reforms, its timetable, or its supervision.

The reasons that Syria's leaders were able to avoid the IMF, however, and to pursue an implicit stabilization program, was not because they possessed the resources to keep the IMF at bay. Opinions differ regarding the depth and length of Syria's economic crisis, but it is widely acknowledged that throughout the 1980s, Syria suffered from "crippling foreign exchange shortages."[18] It ran increasing deficits in its balance of trade and its current accounts, and was unable to pay its debts to the World Bank, accumulating arrears of $210 million by 1990.[19]

The sources of this crisis were several. Syria experienced a dramatic economic expansion following the 1973 Arab-Israeli war, fueling an import boom that was financed by Arab foreign aid and rising world oil prices. When oil markets declined after 1979, Syria both lost revenue directly and suffered from the declining levels of Arab financial assistance. The latter dropped from approximately $1.6 billion in 1980 to about $500 million in the early 1980s, to the point where Syria was reported by the Organization of Economic Cooperation and Development (OECD) to have "paid back to Arab states and lending agencies $9 million more than it received" in 1988.[20] Economic slowdowns in the major Arab oil producing states also meant lower levels of remittances from Syrian workers. After 1979, therefore, greater shares of Syria's import bill had to be financed out of domestic revenues. In addition, low rainfall led to poor harvests from 1982 to 1985, reducing foreign exchange earned from agricultural exports and cutting the supply of raw materials to the manufacturing sector. Trade and service sectors suffered accordingly. And without water, production levels at Syria's hydroelectric power plants declined, further hampering the manufacturing sector and leading to daily power outages in major cities.

Mismanagement and corruption exacerbated problems that were beyond Syria's control. The political allocation of economic benefits, the political character of major investment decisions, and the escalating cost of the regime's extensive patronage networks represented a huge drain on resources, as did inefficiencies associated with Syria's comprehensive system of price controls.[21] Military spending also contributed significantly to the crisis. After 1976, the cost of Syria's military presence in Lebanon rose from $450 million per year to almost $1 billion, while other military spending grew from $900 million in 1976 to $1.9 billion in 1983.[22]

The cumulative impact of these circumstances necessitated Syria's gradual move towards stabilization-style reforms after 1981, but the decision to introduce these policies independent of the IMF was clearly a political decision taken despite the country's limited resources and limited alternative lending sources.

At the same time, and perhaps most importantly, the Syrian regime has pursued stabilization in a highly *selective* fashion. Rather than embark at one time on a full-fledged program of economic rationalization, with its attendant political risks, the Syrian government has managed economic reform as an inherently political process. The logic of politics has shaped the uneven topography of Syria's selective stabilization program as much as if not more than the logic of economic efficiency. Moreover, this very attention to the political dimensions of economic reform has made it possible, I believe, for the Syrian regime to succeed, at least to some degree, in implementing stabilization policies. The logic of politics, in other words, has not prevented the regime from pursuing any form of stabilization, but has instead given rise to a process of selective economic rationalization that is also politically rational.

This process has taken the form of mobilizing the economic participation of sectors previously excluded from the regime's ruling coalition, notably the private commercial, agricultural, and light manufacturing sectors, in order to generate the resources needed to satisfy the demands of politically important coalition members based in inefficient public sector industries, the ruling Ba'th party, the rigidly corporatized trade unions, the state bureaucracy, the military, and the security services. Beginning in 1982 and continuing until the present, elements of the private sector with a high capacity to generate foreign exchange through export and trade and a low capacity to organize in opposition to the regime have benefitted from a gradually deepening process of liberalization and rationalization of their activities. At the same time, the public industrial and state-bureaucratic sectors, which are more important to the regime as sources of patronage and which therefore represent a greater source of potential political instability, have been insulated from the demands of stabilization.[23]

By the end of the 1980s, Syria's rationalizing sectors had become an important source of capital accumulation for the regime as a whole. Between 1985 and 1989, production in the private and joint sectors rose from S£42.6 billion to S£111 billion. Capital formation in these sectors increased from S£6,519 million to S£15,229 million during these years. Between 1986 and 1989, private sector commodity exports rose from S£3,373 million to S£16,189 million, reaching S£19,782 million in the first ten months of 1990, the most recent figures currently available.[24] In 1989 Syria announced its first trade surplus in 30 years, to the skepticism of some observers, and credited the impressive activity of the private sector and newly formed joint sector agricultural enterprises for making the surplus possible.[25]

These sectors now provide, at least in part, the resources needed to sustain those sectors that are politically important, but economically "irrational" and to satisfy the regime's ideological claim to be engaged in some form of redistributive project. Throughout the implementation of this strategy, moreover, the regime's coercive capacity has remained much in evidence, both to ensure that the beneficiaries of stabilization do not attempt to use their economic gains to challenge the regime and to suppress the political pressures that arise from those social groups and classes at the core of the regime's ruling coalition (or patronage system) whose interests are most damaged by the effects of selective stabilization and by competition from those sectors which have benefitted from it.

Over the past decade, private-sector businessmen once identified as a significant threat to the economic and political control of the regime, and thoroughly marginalized as a result, have become an increasingly important component of the regime's economic strategy and have achieved a measure of political clout as well.[26] In parliamentary elections held in May 1990, two members of the Damascus Chamber of Commerce and one of the Aleppo Chamber of Commerce were elected, the first clearly defined "representatives of business" to serve in parliament since 1963.[27] Overall, their numbers, social position, and economic strength have increased, supported by an expanding array of legislative measures and by the relegitimation of the private sector on the part of the regime.[28] As one prominent business leader and successful politician remarked of Syria's private sector in the 1990s, "It has no boundaries."[29]

Despite this sentiment, regime policies continue to restrict the private sector within distinct boundaries. The regime has carefully preserved the privileged position of "national" economic sectors, including petroleum and mining; banking, agricultural processing, cement manufacturing, glass and paper manufacturing, and so on. In these sectors, where workers are heavily unionized, the number of workers per firm is the highest in the country, employment serves political and patronage functions, and the regime has sought to cultivate its political base along highly clientalist lines, rationalization and liberalization have been scrupulously avoided. No set of decrees has been passed encouraging private-sector investment in heavy industry similar to those that have facilitated private investment in trade, light manufacturing for export, agriculture, tourism, and services (and for many reasons it is not clear the private sector would pursue such opportunities were they available). Nor has privatization of inefficient state-owned industries been raised as a strategy, unlike the case of Egypt or many other states.[30]

Insulating politically important sectors from the demands of liberalization, however, has not entirely insulated them from its effects. Employees of the state have watched their fixed salaries lose considerable ground over the past decade to inflation and to the withdrawal or reduction of many state subsidies.[31] Mid-level bureaucrats may earn as little as $60 to $80 per month, university professors $110 per month, and pensioners about $50 per month.[32] Broad popular dissatisfaction is fueled by many sources. Growing discrepancies between public and private sector salaries; continued high inflation; elimination of subsidies on basic commodities such as sugar, tea, and rice; the perception that government policies now favor a "parasitic," "speculative" private sector; and the apparent retreat of the regime from its longstanding populist commitments have generated serious concern among a variety of groups, including the General Federation of Trade Unions, conservative factions within the Ba'th Party, and the much less politically significant Communist Party.[33]

These impacts have caused the regime to devote significant attention to coalition maintenance, but with a distinctive dynamic, one shaped by the character of selective stabilization. Unlike the problems of coalition management associated with full-blown stabilization programs, where regime elites seek to balance the costs of restructuring among all members of the dominant coalition and to ensure that some core set of coalition members remain committed to the process at all times, the Syrian regime has a different, but equally difficult, task.[34] It must simultaneously persuade the private sector of its sincerity and commitment to reform, without which it would abstain from investing, while persuading its clients and beneficiaries that their positions are secure, that they will be protected from the demands of stabilization, and that economic reform will not interrupt their privileges and benefits.

In early March 1990, Minister of Economy and Foreign Trade Muhammad Imadi told the Kuwaiti paper *Al-Anba'*: "The Syrian Government's economic plan sought to support the private sector. It increased its contribution to exports by 300 percent between 1988 and 1989 and allowed it to retain 75 percent of its overall revenues from exports in foreign currency to finance its imports."[35] A week later, Prime Minister Mahmoud al-Zu'bi spoke to the annual congress of the Damascus Workers' Federation, emphasizing "that the public sector will be the principle factor in the national economy and that the government views the private and mixed sectors as complementary to the public sector."[36] These mixed messages, and policies to match, have become a familiar part of the regime's approach to managing economic reform.

Rather than trying to persuade its clients to support stabilization, therefore, the regime seeks to reassure them of their relative immunity from the its requirements and its costs. The regime has not undertaken the political challenge of constructing a grand coalition in support of stabilization, but has in essence cultivated two distinct coalitions, one economic and liberalizing, the other political and populist, and has adjusted the incentives and benefits it provides to each depending on the role defined for it. In this sense, stabilization has not brought about a general renegotiation of the populist "social pact" that has helped to sustain the regime for three decades. It has instead produced a much more limited set of semiprivate bargains. General austerity measures have been introduced, but in a piecemeal fashion. The regime has called on Syrians to reduce consumption and assist in "achieving economic self-reliance" but continues to identify itself as the provider of social welfare. Regime clients have been reassured, but have been made aware, as well, that resources are limited and that they bear the leading responsibility for the country's economic development.[37] Prices paid to farmers for their crops by state purchasing agencies have been raised. To mobilize private-sector participation local and foreign businessmen have been granted guarantees protecting their activities within defined economic sectors. Syria's capitalists have been accorded a limited degree of political recognition, and have benefitted from a consultative role in shaping economic policies that affect their areas of interest.[38]

This strategy is not risk-free. The adjustment costs of stabilization are hard to contain and, as noted above, can spill over into politically important sectors: austerity programs are felt most sharply by salaried workers in the public sector and the state bureaucracy. Even though business groups currently go out of their way to show support for the regime and for the ruling party, it may be difficult to prevent private-sector representatives from acquiring a greater measure of political power than the regime intends and using their positions to support more far-ranging reforms. Moreover, the private sector simply may not be able to satisfy the consumption demands of those groups at the core of the ruling coalition, postponing, but not resolving, the need for structural adjustment. As John Waterbury has argued with regard to Egypt,

> The external resources that might have gone into structural adjustment itself and the attendant remaking of the dominant coalition were used instead to sustain the consumption of the existing coalition, and to add to it at least one new member: private sector interests in imports and banking. At the close of the 1980s, this formula no longer appears economically sustainable. Rents have declined while the claims of coalition partners have expanded, but the productive structure of the Egyptian economy has not been significantly altered.[39]

Syria's strategy has differed from Egypt's in important ways. The regime has made some effort to curb the demands of its supporters, the private sector has become a net contributor to the regime's resources and not simply an additional burden, and the macroeconomic and legal frameworks of the Syrian economy have been altered in meaningful ways to promote substantially higher levels of private-sector activity. These choices have raised the costs and potential risks of the path chosen by Syria's leaders, but they are also less destabilizing than a more broad-based stabilization and adjustment program would be.

MANAGING SELECTIVE STABILIZATION

Regime elites rarely confront the choice between economic restructuring and political survival in a clear-cut fashion. Establishing the necessity of even partial economic restructuring is itself a highly contested process, surrounded by sharp debates and intense political conflicts. Moreover, the process is unlikely to produce a decisive victory for either advocates of reform or supporters of the status quo. Economic decisions are taken slowly and implemented in fits and starts. They are subject to the intervention of factions with conflicting preferences, to sudden acceleration, and to reversal. Economic reform takes place in an atmosphere of uncertainty and ambiguity over ultimate objectives.[40]

At the Eighth Regional Congress of Syria's ruling Ba'th Party, for example, held in January 1985 in an atmosphere of severe economic crisis, debates over economic policy divided those who sought the imprimatur of the party for economic liberalization and those who felt that such measures represented a serious deviation from Syria's path to socialism. The final proceedings of the conference firmly took the middle ground, reaffirming the role of the public sector, calling for improved training for public-sector workers, and for improved public-sector efficiency. They also highlighted the need to strengthen exports, affirmed the importance of the private and mixed sectors, and urged the government to reform exchange rates.[41]

In part, this somewhat divided atmosphere reflects tensions within ruling coalitions about how to respond to economic crises. It is fostered by regimes, to preserve as much flexibility as possible in weakly institutionalized political settings and to reassure constituencies whose support is contingent on the continuation of existing arrangements. It also reflects the limits of administrative capacity, low levels of bureaucratic autonomy, and the inability of such regimes to satisfy all of their many constituents simultaneously.[42] Yet this style of economic policy-making, and the strategy of selective stabilization that ultimately results, reflect above all the crucial dilemma of economic reform in a patronage-based authoritarian regime: under conditions of economic crisis some form of stabilization is necessary to sustain the regime, but to engage in economic stabilization might trigger the political instability that reforms are intended to avoid. If such regimes do not have the choice of doing nothing, they must nonetheless act cautiously.

Regime responses under such circumstances typically emphasize reviving capital accumulation, resurrecting economic activity, and capturing revenues in ways that preserve long-standing (politically rational) institutions and practices. Some of the resulting decisions may lead to more efficient economic and political arrangements and may involve a measure of structural adjustment in addition to stabilization. These might include efforts to improve tax collection, bring the informal economy under state control, and reduce corruption. All of these steps, in theory, promote administrative efficiency and undermine the ability of favored social groups to manipulate the bureaucracy for private gains. Other measures, however, seem to reinforce existing patterns of economic and political behavior—for example by structuring stabilization measures to favor privileged groups, or by expanding the role of the state to ensure compliance with new regulatory regimes—and thus run counter to the argument that economic stabilization is always or necessarily correlated with market-based forms of economic rationality.

Since the capacity of regimes to predict the political or economic consequences of specific decisions is low, stabilization measures have a tentative, trial-and-error quality and are highly sensitive to political feedback.[43] However, opportunities that may exist to fine-tune economic policies are unlikely to emerge if economic technocrats are insulated from their political environment. While stabilization policies enacted under these conditions lack the (potential) coherence of IMF-sponsored stabilization and adjustment programs, they can, nonetheless, achieve (partially) rational economic outcomes that are also politically rational. When this does occur, selective stabilization can provide a patronage-based authoritarian regime with the extractive capacity to sustain clientalist networks, without provoking the zero-sum trade-off between political survival and economic rationality that is often assumed to govern the choices of patronage-based authoritarian regimes.

Selective stabilization has two principal and interrelated dimensions, one based on reshaping domestic macroeconomic policies and the other focused on reorganizing foreign trade and relations with the international economy. At the onset of economic crisis, an initial reluctance to alter existing policies, institutional arrangements, or political conditions is typical of economic policies in both areas. In Syria, this phase occurred roughly from 1982 to 1985. As the crisis deepens, however, this reluctance is replaced by a gradual recognition of the need to make more substantive changes. This recognition, and a more liberalizing approach to stabilization, have existed in Syria since 1985, and continue to define the country's overall political-economic context. This effort to identify distinct phases in the development of Syria's economic policies should not be permitted to obscure a general trend in support of selective stabilization in both periods.

On the domestic front, the initial response of a patronage-based authoritarian regime to economic crisis is to try to revive capital accumulation and to generate new revenues without restructuring; in other words, to rationalize without stabilizing. As in other cases, Syria's leaders adopted a range of policies with this overall aim.[44] They imposed import curbs on luxury and consumer goods in 1982 and devalued the incentive rate of the Syrian pound once the same year, a second time in 1984, and again by 50 percent (from S£11.75 per dollar to S£22 per dollar) in August 1986. In addition, in January 1988 the "official" rate was devalued by 185 percent, from S£3.9 per dollar to S£11.2 per dollar. Beginning in 1982 the regime reduced subsidies on many essential consumer goods and instituted a modest austerity program. Reductions in real spending were accomplished not by cutting budgets, but by limiting their rates of growth to well below the rate of inflation. For almost the remainder of the decade, in fact, nominal budget increases were kept quite small, although some sectors did benefit from real increases in public funding, notably minerals and mining, which includes the petroleum industry, and agriculture. During these years, the (officially unacknowledged) rate of inflation rose from about 15 percent early in the decade to between 40 to 60 percent in the late 1980s.[45]

Syria's leaders also sought to improve the collection of existing taxes, imposed new taxes, and expressed interest in reforming tax structures to encourage investment. In 1982 tax exemptions granted to public-sector enterprises were abolished and tax levels were raised for certain categories of income, taxes, rents, profits, dividends, and interest. Between 1983 and 1986, taxes on business profits doubled. Moreover, the regime began more seriously to provide assistance for the existing activities of the private sector, with a particular interest in generating higher export levels. In August 1983 the government began to permit private-sector businessmen to use up to half of their export earnings to finance the import of goods to be used in production. Additional new measures passed in late 1984 eased access to credit for private-sector importers, once the regime possessed sufficient foreign exchange to make possible a limited resumption of imports. These policies had an immediate and striking effect. From 1985 to 1986 the private sector's share of imports rose from 16 to 25 percent, and of exports from 8 percent to 30 percent in the same period.[46]

The regime focused particular attention on efforts to reduce losses stemming from corruption and to improve the productivity of industrial and manufacturing sectors; new regulations and sanctions were introduced to expand the state's control over the informal economy, notably the black market in Syrian currency and large-scale smuggling from Lebanon, and to capture the gains from informal economic activities, which in some cases rivaled in scope those in the formal economy.[47] These measures had a dampening effect on illegal activities, but never came close to eliminating them. Indeed, the Syrian military units stationed in Lebanon were widely regarded as the largest participants in illegal trade, and official crackdowns on smuggling were often interpreted as attempts to stamp out the competition. Nonetheless, by the end of 1986 a truly repressive system of laws had been put into effect to ensure that Syrian citizens had virtually no legal way to acquire, accumulate, or exchange foreign currency outside of state-controlled channels. Syrians caught exchanging amounts in excess of $100 on the black market were, and still are, subject to a minimum prison term of 15 years and a maximum of 25 years. As these initiatives clearly show, there is no immediate correlation between economic stabilization and economic (or political) liberalization.[48] The former might easily include policies that seek to strengthen the control of the state over the economy in order to enhance the flow of revenues into official channels.

At the same time the regime sought to cushion public-sector and state workers from the effects of these shocks by providing salary increases for employees and pensioners in these sectors in September 1985 of about 20 percent (an increase had been implemented in 1980 as well). Public-sector and state salaries were raised again in November 1987, by about 27.5 percent on average. These efforts were not terribly successful. Between 1980 and 1989 Syria's price index rose by 579 percent, while its GDP increased by only 392 percent, in current prices.[49] According to one source, the effect of Syria's austerity programs in the early 1980s was to reduce Syria's 1986 GDP to below that of a decade earlier.[50]

Externally oriented measures were also introduced in this initial phase, typically aimed at increasing access to foreign capital. Here too, however, the initial intent of Syria's regime was to generate resources without stabilizing or restructuring the domestic political economy. These measures included efforts to increase foreign investment, particularly from the Gulf states and by Syrian nationals residing outside the country, by offering new guarantees for the protection of foreign capital and providing new flexibility for foreign firms to repatriate profits and for nonresident Syrians to open foreign currency accounts in the country. These policy shifts were reinforced by bringing individuals noted for their reformist sympathies into top economic policy-making positions. Among the most important of these appointments was the 1985 return of U.S.-trained economist Muhammad Imadi to the position of Minister of Economy and Foreign Trade.[51]

If these measures are effective—and the administrative reach of weakly institutionalized authoritarian regimes can easily exceed their grasp—they can have a significant cumulative impact on the extractive and revenue-generating capacity of a regime.[52] More typically, however, their effectiveness is quite mixed: reducing domestic expenditures and curtailing illegal activities are difficult, but possible, tasks. Increasing exports or persuading foreign investors to risk their capital in countries like Syria, or indeed in most developing states, are jobs of a different order of magnitude altogether. They usually require more than official expressions of good will, especially in light of the understandably cautious attitude of Syrian and foreign investors toward the Syrian government and the reliability of its commitment to fiscal reform. Similarly, given rather low levels of bureaucratic competence, and the semi-institutionalized corruption that sustains the regime's patronage networks, its ability to improve the country's mid- or long-term economic position through enhanced tax collection and efficiency drives seems highly doubtful. Not surprisingly, Syria's repeated anticorruption drives have acquired a largely symbolic quality that leads many citizens to regard them with more than a measure of cynicism. These institutional constraints and credibility problems have placed even more pressure on the regime to expand those fiscal reforms that are within the rather limited range of its administrative and political capacities.[53]

Whether Syria's regime would have been satisfied with the changes it introduced in the initial 1982-1985 period is uncertain. However, additional declines in the price of oil in the mid-1980s, along with the spillover effects of continuing poor harvests on all sectors of the economy and other factors referred to above, kept Syria's foreign exchange reserves at disastrously low levels through the middle of the 1980s and virtually wiped out the effects of its "phase one" reforms. Policies introduced from 1982 to 1985 continued, but more intensive stabilization measures were introduced alongside them in the period after 1985.

This second phase of Syria's selective stabilization program more closely resembled a formal stabilization program and included several measures that might, under the World Bank definition, qualify as structural adjustments rather than stabilization. Even in this phase, however, Syrian reform policies had select, limited targets and were accompanied by reassurances and protections for the groups that were most important to the stability of the regime. Perhaps most significant was the turn toward a more explicit austerity program, including deeper and more sweeping reductions in subsidies for consumer goods of every kind. In late 1985 price increases of between 7 and 144 percent on 65 consumer items were introduced and the supply of essential commodities dropped precariously. Fuel prices were particularly affected: between June 1980 and the beginning of 1988, kerosene and gasoline prices jumped by 600 percent and gas oil prices increased by 700 percent. Merchants took the opportunity to raise prices, and the Ministry of Supply came under attack for not adequately protecting Syrian consumers. Nonetheless, subsidy reductions continued. In one of his first major speeches to parliament, newly appointed Prime Minister Mahmoud al-Zu'bi singled out the goal of reduced consumption as a leading priority for his new government. "The decrease of public consumption," he said

> requires integrated measures that the government will take. Among these measures are decreasing expenditure and rationalising and organising the use of commodities and services. Increased consumption in some areas is met by a decrease in other areas that are directly connected with certain basic needs. Achieving balance in this regard has become an urgent issue.[54]

Putting Zu'bi's admonition into effect, the 1988 budget reduced the amount available for price-stabilization payments from S£1,400 million to S£900 million.

Mobilizing the private sector also became a more explicit element of the regime's policies in 1985 and subsequent years, particularly in areas that showed high probability of generating foreign exchange and expanding exports. Continuing changes begun in the early 1980s, the regime gave broader flexibility to Syrian residents in the summer and fall of 1985 to import goods to be used in industrial production for which the public sector had previously held an import monopoly, and eased access to credit facilities to finance such imports. These regulations also permitted private-sector importers to use their own foreign exchange to pay for imported goods.[55] In March 1987 the government expanded the categories of businessmen eligible to retain up to half of their foreign-exchange earnings to finance their own imports. And in April 1987 it increased the maximum amount of foreign exchange that could be retained from 50 to 75 percent of earnings for the import of certain categories of items.

Beyond specific import-export reforms, the regime created new categories of activities permitted in the private sector. In February 1986 it introduced Legislative Decree No. 10, which provided for the creation of joint-stock companies in agriculture and tourism with a minimum 25 percent share held by the state. By 1989, 11 new joint-sector agricultural enterprises had been approved. Firms created under this decree receive highly privileged treatment: they are not bound by the constraints of the five-year development plans; they are not required to sell their products to the state; they are exempt from import and export restrictions and taxes; and they are able to hold foreign-currency accounts within Syria, transfer foreign exchange out of the country, and exchange 70 percent of their foreign currency into Syrian pounds at the market rate.[56] Subsequent legislation exempted fruits and vegetables—which became the leading crops grown by joint-sector agricultural ventures—from taxes normally levied on agricultural products and facilitated their export. By 1991, Syria's joint-sector farms had become leading suppliers of these crops to the Arab Gulf states and important contributors to Syria's economic recovery.[57]

As important for the regime as mobilizing the private sector and expanding agricultural production has been its determination to fully and rapidly exploit the country's limited petroleum reserves as the leading source of foreign exchange. Increasingly, "agriculture and hydrocarbons" have become "the twin pillars" of Syria's economic development.[58] Since 1984, discoveries of more marketable grades of oil have raised the level of Syria's proven reserves. Its production of both oil and natural gas has increased significantly, as has the government's willingness to establish joint Syrian-foreign enterprises to carry out oil exploration and production operations. Syria's reserves are too small for it to become a true rentier state, but its leaders are well aware of the political and economic autonomy which accompany oil rents.[59] Indeed, in the push to sell as much oil as possible, one large field was overproduced in 1989 and engineers feared it had been permanently damaged.

Incentives for private-sector investment and export-oriented activities have continued to the present. In 1989 the government authorized Syrian and foreign investors to buy shares in joint-sector firms at a "parallel" market rate of S£42 per dollar. More recently, in May and June 1991, two new laws were passed, Nos. 10 and 20. The former further eased restrictions on private-sector investment and the latter reformed the Syrian tax code to remove provisions that penalized business profits. Private-sector businessmen in Syria have expressed optimism that these recent changes represent a turning point in the liberalization of Syria's economy. After nearly a decade of gradually easing private-sector restrictions, these laws are thought to reflect both how much the regime has come to depend on the private sector and the near irreversibility of the reform process.

A crucial test of the reversibility of reform is now underway, stemming from the inflow of large amounts of foreign exchange during and after the Gulf War. Estimates of the amount of such aid range widely, from $2 to 4 billion. If Syria's selective stabilization process is merely a crisis-generated reaction to a temporary loss of foreign exchange, the resumption of foreign aid would be expected to bring about the rollback of reforms or at least an end to the introduction of new reforms. While it is still too early to reach a definitive conclusion, Syria's regime has not diminished its commitment to reform in the year since the war. Indeed, it has put into effect a number of far-reaching reform measures during this period. Based on this limited evidence, selective stabilization seems likely to remain a part of Syria's overall economic strategy into the postwar period.

CONCLUSION

Over the past decade, Syria's weakly institutionalized, ethnically divided, and patronage-based authoritarian regime has shown a reasonable capacity to implement a set of rationalizing economic reforms. Through a process of selective stabilization of the Syrian economy, it has significantly devalued the Syrian pound, enhanced the incentives for private-sector participation, imposed substantial austerity measures, begun a transition from import substitution to export-promotion industrialization, moved to revitalize agricultural productivity, worked to expand the state's control over informal economic activities, and leaned heavily on the expanding petroleum sector.

These reforms have been introduced without seriously disrupting the patronage-based political arrangements the regime depends on for its survival. Public-sector and state-bureaucratic employees have been among the hardest hit by a decade of austerity, and by their exclusion from the sectoral-specific economic growth enjoyed by private-sector businessmen, who enjoy the increasing support of the regime. Despite their relative decline, however, the public sector and the popular organizations representing workers continue to benefit from a political economy that remains highly command-oriented and from a regime that continues, at least rhetorically, to regard the public sector, and the public industrial sector in particular, as the engine of the Syrian economy, and the truly "national" sector.[60] Despite high levels of overstaffing and capacity utilization rates of 30 to 50 percent overall, the public sector was not subject to serious rationalizing reforms.

Throughout the 1980s the regime affirmed its intent to improve public sector efficiency. In 1988 the government did rescind its pledge of full employment for university graduates. It also reduced the tremendously bloated staff of a prominent construction conglomerate run by the armed forces, Milihouse, from some 80,000 to about 25,000 in the same year. These efforts, however, were exceptions to a general pattern of insulating the public sector from the process of economic reform, and continuing to rely on it as a key source of patronage-linked and politically necessary employment.

Selective stabilization has modified Syria's political economy and has the potential to bring about even more substantive change. Yet as demonstrated by the regime's unwillingness to subject the public sector to the demands of stabilization (and itself to the political consequences that might result) it is important not to overlook just how selective this process has been, and the relatively limited progress it has produced in terms of economic liberalization and economic restructuring. Syria's command economy remains largely intact, though it continues to be plagued by the problems that have affected such economies in other parts of the world. The private sector continues to be restricted to a narrow range of economic activities. Even these are subject to state approvals and, as in the joint agricultural sector, state participation. The private sector's role in imports and exports remains limited and controlled: it suffers from a higher tariff rate than the public sector; it requires licenses for all imports; it is compelled to rely on its own sources of foreign exchange to finance imports, while the public sector continues to enjoy an import monopoly on a wide range of raw materials and essential commodities. Regulations governing the use of private-sector foreign exchange holdings have eased considerably, particularly with the passage of Law 10 in May 1991, but currency markets remain under relatively tight control. Opportunities do exist for the expansion of the private sector into areas of the economy that are currently off limits. But as long as the stability of the regime rests on the exploitation of the public sector as a source of patronage, prospects for the transformation of selective stabilization into a full-fledged, Eastern European-style process of liberalization seem remote.

Selective stabilization did not emerge from a coherent process of economic decision-making by technocrats insulated from the narrow logic of politics. More often, decisions resulted from a politicized process of trial-and-error, a process driven by the ebb and flow of Syria's economic crisis and by the political calculations of a regime whose commitment to reform is limited. Nonetheless, as a result of these changes, by 1989 Syria's economy showed tentative signs of recovering from the 1981-1989 crisis, even prior to the resumption of large scale Arab support following the Gulf War. In 1990 the government announced its second annual trade surplus in a row. Syria's foreign exchange position remains difficult, but it is much improved from the period in 1986 when the IMF reported reserve levels of only $10 million.

Syria's ruling authoritarian regime, in other words, has been able to put in place policies which are both politically and economically rational. This is not to say that the regime has identified a path that is politically neutral, or efficiency-maximizing. Rather, it has established a viable balance between its political and economic requirements. It has managed to bridge the structural conflict between the logic of politics and the logic of economic stabilization.

This balance may not be stable. Syria's economic health remains subject to fluctuations in seasonal rainfall and in world oil markets. It seems inevitable that the changes introduced thus far will bring new pressures in their wake, and thus might serve as the catalyst for unanticipated and unintended changes in the future. As selective stabilization has become more consolidated, however, the possibility appears increasingly distant that Syria's regime will be able to reverse it, and to force the private sector back into its previous, more subordinate role. If full-scale economic stabilization and/or liberalization now seems beyond reach, it appears equally unlikely that the reforms of the past decade can be undone. The political constraints associated with Syria's patronage-based system of rule have not made economic reform impossible, but they do seem sufficiently powerful to prevent selective stabilization in Syria from crossing the threshold between its continuation as a piecemeal process of crisis management and its transformation into a more durable process of reform, and potentially, economic adjustment and liberalization.

NOTES

1. With thanks to Joel Migdal, Stephan Haggard, and Thomas Callaghy for their comments on earlier drafts.
2. One widely quoted study linking successful stabilization to authoritarian rule is Thomas Skidmore, "The Politics of Stabilization in Postwar Latin America," in *Authoritarianism and Corporatism in Latin America,* ed. James Malloy (Pittsburgh: University of Pittsburgh Press, 1977), 149-90. For a more recent example see Robert R. Kaufman, "Democratic and Authoritarian Responses to the Debt Issue: Argentina, Brazil, Mexico," in

The Politics of International Debt, ed. Miles Kahler (Ithaca: Cornell University Press, 1986), 187-217.

3. One particularly noteworthy case is Nigeria. See Julius O. Ihonvbere, "Structural Adjustment, the April 1990 Coup, and Democratization in Nigeria." Paper prepared for presentation at the African Studies Association Annual Conference, November 1990.
4. See William C. Smith, *Authoritarianism and the Crisis of the Argentine Political Economy* (Stanford: Stanford University Press, 1989).
5. On the rise of authoritarianism in response to the strains accompanying stabilization see John Sheahan, "Market-Oriented Economic Policies and Political Repression in Latin America," *Economic Development and Cultural Change* 28 (January 1980). See also Stephan Haggard and Robert R. Kaufman, "Economic Adjustment in New Democracies," in *Fragile Coalitions: The Politics of Economic Adjustment,* ed. Joan M. Nelson, et al. (Washington, DC: Overseas Development Council, 1989), 57-77.
6. See Joan M. Nelson, et al., eds., *Fragile Coalitions,* and Joan M. Nelson, ed., *Economic Crisis and Policy Choice: The Politics of Adjustment in the Third World* (Princeton, N.J.: Princeton University Press, 1990). See also Jeffrey Sachs, ed., *Developing Country Debt and the World Economy* (Chicago: University of Chicago Press, 1989; and Stephan Haggard, "The Politics of Adjustment: Lessons from the IMF's Extended Fund Facility," in *The Politics of International Debt,* ed. Miles Kahler (Ithaca: Cornell University Press, 1986), 157-86. On the Middle East see Ismail Sabri 'Abdallah, "The Current Call for Conversion from the Public Sector to the Private Sector," in *The Public Sector and the Private Sector in the Arab World,* edited collection, in Arabic (Beirut: Markaz Dirasat al-Wihda al-'Arabiya, 1990), 173-93; Said El-Naggar, ed., *Adjustment Policies and Development Strategies in the Arab World* (Washington, DC: International Monetary Fund, 1987), and Said El-Naggar, ed., *Privatization and Structural Adjustment in the Arab Countries* (Washington, DC: International Monetary Fund, 1989).
7. See Karen L. Remmer, "The Politics of Economic Stabilization: IMF Standby Programs in Latin America, 1954-1984," *Comparative Politics* 19, no. 1 (October 1986), 1-24.
8. Haggard, "Politics of Adjustment."
9. See Haggard, ibid., and *Pathways from the Periphery: The Politics of Growth in Newly Industrializing Countries* (Ithaca: Cornell University Press, 1990); and Thomas Callaghy, "Lost Between State and Market: The Politics of Economic Adjustment in Ghana, Zambia, and Nigeria," *Economic Crisis and Policy Choice,* 257-319. In constructing his argument Haggard refers to Callaghy's work on Zaire, *The State-Society Struggle: Zaire in Comparative Perspective* (New York: Columbia University Press, 1984).
10. Reviewing the performance of states which had sought relief through the IMF's Extended Fund Facility (EFF), Haggard found that 24 of 30 adjustment programs experienced some form of compliance problems. All of the

states governed by what he identifies as weak, personalistic authoritarian regimes—Haiti, Guyana, Senegal, Zaire, Zambia—had EFF adjustment packages canceled by the IMF due to noncompliance. "Politics of Adjustment," 157-59.

11. Karen L. Remmer, "New Wine or Old Bottlenecks? The Study of Latin American Democracy," *Comparative Politics* 23, no. 4 (July 1991), 479-95.
12. Yahya Sadowski, "Ba'thist Ethics and the Spirit of State Capitalism: Patronage and the Party in Contemporary Syria," in *Power and Ideology in the Middle East,* ed. Robert J. Pranger and Peter J. Chelkowski (Durham, NC, and London: Duke University Press, 1988), 160-84; Richard T. Antoun, "Ethnicity, Clientship and Class: Their Changing Meaning," in *Syria: Society, Culture, Polity,* ed. Richard T. Antoun and Donald Quataert (Albany: State University of New York Press, 1991), 1-12; and Elisabeth Longuenesse, "Syrie, secteur public industriel: les enjeux d'une crise," *Maghreb-Machrek,* no. 109 (July-August-September 1985), 5-22. She defines Syria's economy in terms of a "social logic based on clientalism and corruption" on p. 16.
13. Callaghy, "Lost Between State and Market," 258.
14. The collapse of Mobutu's political authority in Zaire, in progress as this is being written, illustrates just how politically irrational and destabilizing the unrelenting adherence to economically irrational practices can be.
15. Yahya Sadowski, "Cadres, Guns, and Money: The Eighth Regional Congress of the Syrian Ba'th," *MERIP Reports,* no. 134 (July-August 1985), 3-8.
16. Syria's relationship with the IMF and the World Bank has been strained for several years. In its 1986 annual report the World Bank called Syria to task for failing to "'formulate and adopt a programme for dealing with its structural difficulties.'" Economist Intelligence Unit, *Quarterly Economic Report—Syria,* no. 4 (1986). An IMF delegation visited Syria in late 1988 and held inconclusive talks regarding a structural adjustment program. The Syrian government was due to respond to the IMF's proposal with a detailed plan the following September. Yet by 1991, no Syrian response had been forthcoming. See David Butter, "Syria's Under the Counter Economy," *Middle East Economic Digest* (23 February 1990). Syria is currently regarded as an inactive member of the IMF. On the concept of implicit stabilization see Karen Pfeifer's article in this volume.
17. The World Bank defines stabilization as "managed reductions in expenditures to bring about an orderly adjustment of domestic demand to the reduced level of external resources." Structural adjustment, on the other hand, constituted "changes in relative prices and institutions to make the economy more efficient, more flexible, and better able to use resources, and thereby to engineer sustainable long-term growth." "Adjustment Lending: Ten Years of Experience," *The World Bank Research News* 8, no. 3 (March 1989). Based on these definitions, Syria's experience has combined elements of both stabilization and structural adjustment.

18. A variety of sources have tracked Syria's economic crisis. In addition to the regular reporting in the *Middle East Economic Digest* and the Economist Intelligence Unit publications, see Eliyahu Kanovsky, "What's Behind Syria's Current Economic Problems?" Occasional Papers, Dayan Center for Middle Eastern and African Studies (Tel Aviv: Tel Aviv University, 1985); Longuenesse, "Syrie, secteur public industriel;" Fred H. Lawson, "Liberalisation économique en Syrie et en Irak," *Maghreb-Machrek,* no. 128 (April-May-June 1990), 27-52; Fred H. Lawson, "Political-Economic Trends in Ba'thi Syria: A Reinterpretation," *Orient* 29, no. 4 (December 1988), 579-94; Gunter Meyer, "Economic Development in Syria Since 1970," in *Politics and the Economy in Syria,* ed. J. A. Allen (London: Centre of Near and Middle Eastern Studies, SOAS: 1987), 39-62.
19. The IMF, for example, cited 1986 as a year of modest recovery for the Syrian economy, in sharp contrast to other assessments. The Fund also acknowledged that foreign exchange shortages were among the "most important factors contributing to the sluggish performance of the manufacturing sector." International Monetary Fund, *Syrian Arab Republic: Recent Economic Developments* (March 9, 1988), 4, 12.
20. Alan George, "An Economy Saved by Circumstances," *The Middle East* (December 1988), 27-8; David Butter, "Syria's Under the Counter Economy." During one period in 1986 Syria's foreign exchange reserves were reportedly as low as $10 million. Other estimates suggest much higher levels of aid during the early 1980s but only in the wake of the Gulf War has Arab support resumed at significant levels. See Kais Firro, "The Syrian Economy Under the Assad Regime," in *Syria Under Assad,* ed. Moshe Maoz and Avner Yaniv (New York: St. Martin's Press, 1986), 62.
21. See Volker Perthes, "The Bourgeoisie and the Ba'th: A Look at Syria's Upper Class," *Middle East Report,* No. 170 (May-June 1991), 31-37. According to Sadowski, "Cadres, Guns and Money," 7, Asad made "massive use of patronage" during his struggle against the Muslim Brotherhood to reinforce his popular standing and was unable to curb it after the conflict ended in 1982.
22. Kanovsky, "What's Behind," 6, and Patrick Clawson, *Unaffordable Ambitions: Syria's Military Build-Up and Economic Crisis,* Policy Papers No. 17 (Washington, DC: Washington Institute for Near East Policy, 1989), 7. Clawson does not indicate whether this figure includes the cost of Syria's presence in Lebanon. I assume it does not.
23. On the political character of Syria's public sector see Jean Hannoyer and Michel Seurat, *Etat et secteur public industriel en Syrie* (Beirut: CERMOC, 1979), and Jean Leca, "Social Structure and Political Stability: Comparative Evidence from the Algerian, Syrian, and Iraqi Cases," in *Beyond Coercion: The Durability of the Arab State,* ed. Adeed Dawisha and I. William Zartman (New York: Croom Helm, 1988), 164-202.
24. These figures are from the Itihad Ghurf al-Tijara al-Suriya [Federation of Syrian Chambers of Commerce], *Al-taqrir al-sanawi, 1990* [Annual Report, 1990], 15.

25. David Butter, "Syria's Under the Counter Economy."
26. Fred H. Lawson, "Political-Economic Trends," 590. Lawson records the regime's efforts to keep the activities of private-sector capitalists in check during the late 1970s and early 1980s. He argues that 1981-1985 witnessed a "reassertion of state control" and clamp-down on private-sector mobilization, following the liberalizing trend of the early 1970s. What he regards as a new centralizing effort, however, is interpreted here as the initiation of selective stabilization policies in which attempts to increase foreign-exchange earnings and domestic revenues are compatible with policies seeking to mobilize private-sector participation in the economy.
27. See Volker Perthes, "Syria's Parliamentary Elections: Remodeling Asad's Political Base," *Middle East Report*, no. 174 (January-February 1992), 15-18.
28. Several sources reflect this change. See Perthes, "The Bourgeoisie and the Ba'th;" *Al-taqrir al-sanawi lil-itihad ghurf al-tijara al-suriya, 1990* [Annual Report of the Federation of Syrian Chambers of Commerce, 1990]; and a speech by Minister of Economy and Foreign Trade, Muhammad Imadi, "siyasat al-tijara al-kharijiya fi al-thamaniyat wa-afaquha fi al-tisa'inat" [Foreign Trade Policies in the 1980s and Their Horizons in the 1990s] (Damascus: Damascus Chamber of Commerce, March 1991).
29. Interview, Badia Fallaha, Vice President of the Damascus Chamber of Commerce and member of parliament (one of two from the DCC elected in May 1990), August 8, 1991.
30. Ibrahim Helmy Abdel-Rahman and Mohammed Sultan Abu Ali, "Role of the Public and Private Sectors with Special Reference to Privatization: The Case of Egypt," in *Privatization and Structural Adjustment in the Arab Countries*, ed. Said El-Naggar (Washington, DC: IMF, 1989), 141-81.
31. The price of flat bread has risen 600 percent in recent years, from about S£0.5 per kilo to S£3 pounds per kilo. The black market in tea, sugar, and rice has all but disappeared and these goods are now widely available, but they have become increasingly unaffordable for most Syrians. Basic pharmaceuticals are now more widely available, but even those produced by state-owned enterprises cost between S£20 and S£50, enormously expensive for the vast majority of people whose monthly salaries might range from S£1800 to S£3500.
32. These figures are based on the official incentive exchange rate introduced in mid-1991, as part of Syria's exchange rate reform process, of S£42 per dollar. This rate was sufficiently close to the true (i.e. black market) rate to persuade many who had previously used the black market to shift their transactions to the state-owned banks.
33. See, for example, Itihad al-'Am lil-'Umal fi al-Qutr al-'Arabi al-Suri [General Federation of Syrian Trade Unions], "Mu'tamr al-ibda' al-watani wal-itimad 'ala al-that: al-taqrir al-'am" [Conference on national innovation and self-sufficiency: final report] (Damascus, 1987). The document notes the efforts of union leaders to preserve the primacy of the public sector in the face of growing challenges from the private sector in terms of salary,

productivity, and quality of management. Later, during the parliamentary debate surrounding the 1991 introduction of Legislative Decree encouraging private investment, Communist Party deputies challenged the law as a retreat from the nationalist and populist principles which have guided the Syrian economy. The statement of Communist MP Mahmoud Daoud was reproduced in the newspaper of the Bakhdash faction of the Communist Party, *Nidal al-Sha'b,* No. 469 (Early March 1991). See also a follow-up report in *Nidal al-Sha'b,* No. 470 (Late March 1991), 1-2.

34. John Waterbury, "The Political Management of Economic Adjustment and Reform," in *Fragile Coalitions,* ed. Joan Nelson, 39-56.
35. Foreign Broadcast Information Service (FBIS) *Daily Report: Near East and South Asia,* March 15, 1990, 40.
36. FBIS, *NES,* March 20, 1990, 31.
37. Prime Minister Mahmoud al-Zu'bi, address to parliament on December 28, 1986. Translated in BBC Summary of World Broadcasts, *Weekly Economic Report Part 4: Middle East, Africa, Latin America* (12 January 1987), ME/W0008 A1/6-10.
38. Representatives of the Chamber of Commerce and Chamber of Industry sit on the Committee for the Supervision of Exports and Imports (*Lajnat tarshid al-istirad wal-tasdir*), which is chaired by the Prime Minister and also includes the Minister of Economic and Foreign Trade, the Minister of Supply and Internal Trade, and the Deputy Prime Minister for Economic Affairs. A senior employee of the Damascus Chamber of Commerce singled out the Chamber's representation on this committee as a symbol of the private sector's growing influence. "Whether we agree or disagree with [the committee's] decisions," he said, "we are there in the room and they consult us on every step." Interview, August 10, 1991.
39. Waterbury, "Political Management," 49.
40. As noted in the U.S. Department of Commerce, *Foreign Economic Trends and Their Implications for the United States—Syria,* October 1989, 4:

    > The private sector has benefitted from a number of minor reforms enacted the last two years. There is strong resistance to structural reform on the part of much of the political power structure and a failure to appreciate the extent of economic difficulties on the part of elements of the political elite. There is also a de facto recognition of the failures and mismanagement of the public sector, and the detrimental effect of a lack of investor confidence on the economy. Changes have been enacted piecemeal rather than as part of a comprehensive reform program. The net effect is increased latitude for the private sector. We expect this trend to continue, despite opposition on ideological grounds.

41. The final resolutions of the eighth congress were widely reprinted. My copy came from the monthly journal of the Ministry of Supply and Internal Trade, *Al-tijara wal-tamwin,* no. 33 (February 1985), 16-35. See also Economist Intelligence Unit, *Quarterly Economic Report- Syria,* no. 1 (1985), 11; and Sadowski, "Cadres, Guns, and Money." The importance of the Ba'th Party

in policy-making is a matter of debate. Some argue that it is nothing more than a patronage network par excellence, and that all important decisions are taken by Asad or his most senior advisors. Yet the decision of the regime to permit debate over fundamental economic priorities at the party's most important meeting is an interesting indication of its uncertainty in the face of economic crisis, and its unwillingness simply to use the party to impose a predetermined package of economic reforms.

42. In "Political Management," Waterbury persuasively argues that satisfying all coalition members all of the time is not necessary. However, ensuring that all are not alienated at any particular time is crucial.
43. The general analogy is to Thomas Schelling's thermostat model. See "Thermostats, Lemons, and Other Families of Models," *Micromotives and Macrobehavior* (New York: Norton, 1978), 81-134.
44. These measures are reported routinely in the weekly *Middle East Economic Digest,* and in the Economist Intelligence Unit *Quarterly Economic Report—Syria.* The best summary of the regime's policies during this period is found in Lawson, "Political and Economic Trends," although with a slightly different periodization and a different analytic perspective.
45. For example, budget increases for 1985-88 were 4 percent, 5 percent, 5 percent, and 20 percent, respectively. Even the large 1988 increase represented a real cut in spending.
46. IMF, "Syrian Arab Republic," 46. The following paragraphs draw in part on this document.
47. See Alejandro Portes, Manuel Castells, and Lauren A. Benton, eds., *The Informal Economy: Studies in Advanced and Less Developed Countries* (Baltimore: Johns Hopkins University Press, 1989). Note, however, that where large percentages of the population occupy positions in both the formal and the informal economies, these measures constitute a very important form of restructuring. Moreover, to the extent that informal economic sectors are more likely to exhibit market characteristics than heavily regulated formal sectors, state control of the informal economy can constitute a form of market-restricting activity.
48. According to one Syrian businessman, President Asad has several times refused to repeal Law 24, imposing harsh penalties on the unofficial exchange of foreign currencies. When asked to speculate why the president had refused, the businessman immediately responded, "This law is a weapon against the whole middle class. Anyone who needs dollars must get [the regime's] permission, and they can refuse you for any reason." Interview, August 12, 1991.
49. *Middle East Economic Digest,* February 1, 1991, 22.
50. Meyer, "Syria's Economic Development," 42.
51. Before returning to the ministerial job he held in the 1970s, Imadi worked in Kuwait as director of the Arab Fund for Economic and Social Development. His contacts and good reputation in the Gulf were seen as additional strengths in Syria's efforts to generate Arab foreign investment in Syria.

52. According to the IMF, Syria's "overall fiscal performance improved significantly after 1985 in response to a combination of revenue-enhancing and expenditure-reducing measures. Improvements in tax administration and in the financial position of public enterprises, together with a tightening of expenditures, resulted in a considerable decline in the overall fiscal deficit." International Monetary Fund, *Syrian Arab Republic—Recent Economic Developments* (March 9, 1988), 1.
53. A credible commitment to reform has been identified as one of four key requirements for successful trade liberalization. The World Bank, "Liberalizing Trade: Bank Research on the Hows and Whats" *Research Report* 7, no. 2 (Fall 1986).
54. Statement translated in BBC Summary of World Broadcasts, *Weekly Economic Report, Part 4: Middle East, Africa, Latin America* (12 January 1988), ME/W0008 A1/6.
55. These reforms greatly increased demand for foreign exchange and put the Syrian pound under considerable pressure. As a result, in January and February 1986 the regime launched a major crackdown against illegal currency transactions, arresting hundreds of money-changers.
56. Hans Hopfinger, "Capitalist Agro-Business in a Socialist Country? Syria's New Shareholding Corporations as an Example." Unpublished paper, 1990.
57. One source noted that Syria had replaced Eastern Europe as the source of vegetables and fruit to the Gulf states. He indicated that the biggest problem facing growers was how to respond to the explosion of demand: public-sector transport facilities were inadequate. He said the Chambers of Commerce were considering approaching the government to establish a joint-sector transport company to accommodate the demand for agricultural goods. Interview, Executive Director, Federation of Syrian Chambers of Commerce, July 31, 1991.
58. *Economist Intelligence Unit, Country Report—Syria,* no. 4 (1989).
59. See Hazem Beblawi and Giacomo Luciani, eds., *The Rentier State* (New York: Croom Helm, 1987), and Kiren Aziz Chaudhry, "The Price of Wealth: Business and State in Labor Remittance and Oil Economies," *International Organization* 43, no. 1 (Winter 1989), 101-45.
60. Address by Prime Minister Mahmoud al-Zu'bi, 3 December 1989. Translated in Foreign Broadcast Information Service *Daily Report: Middle East and North Africa,* December 5, 1989.

3

The Engineering of a Heterodox Shock: The Israeli Experience, 1985-1987[1]

Henri J. Barkey

INTRODUCTION

In July 1985 Israel instituted a heterodox stabilization program to combat its high inflation rate. The program has attracted a great deal of attention because it succeeded in bringing down the rate of inflation from over 1000 percent a year to 15 percent, an achievement unmatched by the two other heterodox plans of that time, namely those of Argentina and Brazil. Even though, starting in 1988, there was a marked deterioration in some of the economic indices, unlike the other heterodox partners, Israel has avoided any further bouts of high inflation.

While most of the interest in the plan has focused on its heterodox aspects, that is, the unusual combination of orthodox and nonorthodox economic measures, not enough thought has been devoted to the politics of its implementation. This article argues that, while the mechanics of the measures and the prevailing external conditions were very important, the real key to the success lies in a combination of political factors: a determination by political leaders to make the plan work and strong institutional structures, specifically a strong state apparatus. It is through a careful process of political engineering that the inflationary expectations of a population long accustomed to rapid price increases and to being sheltered through an intricate system of indexation was broken.

ON STABILIZATION MEASURES

Stabilization plans are complex sets of measures of adjustment that require both sacrifices from society and a great deal of coordination among a variety of domestic and foreign economic and political institutions. The ability of an economy to respond to economic stabilization measures improves with the degree of its openness and integration with the world economy. Yet, as Joan Nelson points out, stabilization programs are more often than not postponed, resulting in what most economists would call aggravated circumstances.[2] Crisis conditions are far more conducive to applying stabilization measures than is the simple specter of an imminent crisis.[3] Nelson also contends that while the political reasons for postponements are obvious, what really needs to be further explored are the *inordinate* delays or the *preemptive* actions.[4]

Nevertheless, favorable external conditions or timeliness do not constitute guarantees for success. Just as one government can successfully deal with the circumstances necessitating the implementation of stabilization measures in the first place, another can fail. In fact, in most attempts at stabilization failure constitutes the norm rather than the exception. In the literature, Nelson identifies two common sets of excuses for failures: lack of "political will" on the part of leaders and political obstacles that hamper the implementation of measures.[5] While obstacles and the absence of political will are major factors, their elimination does not always ensure success. In fact, as she points out, numerous other factors enter the equation. This article argues that the Israeli case demonstrates the necessity for political will or leadership even where state capacity and state autonomy are relatively high. In other words, leadership is necessary to exploit the strengths that the state and its institutions provide.

The complexity of stabilization measures requires that a great many decisions be taken and carried through with a high degree of confidence of success. This necessitates proper planning, information, expertise, and a bureaucracy capable of pushing it through.[6] Often, administrative constraints and the ideological orientations of bureaucratic elites against "market-oriented" reforms militate against their successful implementation.[7] For the measures to work, state authorities have to mobilize significant resources to make sure that society complies with the difficult conditions that undoubtedly result from the changes. Clearly, not all states are capable of mobilizing the necessary resources to plan, execute, and carry through such measures. Even when such capacities have been present, few state leaders have managed to resist societal pressures and opposition to stabilization measures and maintain their policies over an extended period of time.

Hence, in addition to enhanced capacities, autonomy is needed. "[T]hrough state autonomy from domestic and outside forces, state officials have sought to act upon their own preferences, making decisions that reshape, ignore, or circumvent the preferences of even the strongest social actors."[8] The more autonomy state leaders possess, the greater the likelihood that they can carry through stabilization policies that are not always to the liking of societal groups. This autonomy, however, is not solely dependent on the state's capacity to mobilize resources,[9] such as means of coercion, taxes, and armies. "A state's capacities in making and enforcing new rules—gaining social control among its population—have depended on its ability to have strategies of survival that it offered accepted by the population."[10]

If a strong state is one that has both the necessary capacity and the autonomy to act, then what are some of its attributes in relation to devising and implementing stabilization measures? Among the most significant are the ability to mobilize resources in the form of taxes, information, and manpower; the existence of a set of competent and experienced local experts acceptable to decisionmakers; the ability to manage the bureaucracy; and, as Nelson also argues, "elite unity" as well as a "support base."[11]

This article argues that the Israeli success can be explained by the combination of two sets of factors: a strong state and a political leadership capable of exploiting the strengths that the state and its institutions provide.

ISRAELI INFLATION: AN OVERVIEW

Israel's rapid, sustained, and orderly pace of economic development came to a sudden stop with the 1973 Yom Kippur War. The war's tremendous costs made an indelible impact on the economy. Not only did the growth rate, which till then had averaged 10 percent of GDP, decline to less than half its previous mark, but the generally low inflation rate which had accompanied this growth was swept away by new annual rates of 30 to 40 percent.[12] The heavy burden of defense expenditures, worsened by the equipment losses and needs of the post-1973 period, together with oil price hikes, accentuated the current account deficits. As a result, inflationary problems coexisted with a chronic balance-of-payments deficit.

The situation would only get worse. After an initial acceleration to over 100 percent following the second round of oil price increases in 1979, the inflation rate in 1983 reached an almost hyperinflationary level. By 1984,

Figure 3.1: Quarterly Consumer Price Increases (%)

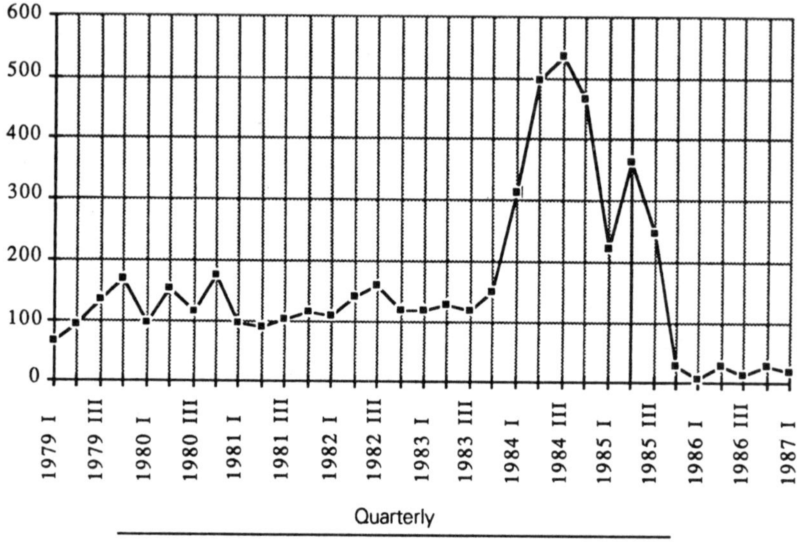

price increases were approaching 500 percent. During this period, the economic growth rate declined to an average of 1.6 percent per annum.

Origins of Israeli Inflation

As Figure 3.1 demonstrates, the Israeli inflation rate experienced sudden and visible jumps followed by periods of remarkable stability at its new-found rate. What accounts for this high rate and its peculiar trajectory?

The Israeli inflationary bout, however, has to be seen in the larger context of an economy deteriorating under the burden of heavy defense expenditures, runaway budget deficits, and balance-of-payments crises. The two most commonly advanced explanations for the persistence of high inflation in Israel are the conventional fiscal approach,[13] which stresses large government deficits as the primary cause, and the balance-of-payments approach,[14] which views high inflation as the product of exchange-rate depreciation, which in turn resulted from balance-of-payments crises.

As Table 3.1 indicates, as a percentage of GNP, the Israeli budget deficits increased consistently from the mid-1960s. The share of spending, which increased by almost 97 percent, eclipsed the 55-percent rise in domestic revenue collection.

Table 3.1: The Israeli Budget, 1960-1984 (% of GNP)

Period	Domestic Spending[a]	Domestic Revenue[b]	Domestic Deficit	Net foreign spending[c]	Defense spending	Base money creation
1960-1964	27.0	28.8	-1.8	1.2	9.4	2.5
1965-1967	32.0	29.6	2.4	2.8	12.5	2.2
1968-1973	41.0	34.4	6.6	6.6	23.6	3.2
1974-1977	56.4	42.1	14.3	3.3	29.3	2.6
1978-1980	60.7	45.5	15.2	2.0	23.9	2.0
1981-1983	61.0	46.5	14.4	-0.3	23.8	2.1
1984	62.9	46.0	16.9	-4.0	24.0	3.2

[a] Includes goods and services, subsidies, transfers, and interest on the public debt.
[b] Includes all direct and indirect taxes and transfers to the government.
[c] Government expenditure abroad (mainly armaments) *plus* interest on debt *minus* unilateral transfers (mainly U.S. government).
Source: Bruno and Fischer (1986); Dornbusch and Fischer (1986).

The dramatic rise seen during the 1974-77 period reflects the decline in the growth rate following the Yom Kippur War, which made the deficits less manageable from the point of view of the overall economy. Also during that same period, the share of defense expenditures reached an all-time high. The high inflation rates further contributed to the size of budget deficits by eroding tax receipts. This led the government to print money and borrow from abroad in order to close the gap in its finances, which in turn magnified the balance-of-payments deficits.[15]

On the other hand, balance-of-payments crises also have had an impact on inflation. Liviatan and Piterman suggest that there is a one-to-one correspondence between balance-of-payments crises and sharp accelerations in the inflation rate. In fact, as they point out, in the nine months preceding the Yom Kippur War, the import surplus had increased by about 6 percent of GNP.[16] The 1983 take-off into hyperinflation followed the government's massive devaluation of the currency which, given Israel's large exposure to foreign trade, led to significant increases in domestic prices.[17] Still, in view of the close linkages between budget deficits and balance-of-payments shortfalls, the long-term solution proposed by both approaches in Israel involved tackling both issues simultaneously.

Finally, as Michael Bruno also points out, inflationary expectations, in general, serve to fuel price increases and as such comprise an added third factor.[18] In Israel, two institutional developments sheltered the public from the ravages of hyperinflation by reducing the sense of urgency and postponing attempts to confront the problem. The first was indexation of wages and assets and the second involved financial assets linked to foreign exchange. Indexation allowed for inflationary expectations to be built into the Israeli economy. Nonetheless, there is no evidence that the indexation of incomes and assets, in existence since 1941, is itself a cause of inflation. Its use, however, complicated the policies designed to stabilize the economy.[19] The 1978 financial reform, which permitted liquid foreign exchange-linked domestic bank deposits, called PATAM accounts, opened the door to the emergence of financial holdings beyond the government's control. In fact, such monetary accommodation weakened "the stabilizing forces in the economy,"[20] by reducing the demand for "base money" and represented "the loss of a monetary anchor."[21]

Pre-1985 Attempts at Stabilization

The hyperinflationary stage reached during the mid-1980s clearly attests to the failure on the part of successive Israeli leaders to combat the inflationary demon. However, this failure does not reflect a lack of trying. There were numerous attempts at stabilization, and this section will look at those adopted following the advent of the high inflationary phase.

The first such attempt came at the end of 1979, when Yigal Hurwitz was appointed finance minister. He proceeded to deal with inflation and the current account deficit "the old-fashioned way, by cutting government demand and restrictive monetary policy."[22] Despite the reduction in subsidies, the cutback in public civilian spending, the general expectation of a slowdown in economic activity, and the increase in unemployment from 2.9 percent in 1979 to 4.8 percent in 1980,[23] the inflation rate did not show any perceptible sign of decline (Figure 3.1).

With the inflation rate rising and elections looming in 1981, the Likud government attempted a populist-type stabilization measure. The new treasury minister, Yoram Aridor, decided to tackle inflation by halting the increase in the price of controlled items. "Subsidies were accordingly increased, import tariffs slashed, and the exchange rate appreciated. . . . The policies had the desired effects, seen most clearly in an 80 percent (real) increase in consumer durable imports, and a fall in the inflation rate during the year (which may in part have been a delayed response to the earlier

Hurwitz contractionary policy)."[24] In fact, real wages increased by 10.4 percent in 1981 after having declined by 3.2 percent the preceding year. The temporary improvement in the inflation rate came, as expected, at the expense of the current account deficit, which worsened steadily over 1981 and 1982. Although the 1981 deterioration was primarily defense-related, by 1982 the civilian (nondefense) import surplus, or trade deficit, was responding vigorously to the continuation of Aridor's program. Following Likud's success in the 1981 elections, Aridor proposed that inflationary expectations be checked by making them predictable and announced that all controlled prices would increase and the exchange rate would be allowed to depreciate at a monthly rate of 5 percent.[25]

Not only did inflation fail to dampen, but 1982 was also the year of the Lebanese War, which by one account cost the economy $1.5 billion in direct expenditures and conceivably $5 billion in total direct and indirect costs.[26] By 1983 the economic situation was out of control and, as Fischer suggested, efforts on the balance-of-payments side were not matched by sufficient reductions on the domestic demand side.[27] A long-delayed devaluation in October 1983 further propelled the inflation rate, and with the announcement of elections in July 1984, the governing Likud, which hoped to repeat its 1981 success at the polls, abandoned all pretense of stabilization.

THE 1985 MEASURES

Immediate Antecedents

The July 1985 heterodox measures were instituted by the Labor-Likud coalition government established following the inconclusive 1984 elections. The National Unity government, as it came to be known, was initially led by Labor leader Shimon Peres. The July program, however, was not the government's first crack at stabilization. In fact, soon after the formation of the National Unity government in September 1984, the first "package deal" was put into effect in November of the same year. Its most prominent feature was a tripartite agreement between the trade union confederation, employers' associations, and the government to freeze prices and wages. The package deal, in effect from November 1984 to January 1985, produced the desired result by slowing "the price advance to 4 to 5 percent a month in December and January [from 24 and 19 percent in the two previous months] and damped inflationary expectations."[28]

Second and third package deals adopted by the government, which aimed at controlling rather than freezing prices, failed to deliver satisfactory results. Concurrently, speculative buying sprees by the public of foreign exchange in anticipation of a large devaluation caused foreign exchange reserves to dwindle at an alarming rate. On May 19, 1985, in what would prove to be a trial run for the heterodox measures, the government met for 13 consecutive hours to decide on budget cuts and on revenue-raising measures. Even then, the question of de-linking the economy, that is, eliminating the indexation of prices and wages, was avoided. Finally, the inability to control inflation with the package deals and the drain on the currency reserves forced the government to take decisive action and on June 30/July 1, 1985, the government, after a marathon 24-hour session, adopted a new economic stabilization plan (ESP).

Features of the Plan

Objectives

Unlike any other previous attempt at stabilization in Israel, the July 1985 plan aimed at remedying two simultaneous diseases: inflation and balance-of-payments deficits. This represented a significant departure from established policy which "hitherto . . . had concentrated on only one of the problems, even if this resulted in the exacerbation of the other one."[29] The two had finally come to be viewed as integral parts of a common problem. A third, but undeclared, objective aimed at getting the economy to resume its growth which, because of the stagflation of the last years, had faded completely.

Unlike previous attempts at stabilization, this comprehensive new effort contained an element of shock. Despite widespread expectations of a forthcoming set of measures and debate in the press regarding the types of measures needed, the June 30/July 1 measures were intended to produce a one-time rapid adjustment that would dislodge inflationary expectations. Gradualism and piecemeal offensives were abandoned because the earlier package deals had failed: the task of periodically revising and calibrating the anti-inflationary measures had proved to be simply impossible. Israeli inflation had thus become inertial in nature, impervious to gradual approaches.[30] The political implications of this therapy will be discussed in greater detail in a later section.

What made the package a "heterodox" one was its digression from standard IMF prescriptions that traditionally concentrate on fiscal restraints to combat inflation. The most significant departure from IMF models was represented by the combination of wage, price, and foreign exchange freezes with fiscal restraint. Such features also characterized the Argentine and Brazilian plans of 1985 and 1986, respectively. Another crucial factor that differentiated heterodox measures from conventional approaches was the importance attached to breaking the population's inflationary expectations. In line with the "rational expectations" approaches to inflation, which stress that the inherent momentum is principally the product of behavioral adaptations by individuals to long-term government policies or regimes,[31] the heterodox approach aims at convincing the public of real changes in government behavior. In the belief that this is what ultimately leads to rapid declines in inflation rates, the wage and price freezes constituted an integral part of the plan's success.

The Economics of the Stabilization Package

The government program's first priority was to reduce the budget deficit to manageable levels so that future economic growth "would entail a gradual reduction in the debt/GDP ratio. This would have required a cut of $2-2.5 billion (10 percent of GDP) in the budget relative to 1984."[32] Resistance to defense budget cuts lowered the goal to $1.5 billion. The cuts were to be effected by reducing subsidies, cutting ministerial budgets, and diminishing public-sector employment by 3 percent or 10,000 persons.[33] The reduction in the deficit was not to come solely from cuts in expenditure but also from increases in revenues and taxes.

As a second step, the Israeli shekel was devalued by 18.8 percent on July 1, 1985, and the exchange rate was fixed at IS1,500 per dollar.[34] By freezing the exchange rate the government hoped to minimize domestic price fluctuations that would result from the depreciation of the currency. This move was designed to further signal domestic producers and consumers of future stability in import prices by removing the fear of periodic devaluations.

Third, a wage and price freeze was instituted, which was followed by the temporary suspension of the cost-of-living allowance arrangements.[35] The government, however, did grant workers a 14 percent wage increase, effective August 1, to compensate for July's inflation. Prices for domestic products and services, after an average initial increase of 17 percent, were also frozen.

On the monetary side, the government and the Bank of Israel, in order to reduce domestic demand, maintained high real interest rates, raised reserve requirements and, to regain control of some monetary instruments, prohibited any *new* money from flowing into PATAM accounts. The general expectation was that once the exchange rate had been fixed, PATAM accounts would lose their importance as funds would flow from them into regular bank deposits. This expectation was fully realized as the public liquidated some $150 million in PATAM deposits on the day following the announcement of the plan.

Results

The measures proved remarkably successful. Within a few months, the inflation rate was reduced to 1 to 2 percent a month. The budget deficit was cut sharply and, by 1986, reduced to zero as a percentage of GDP. The price freeze worked so well that the public did not experience any shortages, despite the fact that very little effort was put into its enforcement.[36] Real wages also declined and "in January 1986 [they] were 13 percent lower than in June 1985, and 24 percent lower than the all-time high of April 1985."[37] As Figure 3.2 demonstrates, the unemployment rate, the great fear of all Israeli politicians and labor leaders alike, did not increase dramatically: from 6.5 percent during the second quarter of 1985, it reached a peak 7.9 percent during the second quarter of 1986.

On the balance-of-payments side substantial gains were recorded. Although Israel benefitted from a $1.5 billion emergency loan from the United States, which was paid in two equal installments over two fiscal years, export figures also improved significantly in the three years starting in 1985. As a result not only did foreign reserves improve, but Israel's total foreign debt showed very slight signs of declining from a high of $19.7 billion. By 1986 the current account had a surplus of $1.1 billion. Thus, on the balance-of-payments side, the indications were that the economy was holding its own and the tremendous pressure was easing somewhat.

Two significant exogenous factors that contributed to the success of the measures were the aforementioned U.S. administration's decision to help Israel with an emergency aid package and the worldwide decline in the price of oil. The aid package provided Israel with foreign currency reserves necessary to implement the devaluation and also helped stem the outflow of foreign currency. From another perspective, the U.S. aid represented a vote of confidence in the plan and thus bestowed it with an element of credibility. Similarly, the decline in oil prices delivered an unexpected bonus to the current account balance. Barkai estimates that, in 1986 alone, the cost of oil imports dropped by $500 to 600 million.[38] Two other factors that contributed

Figure 3.2: Israeli Quarterly Unemployment Rate (%)

to the external economic climate were the relative decline of the U.S. dollar vis-à-vis European currencies and the decline in interest rates. The shekel, which was tied to the dollar, also depreciated in relation to European currencies, thus giving an added boost to Israeli exports in their most important markets. In all, between the third quarter of 1985 and the last quarter of 1986, the shekel lost some 15 percent of its value against a five-currency basket.[39] The final factor, though of less significance, was the lowering of worldwide interest rates, which helped reduce the cost of servicing that part of the foreign debt tied to market interest rates.[40]

Finally, by the end of 1987, the economy's growth rate appeared to be partially restored. Real GDP growth for 1985, 1986, and 1987 was 3.7, 3.3 and 5.2 percent, respectively. More significantly, the business sector GDP growth for the same period was 5, 5.3 and 6.9 percent.[41]

The success of the 1985 program did not mean that Israel had climbed out of its economic crisis. In fact, the results of 1988 and 1989 indicated that the process of stabilization is an ongoing proposition and the sustainability of the changes depends on other reforms. The Israeli economy was (and still is) in need of structural reforms, and as Fischer suggested, "the ending of inflation was a necessary precondition for dealing with the economy's real problem."[42]

ENGINEERING THE MEASURES

When, on July 1, 1985, the National Unity coalition announced the heterodox package, neither the public nor the government were convinced of the program's long-term viability. The coalition had come to power in September 1984 with a mandate to extricate the country from the Lebanese morass and hyperinflationary conditions. Despite the withdrawal from Lebanon, the government's credibility had been tarnished by its less-than-impressive economic record. Although the government had the outline of a plan similar to the July heterodox package in its possession in October 1984, it opted for a series of three package deals that lacked the comprehensive nature of the July plan.

By July 1985, the government had run out of options. More than inflation, the most troubling sign on the immediate horizon was the precipitous decline in foreign exchange reserves. Some estimates had Israel running out of foreign exchange reserves within two months. For an economy as open and as dependent on imports as Israel's, this was an intolerable situation. The exigency of the foreign exchange situation was shared not only by the business sector and some government agencies but also by the Histradut, the main labor confederation.

Despite the urgency of the situation, there remained a great many obstacles to overcome. Some of these constraints on the decisional latitude of the leadership were unique to Israel, while others were typical of societies experiencing similar difficulties.

Constraining Factors

Among the unique and structural constraints, the most visible is the permanence of external insecurity, which has had three significant effects. The first is the extraordinary economic cost of the defense burden. Israel spends almost a quarter of its GNP on defense-related needs. Even though Israel has benefitted from U.S. largesse, which has helped defray some of these expenses, other not immediately visible costs resulting from the stockpiling of food and equipment and land use,[43] and the opportunity cost of idle labor during extensive periods of reserve duty or military service imply that the real costs of maintaining a vigilant defense posture have been underestimated. Second, this necessary posture has made the defense budget, the single largest item in the overall budget, politically very resistant to cuts.

Unemployment, though not unique in its own right, presents Israel with a special political and ideological challenge. Electoral consequences notwithstanding, the unemployment question directly engages the Histradut, the main trade union organization, which represents 90 percent of the labor force.[44] The Labor Party in particular has been sensitive to the Histradut, especially following the party's electoral defeat in 1977 and consequent loss of its political preeminence in Israeli society. The erosion in the party's support, especially among Sephardi (Eastern) voters, began in the 1969 elections, which followed the 1965-67 recession.[45] Labor, therefore, could ill afford to alienate a core constituency by advocating or resorting to policies that could lead to increased unemployment.

Given the importance attached to the absorption of immigrants, unemployment has had an ideological significance ever since the prestate years. This ideological component was accentuated by the 1965-67 recession, which led to an upsurge in emigration and, thus, a seeming failure of the dream of Labor Zionism. Since the 1965-67 experience, successive Israeli governments have had to fight inflationary or balance-of-payments problems with one hand tied behind their back—that is, without recourse to restrictive fiscal and monetary policies that cause unemployment.

Third, foreign affairs and security considerations have captured the attention and energy of Israeli leaders, so that economic decision-making is often relegated to lesser-known functionaries or politicians. Therefore, economic decision-making is deprived of forceful and visible advocates. This problem was most acute during the Likud administrations, when not only was Prime Minister Begin completely uninterested in economic issues, but economic stewardship was given to a member of a minor coalition partner, who, lacking broad-based support, was easily jettisoned at the first hint of trouble. This was Hurwitz's predicament as finance minister in 1980.[46]

This lack of political leadership has enabled individual ministries to gain a great deal of autonomy in the disbursement of funds; not surprisingly, they could always be counted on to resist attempts at reducing their budgets. In fact, during the high inflationary period, individual ministries routinely dispensed their budgetary allocations well in advance of the transfer of Treasury funds into their accounts. In so doing, they maximized the value of their expenditures, which were worth more than their delayed receipts, and thereby further contributed to budgetary deficits.

Among the immediate political constraints two figured prominently: intercoalition and party conflict and absence of general credibility. The Labor-Likud coalition government, which joined the two traditional rivals, commanded an impressive majority in the Israeli parliament, the Knesset.[47] The formation of such a broad-based coalition following the inconclusive 1984 elections was necessitated by the wide-ranging problems facing the country at the time, of which hyperinflation was by no means the most serious. The coalition agreement stipulated that during the first 25 months, Shimon Peres, leader of the Labor Party, would assume the prime ministership, with Yitzhak Shamir, his Likud counterpart, following him for the second half. During the course of the first few months, it quickly became clear that the Likud block, specifically Shamir himself, would let Peres and Labor handle the most difficult issues: extrication from Lebanon and economic stabilization. In fact, it was a calculated gamble on both sides. Peres, if he succeeded, could claim that his stewardship had accomplished the task(s) and then expect to be rewarded at the polls by the electorate. If Peres failed, Shamir could claim that he was simply a junior partner who was not allowed to share in many of the decisions taken by the cabinet. In effect, Shamir's stance during the adoption of the stabilization package confirmed his contentment with this strategy.

Complicating matters further were the internal squabbles within each of the coalition partners. This was particularly evident in the Likud, where Shamir's leadership was seriously challenged by two mavericks and populists: Ariel Sharon and David Levy, both of whom had cabinet responsibilities. On the Labor side, the party had traditionally been divided into many factions, including those centered around the two main personalities and long-standing rivals, Yitzhak Rabin, the then defense minister, and Peres. Hence, despite the general rules regarding cabinet responsibility and party discipline, the coalition lacked cohesion and was riddled with internal tensions, rendering its impressive parliamentary majority illusory.

After years of accelerating inflation, the government's ability to tackle inflation was highly dubious, even according to its own members. Given earlier failed expectations and continued indications by all leaders, including Peres, that inflation would not be fought with increased unemployment, there was little reason to believe that the coalition government could maintain a policy even if one could be formulated.

This absence of faith permeated the initial calculations and response of the different participants in the program. Employers, for instance, with the economic team's acquiescence, granted the Histradut wage increases in advance for the three months beginning in December 1985 of 4, 4, and 3.5 percent.[48] Both the Histradut's and employers' behavior indicated that the struggle against inflation would, at best, produce temporary gains.

Preparing the Measures

This section discusses the steps taken by the coalition, specifically by Peres, to circumvent the above-mentioned constraints.

The prime minister's decision to personally get involved in the process was most significant in providing political credibility to the measures. In view of the conspicuous absence of decisive political leadership in economic affairs, this step represented a crucial break with the past. There were two distinct phases to Peres's role in the process. The initial stage consisted of fact-finding and exploration. In the second, his commitment deepened as he put his prestige and that of his office behind the plan. The latter will be explored in a later section on implementation.

During the first phase, Peres held frequent and lengthy late-night meetings at his private residence, where he entertained various players from the economic arena with the purpose of obtaining as many diverse views as possible. Soon after taking office, he had set up an economic and social committee designed to encourage tripartite cooperation between the government, the private sector, and the Histradut by creating an atmosphere of reduced tension in which the various actors learned to talk to each other about pressing economic issues. This device had proved useful during the earlier package deals. In addition to the prime minister, the roundtable members included the leaders from the Histradut and Manufacturers' Association; the ministers of finance, trade and industry, and economics; and ad hoc guests. By the time the heterodox measures were announced, this group had been active for close to nine months.[49] It is not surprising, therefore, that Yisrael Kessar, the Histradut leader, commended Peres on being one of the few prime ministers who had involved himself in economic matters, producing positive results.[50] Similarly, while some members of the Manufacturers' Association objected to the imposition of a price freeze, it was ultimately the association's leadership that carried the day in support of the freeze. In effect, Peres succeeded in creating "an economic coalition," that is, an alliance composed of business, labor, and certain government ministries in opposition, if necessary, to other political bodies.

Also cooperating with Peres was the U.S. administration, which was clearly worried over the course of the Israeli inflationary process. A committee, the Joint Economic and Development Group (JEDG) was formed under the aegis of the U.S. State Department and composed of senior State Department and Israeli finance ministry officials joined by some preeminent U.S. economists. It served two purposes. On the one hand, it kept the U.S. and especially Secretary Shultz, who took an active and personal interest in the matter, apprised of Israeli moves, especially those concerning Israeli promises to end the printing of money and to reduce budget deficits. This link, given the U.S.'s financial commitment in the form of two $750 million aid packages, would become important as the U.S. administration expressed its frustration with lack of improvement, thus strengthening Peres's hand against domestic recalcitrance.[51] Another of the JEDG's functions was to provide the prime minister with impartial analysis of the developments in the Israeli bureaucracy.

The heterodox plan itself was devised by a small of group of officials and academics working in secret. The group led by Emmanuel Sharon, the director of the ministry of finance, included Amnon Neubach, the prime minister's economic advisor; Mordechai Frenkel, head of the research department at the Bank of Israel; and two outside economists, Eitan Berglas and Michael Bruno, the future governor of the Bank of Israel. Although responsible to the prime minister and the minister of finance, the group operated with great discretion and was insulated from other societal and political pressures. Even the Bank of Israel, one of the state's most important institutions, had to be kept in the dark because of its governor's (Moshe Mandelbaum) potential political liability resulting from the investigation into his role in the 1983 Bank Shares scandal.[52] Once the plan was put into effect, this group remained in charge of monitoring its performance. For the most part, the prime minister did not interfere with the workings of the group except when he lowered the recommendation on the extent of the devaluation.

To help ensure the plan's implementation, the economic team proposed the invocation of emergency legislation. Such legislation enabled the government, if necessary, to annul collective wage agreements and circumvent some restrictions such as the requirement to notify an employee of his dismissal 90 days prior to taking the action. As such, the emergency legislation was anathema to the labor movement and its leadership. Nonetheless, it was designed to force the Histradut to negotiate with the Manufacturers' Association. In fact, it was an ace the team and Peres had dealt themselves to use as a bargaining chip. They were quite willing to abandon it—as they ultimately did—in exchange for concessions.[53] The emergency legislation also hastened the process of ratification in the Knesset, where the finance committee alone was capable of delaying the package indefinitely—as it had done so many times in the past.

Despite the Histradut's dislike for emergency measures, its leadership could not fault Peres for being reckless. In the past, he had been mindful of their needs, making sure that government initiatives did not conflict with their timetables and elections. In May 1985, for instance, he had waited until after the conclusion of Histradut elections, in which Kessar had emerged victorious, before initiating a new round of government cutbacks and belt-tightening policies. The whole heterodox plan was delayed by the Histradut elections, primarily because Peres did not want to force Kessar into opposing his economic plans. Peres expected to gain from both Kessar's indebtedness and his increased majority within the union.

The emergency legislation was not the only negotiable aspect of the plan. The price freeze and the 3 percent cut in the public-sector workforce were not necessary to the program's success. In this respect the plan was overdetermined. The price controls were instituted to gain credibility and support among the population at large.[54] These controls enforced the notion that sacrifices were being made at all levels of society and not only by labor.

In the final analysis, to establish credibility a government needs to put its own house in order by cutting expenditures and, ultimately, by holding the line against the parochial demands of interest groups. In this regard, by distributing the burden equally, the wage-price freeze foreshadowed and prevented some of the opposition to the plan. More importantly, the wage-price freeze was an attempt at short-circuiting the unemployment issue, since while a wage-price freeze does not necessarily eliminate "the credibility dilemma—for controls have to ultimately be lifted—it does give the governments more time to demonstrate that they have made fundamental changes in policy."[55] In this case, as people sensed that prices were not increasing—an awareness helped not only by an exchange rate that demonstrably did not budge from day to day but also by a new practice of publishing the consumer price index twice a week—the government earned its breathing space.

In a significant step that helped improve the credibility of the monetary institutions, the Bank of Israel was prohibited from making loans to the government. Thus, by assuming some control over the money supply, both the public and creditors were assured of the limits to government borrowing.[56]

Implementation

The successful implementation of the measures, however well prepared they may have been, still depended on the reactions of the coalition, the Histradut, and the general public.

The National Unity coalition, although devoid of the traditional fringe party interests, was far from being harmonious. In the first place, the evolution of hyperinflation had occurred during Likud's watch—a fact underscored not only by Labor ministers, but also by the Histradut leader Yisrael Kessar and the head of the manufacturers' organization.[57] In its defense, the Likud held on to its consumption-oriented "populist" positions. On the eve of the measures, Shamir publicly stated that the Likud ministers would oppose any attempt to lower wages and fire workers,[58] a position underscored by others in his party.

The cabinet meeting of June 30/July 1, 1985, which lasted more than 24 hours, was an endurance test where ministers were confronted with a stark choice: continuation of the status quo or the heterodox plan—the only suggested alternative.[59] Peres, on at least three occasions when the negotiations got bogged down, threatened to resign if the stabilization package was not approved. While Levy, Shamir's principal opponent and deputy prime minister, led the charge against the measures, Shamir remained quiet during the deliberations and failed to deliver Peres the needed assistance. In the final vote, seven Likud ministers voted against the measures and only three, Shamir, Haim Corfu, and Yitzhak Moda'i, who along with Peres had been pushing the plan forward, voted in the affirmative. Given the shakiness of the coalition and Peres's clear willingness to break the agreement over this issue, Shamir had to make sure there was minimum support from his party.[60] By contrast, Peres delivered all his ministers, even though many were voting against their best judgment. The sole exception was Rabin who, unhappy about defense cuts, abstained.[61]

As recriminations not only against Labor and Peres but also against one of their own, Moda'i, were amply aired in public and at party meetings, it became quite clear that the Likud intended to sit on the fence on this issue. Some, like Levy and Moshe Arens, minister without portfolio, claimed that Moda'i and Peres had failed to inform them and Shamir of the contents of the package until the cabinet meeting. Despite Moda'i's protestations to the contrary, Shamir also claimed that he was only vaguely aware of some of its general principles and expressed his belief, along with Arens, that the plan (for which he had voted) presented many dangers and would not solve Israel's economic problems. Likud, he argued, had to prepare a plan of its own in the event that this one collapsed.[62]

With less-than-total Likud support for the package, it was left to Peres and to a lesser extent the Labor Party to carry the burden. Even though the measures were approved by the Knesset, on a 70 to 19 party vote with many abstentions and absences (including Levy, who failed to show up), the Labor Party found itself on the defensive. The delicate nature of inner cabinet relations was evident in Shamir's inability (and unwillingness) to curtail Levy's criticism of Peres. Levy, on a populist spree, went around the country claiming that he had an alternative, one that was never elucidated, and that Peres had ignored his advice.[63]

If the Likud clearly resisted the measures, the Labor Party too harbored its doubts and divisions. The most important concern for Labor was the measures' potential impact on wage rates and the country's standard of living. Its leadership found itself in a difficult predicament: it was caught, on the one hand, between the Histradut and its head, Kessar, himself a Labor member of the Knesset, and his allies who formed the "social lobby" within the Labor Party, and, on the other, the dovish middle-class voters of Ashkenazi origin who favored the package. The adverse impact on wages and especially the use of emergency measures in their implementation pitted Kessar against the other wing of his own party.[64] In the emergency measures, Kessar and his Histradut membership saw an attempt to tamper with the right of workers to negotiate binding agreements with employers.

The Histradut's immediate reaction to the measures was to call for a one-day general strike, which brought the country to a complete standstill on July 2, 1985. The Histradut promised further action. Kessar's debt to and admiration for Peres notwithstanding, he was forced to go along with a strike because of the precedent created by the emergency legislation and pressure from the rank-and-file and radical union members. The latter, in general, were disappointed with the moderate tone adopted by Kessar in his criticisms of the reform package. This was especially true of the "Big Thirteen," the most radical of the workers' committees, which promised further industrial action unless the negotiations undertaken by Kessar with Peres did not quickly produce satisfactory results.[65]

Initially, the general strike seemed to have achieved some results. Peres, in what appeared to be his first public concession, temporarily delayed the implementation of some of the stabilization measures' components, including the freeze on wages, dismissal of workers and the cutting of the cost-of-living adjustments. More importantly, he promised not to invoke the emergency rules if the Histradut and representatives from the employers' organization were to come up with a satisfactory wage agreement. With the two-week deadline for devising a voluntary agreement, negotiations with the manufacturers were concluded to the satisfaction of the economic team that was monitoring them closely. In some ways, forcing employers and labor to face each other separately was a correct tactic: both parties had had years of experience in negotiations and felt quite comfortable with each other. The emergency measures, whether intended as a bluff or as a real threat, proved to be a potent bargaining weapon.

Peres also promised to initiate a new dialogue with the Histradut regarding his request that public employment be trimmed by 3 percent and that public-sector employees also take a 3 percent cut. By the end of July, talks with the Histradut on this issue had collapsed and Peres threatened to unilaterally dismiss 6 percent of the public workforce. In the end, the government and the Histradut reached a compromise whereby the government promised to carry out the dismissals according to collective bargaining procedures, thereby electing not to use the discretionary power obtained through the invocation of emergency measures. The 3 percent wage cut was also abandoned. The Histradut, on its part, agreed to reduce the duration of the dismissal procedures.

While the Histradut negotiations were important to start the process, Peres and Moda'i also made sure to signal that they were prepared to hold the line whenever necessary. They made this point clear by adopting an uncompromising attitude toward workers at ATA who had undertaken a visible campaign for state intervention to save their jobs in one of the largest Israeli textile firms, which had been forced into bankruptcy by bad management. Similarly, the government stood firm on new price increases. Since price increases were only allowed for new products, manufacturers tried to "circumvent price controls by introducing 'new' products only marginally different from current ones but at higher prices . . . the Ministry of Industry and Trade . . . stood firm by honoring only a few requests for such price increases."[66]

The most important steps taken by the government in establishing credibility were those aimed at reducing the budget deficit. As shown earlier, the government was successful in reducing the budget deficit to zero percent of GDP within a year. In 1986 alone, defense expenditures were cut by 8 percent and the share of defense expenditure as a percentage of GNP was reduced from 14 or 15 percent to 12 percent in 1986.[67] Given the sensitivity of defense cuts, the willingness of the government to go ahead with them helped establish the seriousness of its intentions and credibility of the measures. Despite the apparent success in reducing the defense burden,[68] considerable difficulties were encountered: it would, for instance, take another two years for the Lavi project, an Israeli-made fighter aircraft, a favorite of the defense establishment and some Likud politicians such as Arens, to be dismantled. These tasks fell on Peres's shoulders. Even before the promulgation of the heterodox package, finance minister Moda'i had made it clear that the only person who could ensure that the budget cuts were actually made was Peres, since the government's fate rested in his hands.[69]

Once in effect, the plan was continuously monitored by a "Follow-up Committee" composed mostly of those advisors who were on the original economic team. This committee identified bottlenecks in advance and warned the two concerned ministers of future problems and the need to synchronize processes. In addition, the government, through the prime minister's office, launched a sophisticated press campaign designed to educate the public on the plan and inviting it to help monitor prices. "Maximum prices were established for 40 percent of all goods and services, and the list of prices was distributed free so the public could compare prices in the market to the list."[70] Public participation was crucial since only 54 people were involved in monitoring prices.

In August, the Bank of Israel announced that as of January 1, 1986, it would be introducing a new currency. This was not an action initiated by the economic team in charge of the stabilization plan, but by the bank, which was still under the control of Mandelbaum. The team had considered introducing a new currency with the July plan but then had abandoned the idea because it was decided that it would not necessarily inspire any new confidence, given that the currency had recently been altered by the Begin government. In addition, the team had also been misinformed by Mandelbaum regarding the existence of a reserve currency. Although the introduction of a new currency was initially viewed with alarm by the economic team, its official appearance in January was sufficiently distant to allow the stabilization plan time to prove its prowess. Thus, despite the fact that it was an glaring example of a breakdown in bureaucratic cooperation, in the long run, it even proved to be helpful.[71]

Finally, the heterodox package of July 1985 did not come as a shock to the Israeli public. Discussions regarding the details of the program had leaked to the public even before the specifics had been finalized, and the government felt constrained by all the disclosures in the press. A second reason why the public was not surprised by the announcement was because of the obvious failure of the gradual approach. By June 1985, all the package deals had to show for themselves was disillusionment. Clearly, Peres derived some of his strength and resiliency from this fact.[72] Within a month of the July measures, opinion polls showed a marked decline in the public's opposition to the program.[73] The stock market soared on the day following the announcement of the measures.

State Strength and Stabilization Measures

A crucial factor for the July 1985 heterodox plan was the relative strength of the state. The Israeli state has repeatedly demonstrated its ability to mobilize its population to confront its external dangers and simultaneously construct a modern welfare state. While Israel has always relied on external sources of funding to alleviate the defense burden, the Israelis remain the most taxed people in the world. "In 1986, 79.3 percent of those employed were salaried, and that figure has been growing. More than 75 percent of the working population tend to be in a dependent financial situation within relatively easy grasp of the tax authorities."[74] Additionally, as Halevi and Baruh also demonstrate, since the early years, state authorities have gradually liberalized the foreign trade regime in opposition to private sector and Histradut wishes.[75]

Migdal argues that the strength of the Israeli state is the direct result of the state-building process and activities of state elites during the pre-independence period. He argues that state elites face three potential threats: (1) from the remnants of the old regime (or old rulemakers), (2) from potential rulemakers (internal rivals) and (3) from potential statebreakers (neighboring states and world powers).[76] The absence of an ancien regime with which new elites had to contend, the ability with which Ben-Gurion and the Labor Zionists successfully forestalled competing ideological groups from shaping the institutions of the new state and, finally, the ability of these same leaders to turn the threat from neighboring states into an occasion to mobilize resources and consolidate institutions helped fashion a strong Israeli state. The Histradut, from its inception, was more of a political organization than a trade union[77] and, therefore, its dominant role in society is not an accident. Its leadership is closely knit with the state elite—especially with the Labor Party. In 1985, despite the initial friction with the government, the union's overwhelming share of the representation simplified the negotiations and helped rein in centrifugal societal forces that are often unleashed by such drastic changes.

Ironically, Migdal also points out that this same strong state capable of fashioning the new rules has failed in one important respect: ability to reformulate and change existing rules.[78] This is nowhere more evident than in the electoral system, which has tended to favor fringe and especially religious parties. They, by virtue of their contribution to the minimum winning coalitions governing Israel, have impeded many reforms, including, of course, electoral ones. This inability to effect changes in the rules has clearly eroded some of the state's strength and its control of socioeconomic and political events. The spiraling inflation, the state's acquiescence to PATAM type of accounts and the bank shares scandal, which occurred under the very eyes of the minister of finance and the governor of the Bank of Israel, are all examples of this erosion.

In part, the relative decline in state strength can also be ascribed to the Likud's accession to power in 1977. Historically, the Likud had been more focused on ideological than on organizational approaches.[79] Consequently, it was ill prepared to govern and was also interested in undermining the very institutions created by its arch-rival, Labor, which were precisely the ones that injected the state apparatus with the necessary strength. Chief among the targets was the Histradut.[80] In addition, the Likud, upon assuming power, engineered a switch in state priorities away from investment-oriented goals towards more emphasis on "consumption" and, hence, staked a "populist" position in Israeli politics.[81]

What the National Unity government achieved, even if in appearance only, was to restore elite unity at the state level. As such, it relayed a powerful message to society regarding state intentions and allowed for state elites to exploit the state's inherent strength. In fact, Peres's accomplishment in 1985 was to resurrect those powers of the state that only Labor, for organizational and ideological reasons, could mobilize. Ultimately, just as he was propelled by the looming crisis—a crisis made potentially worse by the degree to which the Israeli economy is open to the international market—he successfully used the crisis as the glue that bound the different parts of the state together. This also allowed for the smooth functioning of interagency cooperation. For instance, crucial to the success of the 1985 stabilization measures was the ministry of trade and industry, within whose domain the price control mechanisms resided. Despite the fact that its head, Ariel Sharon, vigorously opposed the stabilization plan and voted against it, the ministry apparently cooperated efficiently and effectively with the rest of the economic team to implement the price control mechanism.

Finally, the credibility of the domestically generated analyses of the crisis enhanced the political elite's abilities. As Bruno demonstrates, this was primarily the result of the existence of a significant and well-trained group of Israeli economists with experience in policy formation and critique and hence with considerable impact on government decision-making.[82] The existence of such assets strengthened the hand of political elites, especially when external pressure for reform was imminent.

POSTSCRIPT

The Israeli program, which in 1985, 1986, and 1987 was heralded as an example to all others, eventually ran out of steam in 1988. By 1989, inflation had picked up again, although not at the same hyperinflationary level, and the growth rate, which in 1987 had surpassed the 5 percent mark, had declined to a trickle. More importantly, by 1989 the unemployment rate climbed to over 9 percent. In January 1989, the government had to reinstitute another harsh stabilization plan. Again, it was Shimon Peres who was given the charge of implementing, except this time he was no longer the prime minister, but the minister of finance.

Some of the problems experienced by Israel starting in 1988 were none other than the delayed reaction to the 1985 stabilization measures. The plan had been based on four anchors: budget cuts, price and wage freezes, an exchange-rate freeze, and monetary aggregates. Of the four, the monetary one became the linchpin to which the other three in turn were fastened. Budgetary improvements, especially if they take the form of increased taxes, require time to become effective, just as the price, wage, and exchange-rate freezes take time to bring about results. In the meantime, credibility was assured by a contraction in monetary aggregates. Bank credits were drastically reduced, forcing real interest rates to higher levels. The private sector, as well as some of the large Histradut enterprises like Koor felt the brunt of the increased interest rates. Many firms that continued to operate in the red during 1985 and 1986—either because of bookkeeping errors or the assumption that the situation would improve—finally started to make their adjustments in 1987 when layoffs began. Business was hurt by both the lack of money and the 4-4-3.5 percent arrangement negotiated with the Histradut, which did not result in the planned retrenchment in real wages. In the end, the Israeli stabilization plan did result in increased unemployment, but it was a delayed reaction.

The economic team and the political leadership were to some extent victims of their own success. They were unprepared for the speed with which inflation would come down. In fact, most of their preparations indicated that they expected inflation to rage on for a while. The 1985 program was a solution to an immediate problem: hyperinflation and the related possibility of an economic collapse. It did not address some of the major fundamental issues confronting the Israeli economy. In some respects, some of these are here to stay as long as the quasi-state of war continues to exist. In addition to the defense burden, the Palestinian *intifada* has added another set of costs to the economy—ranging from increased direct military expenditures to reduced tourism revenues.

On the other hand, the government- or Histradut-related enterprises, with their bloated budgets and inefficient practices, were not brought under control by the 1985 program. By 1989 their economic condition had deteriorated to such an extent that it threatened the integrity of the public and quasi-public sector that the Histradut enterprises represented. Thus, the government, and specifically the Labor wing of the coalition, was confronted with the difficult decision of whether to save these enterprises. For the Labor Party, unable to emerge victorious from the 1988 elections, this crisis of the public sector symbolized the potential undoing of the most significant part of its already diminished power base, a fact that also explains Peres's agreement to take over the finance ministry and thus assume a junior role in a new Likud-Labor coalition.

The 1985 program's achievements, somewhat indebted to the convergence of favorable external events, should not be taken for granted. As finance minister Moda'i would admit later, during the 1984 coalition negotiations the government was provided with a blueprint for the heterodox measures but concluded that it was politically too weak to implement them.[83] By July 1985 the task facing Peres was more than simply implementing measures but rather the restoration of state authority.

For Peres the 1985 program was both a significant accomplishment and a failure. Having also skillfully extricated the country from Lebanon, he was unable to translate these successes into an electoral mandate in the 1988 elections or break up the coalition agreement before the rotation went into effect. Here his skills abandoned him. It was the Likud that really benefitted from Peres's exploits. When the rotation agreement was implemented, Peres assumed the foreign ministry while Shamir became prime minister. As Peres increasingly turned his attention to foreign affairs, where he competed with Shamir, the economy was deprived of the resources of a forceful and attentive leadership.

NOTES

1. I would like to thank Lehigh University for providing me with a Faculty Research Grant and the Philip and Muriel Berman Center for Jewish Studies and the Center for International Studies for the additional support which allowed me to conduct the necessary interviews and research in Israel.
2. Joan M. Nelson, "Introduction: The Politics of Economic Adjustment in Developing Nations," in *Economic Crisis and Policy Choice: The Politics of Adjustment in the Third World*, ed. Joan M. Nelson (Princeton: Princeton University Press, 1990), 13.
3. In fact, one can argue that preventive measures in the absence of crisis conditions can easily backfire for a government attempting to implement them. Such was the case of Turkey in 1970 when the Demirel government put together a plan that anticipated shortfalls in foreign exchange reserves and government revenue. It cost the government dearly in electoral support. See Henri J. Barkey, "State Autonomy and the Crisis of Import Substitution," *Comparative Political Studies* 22, no. 3 (October 1989).
4. Nelson, "Introduction: The Politics of Economic Adjustment in Developing Nations," 13.

5. Nelson, "Introduction: The Politics of Economic Adjustment in Developing Nations," 24-25.
6. Of these, an often overlooked factor is the presence of competent and experienced local experts. These are crucial because, unlike external experts, such as IMF-sponsored ones, their analyses command a certain degree of credibility and legitimacy with national decision-makers.
7. Stephan Haggard, "The Politics of Adjustment: Lessons from the IMF's Extended Fund Facility," in *The Politics of International Debt,* ed. Miles Kahler (Ithaca: Cornell University Press, 1986), 184.
8. Joel S. Migdal, *Strong State and Weak Societies: State-Society Relations and State Capabilities in the Third World* (Princeton: Princeton University Press, 1988), 18-19.
9. Societal opposition generated toward stabilization measures, especially in democratic societies, has led many to the conclusion that only authoritarian states can marshall the requisite will and capacities to implement them.
10. Joel S. Migdal, "The Crystallization of the State and the Struggles over Rulemaking: Israel in a Comparative Perspective," in *The Israeli State and Society: Boundaries and Frontiers,* ed. Baruch Kimmerling (Albany: State University of New York Press, 1989), 8.
11. Joan M. Nelson, "The Political Economy of Stabilization: Commitment, Capacity and Public Response," *World Development* 12, no. 10 (1984), 991.
12. Michael Bruno, "External Shocks and Domestic Response: Macroeconomic Performance, 1965-1982," in *The Israeli Economy: Maturing through Crises,* ed. Yoram Ben Porath (Cambridge, MA: Harvard University Press, 1986), 276-277.
13. Michael Bruno and Stanley Fischer, "The Inflationary Process: Shocks and Accommodation," in *The Israeli Economy: Maturing through Crises.*
14. Nissan Liviatan and Sylvia Piterman, "Accelerating Inflation and Balance of Payments Crises, 1973-1984," in *The Israeli Economy: Maturing through Crises.*
15. Bank of Israel, *Annual Report 1985* (Jerusalem: Bank of Israel, 1986), 67.
16. Liviatan and Piterman, "Accelerating Inflation," 333.
17. Liviatan and Piterman, "Accelerating Inflation," 336.
18. Michael Bruno, "Sharp Disinflation Strategy: Israel 1985," *Economic Policy* (April 2, 1986), pp. 379-402.
19. Fischer argues that the existence of indexation mechanisms can help stabilization attempts by providing an obvious avenue for bargaining for changes. He points to the fact that often workers were asked to forego cost-of-living adjustments as part of stabilization attempts. Stanley Fischer, "Inflation and Indexation: Israel," in *Inflation and Indexation: Argentina, Brazil, and Israel,* ed. John Williamson (Washington DC: Institute for International Economics, 1985).
20. Bruno and Fischer, "The Inflationary Process: Shocks and Accommodation," 349.
21. Michael Bruno, "Sharp Disinflation Strategy: Israel 1985."

22. Bruno and Fischer, "The Inflationary Process: Shocks and Accommodation," 363.
23. Bank of Israel, *Annual Report 1980* (Jerusalem: Bank of Israel, 1981), 78, 56.
24. Bruno and Fischer, "The Inflationary Process: Shocks and Accommodation," 364-65.
25. Aridor would eventually go one step further an argue for the dollarization of the economy. The backlash against his proposal was such that he resigned the same day he proposed it.
26. Haim Barkai, "Reflections on the Economic Cost of the Lebanon War," *Jerusalem Quarterly* 37 (Winter 1986), 95-106.
27. Fischer, "Inflation and Indexation: Israel," 79.
28. Bank of Israel, *Annual Report 1985* (Jerusalem: Bank of Israel, 1986), 1.
29. Bank of Israel, *Annual Report 1985,* 4.
30. Mario Blejer and Nissan Liviatan, "Fighting Hyperinflation: Stabilization Strategies in Argentina and Israel, 1985-86," *IMF Staff Papers* 34 (September 1987), 410.
31. Thomas J. Sargent, *Rational Expectations and Inflation* (New York: Harper and Row, 1986), 40-47.
32. Michael Bruno, "Sharp Disinflation Strategy: Israel 1985," 390.
33. The announced breakdown of the cuts was as follows: $400 million in cuts in subsidies, $350-400 million in tax increases and the remaining $750 million in increased charges for government services and reduced social allowances. Only $250 million would come from cuts in the ministries themselves. *Jerusalem Post,* July 3, 1985.
34. With the adjustments made to the shekel a few days earlier, the actual devaluation amounted to almost 25 percent, Michael Bruno and Sylvia Piterman, "Israel's Stabilization: A Two Year Review," in *Inflation Stabilization: The Experience of Israel, Argentina, Brazil, Bolivia and Mexico,* ed. Michael Bruno et al. (Cambridge, MA: MIT Press, 1988), 7.
35. A new cost-of-living agreement would go into effect in October which provided for wage increases to amount to no more than 80 percent of the previous month's inflation (this provision was unchanged) and to be paid when prices went up by 4 percent or after a three-month period, whichever came sooner.
36. Haim Barkai, "Israel's Attempt at Economic Stabilization," *Jerusalem Quarterly* 43, (Summer 1987), p. 10.
37. Barkai, "Israel's Attempt at Economic Stabilization," 11.
38. Barkai, "Israel's Attempt at Economic Stabilization," 13.
39. Bruno and Piterman, "Israel's Stabilization: A Two Year Review," 30. This decline in the shekel's value, on the other hand, had its adverse effects. It contributed to a higher rise in the consumer price index (CPI). As Bruno and Piterman argue, had the August 1986 repegging of the shekel from the dollar to a five-currency basket occurred earlier, the CPI would have increased by only 13 percent rather than the actual 20 percent.

40. Included in this were obligations the Begin government had undertaken during the relocation of military installations at the time of the Israeli-Egyptian peace treaty in 1979. Although offered by the U.S. at discretionary interest rates, Begin, in a burst of national pride, refused and instead borrowed the money at current and fluctuating rates. The terms of this agreement were finally renegotiated in the summer of 1988.
41. Bank of Israel, *Annual Report 1987* (Jerusalem: Bank of Israel, 1988), 2.
42. Stanley Ficher, "The Israeli Stabilization Program, 1985-86," *AEA Papers and Proceedings* (May 1986), 278.
43. Eitan Berglas, "Defense and the Economy," in *The Israeli Economy: Maturing through Crises.*
44. The Histradut, a multifaceted organization, also runs the country's largest health care system and is engaged in the manufacturing sector through its numerous directly owned corporations.
45. Michael Shalev, "The Political Economy of Labor-Party Dominance and Decline in Israel," in *Democratic Oddities: One Party Dominance in Comparative Perspective,* ed. T. J. Pempel (Ithaca: Cornell University Press, 1988), 122. The recession was induced by the government's determined attempt at reducing the then high inflation rate of 10 percent which, in turn, edged up the unemployment rate to 9 percent. Fischer, "Inflation and Indexation: Israel," 62.
46. Fischer, "Inflation and Indexation: Israel," 78.
47. The coalition controlled 96 out of 120 seats in the Knesset. Although other parties also joined the coalition government, the main players were the Likud and Labor parties.
48. This was also viewed as the price to pay for obtaining the Histradut's collaboration. See Bruno and Piterman, 8. Yet the Histradut would have probably gone along with an earlier but smaller increase, an action which by reducing the population's consumption expectations, would have forced the economy to make adjustments earlier.
49. Although this group was to be composed of three representatives from each of the three groups, it often included many more. Sometimes open to the press, its efficacy has been doubted by some of its participants.
50. *Jerusalem Post,* June 28, 1985. Peres, who was not renowned for his economic background, made a committed effort to improve his knowledge in this regard. As a result, by the time the new measures were being implemented, he was widely acclaimed as the first prime minister since Levy Eshkol in the 1960s to really understand economics.
51. A senior U.S. delegation that had visited Israel in early June to discuss economic cooperation also pressed the government to adopt a recently published IMF report calling for the end of indexation, sharp budget cuts, devaluation, and erosion of real wages. *Jerusalem Post,* May 31, 1985.
52. He would not resign because doing so would have diminished his credibility in the eyes of the public and the investigating Beiski Commission. Mandelbaum did not believe in the plan, the new budget figures, or the capacity to reduce the rate of inflation. This was made evident by his

insistence on the high real interest rates and in the new currency announced in August, where the size of the new denominations made it clear that the bank expected inflation to rage on unabated.

53. Some thought that the emergency legislation was actually a bluff devised by the government and that Peres could have never used it. There were clear disagreements over the constitutionality of this move; not only did the Histradut object on these grounds but even the attorney general thought that wartime measures could not be applied to a peacetime crisis. On the other hand, there was considerable concern regarding the impact of prolonged hyperinflation on a society's democratic institutions.
54. Ironically, the price controls were not part of the original draft but were introduced by the minister of finance, Moda'i, an unlikely originator given his Liberal Party and free enterprise background. See Emmanuel Sharon, "Israel's Stabilization Program: Lessons in Political Economy," paper presented at a conference on hyperinflation at Instituto Fernand Braudel de Economia Mundial, Sao Paolo, Brazil (August 28-31, 1989), 6.
55. Rudiger Dornbusch and Stanley Fischer, "Stopping Hyperinflations: Past and Present," *Weltwirtschaftliches Archiv* (January 1986), 44.
56. The initiative for this reform came from within the central bank and not from the economic team. Nonetheless, the team would have insisted on this reform had the bank not acted on time.
57. *Jerusalem Post,* June 28, 1985.
58. *Haaretz,* July 1, 1985.
59. Those ministers who dozed off found, upon waking up, that their budgets had been cut.
60. In fact, this is what some of Shamir's opponents within the party probably wanted, since a coalition breakdown would have led to a showdown in the party over leadership. Haim Corfu, known as the most loyal of Shamir's party members, went along only because his party chief wanted him to.
61. *Jerusalem Post,* July 3, 1985.
62. *Haaretz,* July 11, 1985.
63. Clearly challenging Peres's call for a reduction in the country's standard of living, Levy argued that there were more important issues than the economy's recovery—feeding children for instance. *Haaretz,* July 12, 1985. In the final analysis, it was left to Peres to figure out the means by which Levy could be reined in. Peres offered Levy an olive branch of sorts which allowed the latter to also save face.
64. *Jerusalem Post,* July 3, 1985.
65. *Jerusalem Post,* July 3, 1985. Some local committees, such as those of the port city of Ashdod, struck out on their own regardless of the national leadership's wishes.
66. *The Israel Economist,* December 1985. In general, relations with the private sector were easier, given that it had been demanding that the economy be de-linked and measures be taken. Peres, nonetheless, had made it clear that he would be unwilling to grant concessions to the business sector. At one

point, when confronted with private-sector demands and ultimatums, he was reported to have simply said, "Perhaps I am getting a little deaf."

67. Bank of Israel, *Annual Report 1986* (Jerusalem: Bank of Israel, 1987), 64.
68. Some charged that the defense cuts were somewhat illusory because the defense establishment had run down stocks and reduced training missions in an effort to reduce outlays.
69. *Jerusalem Post,* June 28, 1985.
70. Emmanuel Sharon, "Israel and the Success of the Shekel: The Key Years, 1984-1987," in *Inflation: Are We Next? Hyperinflation and Solutions in Argentina, Brazil and Israel,* ed. Pamela Falk (Boulder, CO: Lynne Rienner, 1990), 16.
71. An earlier introduction, such as in Argentina, would have not only complicated the measures but would have failed to protect the new shekel from the immediate and inevitable vagaries of the inflationary process. In Argentina, the austral was introduced with the old peso, indexed to the inflation rate, losing value daily against the new currency. Daniel Heymann, "The Austral Plan," *AEA Papers and Proceedings* (May 1987), 285.
72. Soon after the measures were announced he remarked, "I don't expect them [the public] to applaud, I know in their hearts they understand there is no choice." *Jerusalem Post,* July 7, 1985.
73. Bruno, "Sharp Disinflation Strategy: Israel 1985," 394.
74. Asher Arian, *Politics in Israel: The Second Generation* (Chatham, NJ: Chatham House, 1989), 47.
75. Nadav Halevi and Joseph Baruh, "Israel," in *Liberalizing Foreign Trade: The Experience of Israel and Yugoslavia,* ed. D. Papageorgiou, M. Michely and A. Choksi (Cambridge, MA: Basil Blackwell, 1991).
76. Migdal, "The Crystallization of the State and the Struggles over Rulemaking," 4-5.
77. Shalev, "The Political Economy of Labor-Party Dominance and Decline in Israel," 91-92.
78. Migdal, "The Crystallization of the State and the Struggles over Rulemaking," 25.
79. Myron J. Aronoff, "Israel under Labor and the Likud: The Role of Dominance Considered," in *Democratic Oddities: One Party Dominance in Comparative Perspective,* 264.
80. Yonatan Reshef, "Political Exchange in Israel: Histradut-State Relations," *Industrial Relations* 25, no. 3 (Fall 1986).
81. Richard Weisskoff, "The Political Economy of the Israeli Inflation," in *Inflation: Are We Next? Hyperinflation and Solutions in Argentina, Brazil and Israel,* 140.
82. Michael Bruno, "Economic Analysis and the Political Economy of Policy Formation," *European Economic Review* 34 (1990), 281.
83. *Jerusalem Post,* July 4, 1985.

Part II

Economic Reform and the Politics of Controlled Change

4

Survival Strategies vs. Democratic Bargains: The Politics of Economic Reform in Contemporary Egypt[1]

Daniel Brumberg

INTRODUCTION

> Let our IMF accord be a prologue to candor at the polls. The peoples of the world have learned the bitter truth that there can be no economic reform without political reform.[2]

In the above statement, issued one month before parliamentary elections, an Egyptian economist challenged the regime to galvanize support for economic reforms through an open poll. But instead of heeding this advice, the regime enacted a new election law that provided few safeguards for a free election. After the November 1990 poll, which all but one opposition party boycotted, the regime adopted economic reforms that imposed hardships on the population.

This development may represent a watershed. From 1974 to 1989 Egypt's leaders avoided promoting substantive economic reforms, whether by authoritarian or democratic means. By 1990, however, Cairo appeared to be moving towards a more exclusionary system.

Not long ago, both Marxist and conservative scholars were predicting this type of development, suggesting that authoritarianism offers an effective way to foster accumulation and savings. Yet recent events in Eastern Europe and the Third World suggest that a "democratic bargain" may provide a better alternative to "authoritarian accumulation." This "bargain" entails an exchange by which regimes offer a degree of substantive—if limited—democratic reforms in return for popular support or acquiescence to painful economic reforms.

Democratic bargains, I argue, are secured through electoral procedures and institutional arrangements that allow reformists to mobilize "winners" of reform and marginalize "losers." However, because the number of potential losers in command economies have often outnumbered the potential winners, the forging of such bargains has often proved difficult.

This is particularly true in populist authoritarian states. In these states ruling elites have tied their fates to groups that have an interest in retaining statist economic programs. Unwilling to antagonize these groups, reformers have pursued a "survival strategy" by which they promote limited economic changes without permitting substantive democratization.

This chapter examines the genesis and transformation of "survival strategies" in Egypt. I argue that neither Sadat nor Mubarak have been able to totally dismantle the legacy of established populist authoritarianism. Sadat, far from being an agent of a reemerging bourgeois class, tried to recast many of the social, political and ideological structures of Nasser's state in an effort to retain, at least in part, its populist orientation.

Towards this end Sadat tried to widen his popular support by expanding higher education and by retaining public-sector industries. He also promoted limited economic reforms to satisfy middle-class demand for consumer goods. By 1977 this dualistic approach to reform compelled Sadat to initiate stabilization measures. He failed, however, to bolster these steps by forging a democratic bargain. Instead, he repressed groups that would have made natural supporters of economic liberalization.

In contrast, Mubarak sought a tacit understanding with opposition groups regarding the bounds of economic reform. Yet while "pluralist accommodation" provided for a degree of openness and a relatively more productive orientation, it did not advance substantive economic reform. In fact, it created a stalemate between the regime and the opposition that limited the former's ability to address the structural causes of economic decline in Egypt.

This inertia was sustained by the growth of a quasi-rentier economy. But with the onset of the oil glut of the mid-eighties, revenues from oil, foreign remittances, and the Suez Canal fell as creditors pushed for reforms. Pressed, Cairo flirted with a more genuine democratic bargain. But resistance to reform in the ruling party, combined with the failure of the opposition parties to mobilize grass-roots support, undermined this effort. By 1990

Egypt appeared to be pursuing far-reaching economic reforms without securing a political base for them.

THE "AUTHORITARIAN" LOGIC OF ACCUMULATION?

During the seventies a consensus emerged in academia that the exigencies of economic development make Third World countries prone to authoritarianism. "Institution-building" theorists held that in the absence of cohesive civil institutions that can absorb popular demands, single-party states must impose order from above.[3] Marxist dependency theorists argued that the attempts by populist regimes to overcome the constraints of dependency via import substitution created new economic crises that obliged dominant groups to advance economic growth by authoritarian means.[4]

Although this pessimistic consensus held sway for more than a decade, subsequent studies showed that some democracies might provide a more sound *long-term* basis for economic liberalization than authoritarian regimes.[5] For example, Stephan Haggard and Robert Kaufman found that of "new democracies," all but one case in their sample had limited government spending.[6] Similarly, in her study of stabilization in Latin America, Karen Remmer concluded that to "the limited extent that regime differences are significant, the edge appears to be with democracies."[7]

From "Ruling Bargain" to "Democratic Bargain"

The most important explanation for this remarkable course of events lies in the failure of authoritarian regimes in Eastern Europe, Africa, and the Middle East to sustain the "ruling bargain" by which popular social groups obtained social welfare guarantees from the state in return for their political quiescence.[8]

To finance this authoritarian compact some regimes relied on oil rents while others depended on import-substituting industrialization (ISI) strategies, inefficient public-sector industries and bloated bureaucracies. But with the decline in oil revenues in the mid-eighties, the paralysis of command economies, and pressures from Western creditors, reformists were compelled to offer a new, "democratic bargain": in return for popular support or acquiescence to harsh economic reforms, they offered a measure of political openness and democratic reform.[9]

Such democratic bargains are neither purely voluntary nor coercive enterprises: they are secured through political mechanisms and processes that facilitate the mobilization of the winners in the economic reform contest and the marginalization of potential losers.[10]

Latin America's experience suggests that this process of strategic mobilization is affected through electoral and party reforms that favor dominant groups.[11] Similarly, the cases of Sri Lanka, Jamaica, and the Philippines indicate that democratic bargains obtain when executive institutions are united behind economic-reform programs and relatively removed from popular pressures.[12]

However, to be effective, democratic bargains must also secure a modicum of support for reforms from popular groups as well. They do this by abolishing corporatist controls over labor and by creating pacts between labor and government that at least temporarily limit the economic demands of popular groups.[13]

In sum, democratic bargains are forged through mechanisms that allow newly elected governments a means of reaping the political legitimacy and organized support derived from democracy while minimizing the constraints that competitive politics often entails.

Populist Authoritarianism and Dilemmas of Economic Reform

Reformists in all authoritarian regimes face daunting challenges in their quests to devise the institutions and coalitions required for democratic bargains. The most trying task is to mobilize supporters of reform—export-oriented manufacturers, independent artisans, skilled laborers, and so on—when the former are outnumbered or out-organized by potential losers—public sector bureaucrats and workers tied to import-substituting firms, students, white-collar state employees, and so on.[14]

Populist authoritarian systems are especially resistant to the challenge of economic reform. Three attributes of these regimes account for this resistance: (1) they are based on a broad, popular coalition that embraces, to various degrees, workers, peasants, professionals, and "national" capitalists; (2) they promote eclectic economic policies designed to satisfy as many members of the coalition as possible; and (3) they subordinate these social groups through corporatist and patron-client mechanisms that give the latter privileged access to policy-makers in return for their political quiescence.

The significance of the above three attributes is that together they link the state to powerful social groups that have an interest in maintaining the benefits that statist economies are said to deliver. The resulting *absence* of state autonomy makes it difficult for reformists to extract the state from the intricate web of commitments and alliances it has woven with such groups.

For if reformists try to impose changes, they will face resistance from former allies who have the means to mobilize against the state. If, on the other hand, reformists want to forge a democratic bargain, they must gain new allies; or where such allies are lacking, they must fashion links with traditional allies via corporatist institutions. But because such institutions have often promoted statist policies, they make poor arenas for negotiating democratic bargains.

Given that the transaction costs of moving towards greater authoritarianism or a democratic bargain are both very high, pro-reform elites often adopt the path of least resistance: instead of investing resources in the hazardous enterprise of political and economic engineering, they employ the institutions, coalitions, and ideologies *already available to them* to contain pressures for dramatic economic and political reforms. The result is an economic policy driven by the basic political instinct to survive.

"Survival Strategies" and the Legacy of Populist Authoritarianism

For our purposes we can distinguish between the economic and political aspects of survival strategies. In the political domain, survival strategies entail limited political "openings" designed to attract the support from professionals, intellectuals, and entrepreneurs without affording these groups sufficient political space in which to mobilize against the regime. To effect these openings reformists employ the party machines, such as Mexico's Institutionalized Revolutionary Party (PRI), to engineer electoral "victories."[15] They can also mobilize groups such as corporatist federations against advocates of democracy, a tactic that the leaders of Egypt and Mexico used in the seventies.[16]

The goal of the economic strategy is to effect a minimal degree of reform without harming the basic interests of popular groups. To achieve this, reformists delegate limited economic tasks to groups in the private sector or in corporatist institutions. Syria's leaders used this method in the eighties.[17] Similarly Egypt's leaders promoted compartmentalization by dividing economic activities between the state, private sector, and state-linked groups.[18] Where these approaches prove insufficient, leaders can adopt limited reform programs aimed at stabilizing the economy *without* punishing regime allies. "Heterodox shock" programs, such as Brazil's 1986 "Cruzado" package,[19] typify such approaches.

Such strategies can buy leaders some time. However, because they do not address structural inefficiencies in command economies, their success *depends on the provision of an external source of income,* from rents or from foreign aid in the form of grants or loans. When these sources diminish and economic crisis intensifies, strategies such as compartmentalization become, as Robert Bianchi points out, a poor "substitute for a 'new social contract.'"[20] At this critical juncture, when the state is obliged to withdraw the benefits that had financed the "ruling bargain," it must choose between escalating repression or forging a genuine democratic bargain.

Populist Authoritarian Legacies and Survival Strategies

In recent years Algeria has faced this moment of truth, while Egypt skirted it for decades. Why did Egypt sustain survival strategies while other states did not? Part of the answer lies in differences within populist authoritarian regimes. Two variables are critical: the relative heterogeneity of coalition membership and the relative malleability or heterogeneity of interest representation. We can conceptualize the relationship between these two variables and survival strategies as follows:

1. The more heterogeneous the founding populist coalition in terms of class and social group, the more room there will be for reformists to manipulate new social alliances to sustain survival strategies.
2. Conversely, where founding coalitions are narrowly based, it will be more difficult to break loose of the state and advance survival strategies.
3. The more mixed and flexible the interest-group system, the easier it is to combine limited political openings with corporatist controls. The more flexible, the easier it is to create channels through which approaches such as compartmentalization can be sustained.
4. Conversely, the more homogeneous and exclusive the interest-group system, the more difficult it is to mobilize support and the harder it is to affect and sustain economic delegation and compartmentalization.

With these four propositions in mind, we can place Arab states along a spectrum moving from more radical and homogeneous on the left to more traditional and heterogeneous on the right.[21]

On the left are Iraq, Syria, and Algeria, states in which the original populist coalition was narrowly based, excluded or minimized domestic and foreign bourgeoisies, and institutionalized representation in closed systems that provided limited autonomy. In these states there is little "space" in which to effect survival strategies. Moving to the right are Tunisia, Jordan, and Egypt. To varying degrees, they have a greater heritage of economic and political pluralism. *As long as external sources of income are available,* this

Radical ←——————————————→	**Traditional**
Iraq Syria Algeria Tunisia (Jordan?)	Egypt
Homogenous ruling coalitions and representation systems	Heterogenous ruling coalitions and representation systems

eclectic legacy can be manipulated by elites seeking to avoid the brutality of bureaucratic authoritarianism or the fragility of democratic bargains.

SURVIVAL STRATEGIES IN EGYPT

The Genesis of Survival Strategies in Nasser's Egypt

Nasser's populist authoritarian state emerged in its fullest form with the 1961 socialist measures. It was based on a broad coalition consisting of the rural middle class (the "peasantry"), labor, "productive" urban capitalists, intelligentsia, and the military. These groups were organized in a loose or "unruly" system that was distinguished by a mix of control mechanisms, including corporatist federations and informal patron-client networks.[22] These channels provided the arena through which the state pursued both economic growth and social equity.

In an effort to achieve these two competing goals, the regime promoted land reform, price controls, import-substitution, an expanded public sector bureaucracy and "productive" capitalists[23]—whose representatives were linked to Cairo via clientalist networks.[24] This eclectic economic program was enshrined in the 1962 "Charter of National Action" and its amorphous doctrine of "Arab Socialism," both of which advanced a corporatist notion of peacefully "melting" class differences through a "national alliance of working forces."[25]

Partly due to its competing social commitments, Nasser's regime constantly engaged in a process of economic improvisation that by its very nature produced neither growth nor equity. From 1959 to 1965, income distribution barely changed. As for "deepening," with the exception of engineering and metallurgy, there was no appreciable sign of industrial growth.[26]

The failure to engender industrial growth reflected the primacy of redistributive policies. The public sector served one primary purpose, employment. From 1960 to 1965 the work force grew some 22 percent. During this period the share in the labor force accounted for by industry and the service sector grew from 9.8 to 11.4 percent and 35 to 38 percent, respectively, whereas labor productivity began declining from 1962 on.[27] At the same time, total final consumption remained at 85 percent of GNP, gross domestic savings stagnated, exports fell, and imports increased.[28]

This familiar syndrome put a severe strain on Egypt's economy as early as 1962, when Nasser negotiated a standby agreement with the IMF in return for a pledge to reduce internal demand, lower government spending, and devalue the pound. However, Nasser did not honor the first two pledges, while he cushioned the effects of devaluation through subsidies. These policies helped create a foreign- exchange crisis in 1964, and the beginnings of economic retrenchment or *inkimash*.

We can discern in the policy of *inkimash* the contours of the survival strategies adopted by Nasser's successors. Unwilling to anger popular groups, Nasser refused to enact the stabilization program demanded by the IMF. Instead, he took limited steps to reduce consumption and expenditures. As the latter proved ineffective, he turned to foreign loans. From 1965 to 1970 Egypt's external debt grew by a factor of five. By the time of his death, Nasser had sown the seeds of Egypt's dependency.[29]

These measures were paralleled by cosmetic efforts at political liberalization. Following the 1968 student riots, Nasser announced his "March Program." The purpose of this program was to neutralize the regime's critics rather than advance democracy. Nasser tried to discredit the students by insisting that they were led by "counter-revolutionary elements," whose demands for political pluralism threatened the "gains" of the Revolution.[30] He then rigged the Arab Socialist Union's (ASU) elections. In the three succeeding years the economic system ground to a halt.

Sadat and the Political Economy of Survival

Sadat's economic policies were not, as some have argued, determined by the nefarious influence of a reemerging bourgeoisie, which pushed "post-populist" Egypt towards an alliance with the global capitalism.[31] Rather, they grew out of the political, social, and institutional constraints that were deeply embedded in Nasser's populist authoritarian state.

These constraints became apparent in the fall of 1973, when the Egyptian Trade Union Federation (ETUF), responding to a government proposal to sell public-sector shares, declared that it supported "any initiative from private local, Arab, or foreign capital," so long as such initiatives did not threaten the public sector.[32] In the ensuing years, this "dualistic approach" (see below), became the hallmark of Sadat's opening or *infitah*.[33]

In addition to labor, Sadat had to consider other organized players such as white-collar public-sector workers represented by professional syndicates, and managers of parastatals linked to the Chambers of Commerce and Industry—two organizations that had served as "agents of regulation" in the sixties.[34] These groups, together with labor, formed a formidable block by comparison to the more disparate advocates of reforms.

Faced with an array of organized "losers," and lacking a coherent "winners coalition," Sadat took a cue from Nasser by trying to promote limited economic and political reforms without provoking an upheaval that might threaten the regime's survival.

The Politics of Survival

On the political plane, Sadat sought to create a degree of reform that would pacify advocates of political liberalization without giving middle-class forces sufficient space in which to collectively undermine the ruling elite's hegemony. To achieve this he attempted to squeeze middle-class groups between the upper echelons of rural land-owners from above, and "popular" groups such as labor, peasants, and students from below.

This strategy became apparent during the 1974 "Listening Committee" hearings at which the regime trotted out an array of corporatist groups that promptly denounced the intelligentsia's call for democracy. To bolster its populist credentials, the regime expanded university enrollment from 161,000 in 1970 to 455,000 by 1975. This "democratization" of education was achieved by admitting nearly all high-school graduates, in contrast to Nasser's time, when the universities were the preserve of the middle class.[35]

As Sadat expanded his "popular base" from below, he forged an alliance with the big landowners from above. The latter were galvanized during the 1971 "Corrective Revolution" purge of the ASU and the 1976 parliamentary election.[36] With their power sanctified by "elections," Sadat's allies enacted a series of restraining laws that the regime subsequently used (and expanded upon) whenever it held its opponents responsible for violating the bounds of "acceptable" dissent.

Sadat defended these repressive laws by invoking the corporatist themes of Nasser's "Arab Socialism." In his 1974 *October Working Paper*,[37] and in other statements, he argued that by placing limits on democracy, he would protect the values of "peaceful" social change that had defined the Revolution.

The Economics of Survival

Just as Sadat had exploited Nasser's ideologies and social alliances to impose controls on democratic reform, so he used these structures to forge an experiment in limited economic reforms. These reforms were designed to respond to the "objective" push for economic reforms without destroying Nasser's populist legacy.

Sadat's outlined this "dualistic" policy in his 1974 *October Paper.* While he pledged that the public sector would remain predominant, he noted that even in Nasser's state, productive capitalists had a role. The *Charter of National Action,* he observed, had stated that "foreign aid is a duty for developing countries," so long as it was provided unconditionally. Thus, Sadat argued, an opening to foreign capital would *realize* Nasser's vision, while the "fears" of those who "alleged that we want to . . . go back on our socialism" were baseless.[38]

This foundation for this dualistic approach was Law 43, passed in June 1974. The law was designed to promote both import substitution of capital goods as well as Egyptian exports. Foreign firms were invited to invest in the private sector, in which case they could have a majority interest, or to invest in public-sector firms, providing the latter retained majority share of equity. Yet public-sector firms participating in joint ventures benefitted from many conditions that applied to the private sector: they were not subject to the labor laws, profit sharing schemes, or worker representation on "management boards."[39]

As a further incentive to foreign investment, Law 43 created free zones, which were not subject to Egyptian taxes, and in-country projects, which obtained similar advantages. However, these firms were only allowed, at least initially, to use their own foreign-exchange holdings to repatriate earnings—a provision that discouraged investments.

The other innovation that played a key part in *infitah* was the "own-exchange" system, introduced in June 1974. Its purpose was to encourage the importation of production inputs for the private sector by permitting importers to obtain foreign exchange without converting it in Egyptian banks. It was assumed that importers would obtain foreign currency at prices higher than the official rate by buying it from expatriate Egyptians workers, whose oil-boom savings rose from $250 million in 1974 to $1.7 billion by 1976.[40]

The significance of the above measures derived as much from what they did not say as what they said. They did not provide for devaluation of the pound, the deregulation of interest rates and exchange rates, or a reduction in government spending. They also left the public sector alone—despite increasing calls from within the administration for privatization.

The administration responded to these calls during the summer of 1975 with two initiatives. Presidential Decree 262 authorized that public-sector shares be offered for private subscription. Law 111 abolished the "General Organizations," which had supervised public-sector firms. It set out procedures by which private-sector experts sat on public-sector management boards, and by which public-sector shares were to be offered. However, to soften the effects of Law 111, an additional Clause 10 was added. It stipulated that share sales be limited to public-sector firms that already had some private participation, and the state's overall shares in these joint companies could not be reduced through subscriptions.[41]

The leaders of the ETUF applauded the addition of Clause 10, knowing full well that it denuded Law 111 of much of its potency. The public sector would not be sold off when so many social groups had a stake in the survival of the public sector.

The Effects of Dualism: From Bad to Worse

In the absence of any deregulation of exchange and interest rates, or the diminution of public-sector control over joint ventures, neither domestic nor foreign investors had much incentive to risk their capital in domestic enterprises. By the close of 1978 the regime had approved only 134 joint ventures. These projects barely touched the labor market; they employed some 13,553 Egyptians, far short of the 139,000 expected to work in such projects by the end of 1979.[42]

Moreover, the little investment that did transpire was concentrated in the financial and service sectors; of the 2.1 billion Egyptian pounds capitalized in joint ventures by the end of 1983, 54 percent went to banking and financial services, while only 23 percent went to industry.[43] This debilitating trend was brought about by the lethal combination of the "own-exchange" system, which together with an overvalued pound, fed the black market and new commercial banks; and the halfhearted provisions of Laws 43 and 111, which encouraged Egyptians to invest in avenues that offered the quickest returns. The result was a class of profiteers, the *munfatihun* or "openers," who sought quick killings in the import of consumer goods, in banking and currency, or in real estate speculation.

The *munfatihun* benefitted from pent-up middle-class consumer demand, which exploded in the seventies: the share of the total import bill comprised by own-exchange imports rose from 3.5 percent in 1975 to 21 percent in 1979, while the share of total imports represented by consumer goods rose from 10 percent in 1969, to 28 percent in 1973, and 34 percent by 1977.[44] Meanwhile, the commercial-banking sector became a huge foreign-currency siphon: by 1978 an estimated 58 percent of all deposits in joint-venture banks had been shifted to parent banks, while only 23 percent of the former's loans went to Egyptian industry.[45]

Within three years this trend exacerbated Egypt's economic crisis. The inflow of dollars and speculative activities heated up the economy, producing a 30 percent inflation rate. To compensate state employees and other vulnerable groups, the regime raised subsidies, which cost some $1.28 billion a year by the close of 1976, 30 percent of central government expenditures.[46] This contributed to a $4.659 billion balance-of-payments deficit as compared to $2.564 billion in 1975, and to a $1.092 billion current account deficit, as compared to $1.035 billion in 1975 and $524 million in 1974.[47]

As the situation worsened, the IMF pressed Cairo to accept a deal: it would lend Egypt $300 million over three years to ease its balance-of-payments crisis in return for stabilization measures. This was followed by months of haggling, during which Cairo put up a determined fight, particularly against the demands for devaluation.

At first the cabinet, rent by internal divisions between pro- and anti-reform elements, rejected the IMF's demands. But with the appointment of Abdel Monem al-Qaisouni as Minister of Economy in November 1976, the cabinet moved.[48] In December Prime Minister Mamduh Salem announced to the Peoples Assembly that the government would adopt measures such as reducing subsidies from $1.282 to $1.218 billion. In turn, the IMF promised to provide $450 million standby credit and reschedule Cairo's $11.846 billion foreign debt.[49]

A month later the government announced that it would cut $123 million from commodity supports. In addition, the regime indicated that it would raise customs duties on imported electrical household goods by 100 percent and those on imported textiles by 50 percent.[50] The announcement led to two days of bloody rioting on January 18 and 19, during which at least 100 people died and 1200 people were arrested.

Sadat's *Infitah:* A "Lose-Lose Game"?

When the smoke cleared, it turned out that the most controversial cuts, those on rice, sugar, and bread, amounted to only $28.2 million out of the $123 million in total commodity cuts sought by the regime.[51] Most of these cuts concentrated on "luxury" goods such as fine flower, unbroken rice, and granulated sugar.

The modest scope of the subsidy cuts indicated that the violent reaction to them had more to do with political symbolism than financial hardship; they were seen by groups such as salaried state workers and students as a symbol of the inequity and corruption that accompanied *infitah*.

The regime might have cushioned the political effects of the cuts by preparing the populace for them. But except for Salem's December Peoples Assembly speech, which gave little cause for concern, Sadat did not seek the support of groups such as the labor federations or professional syndicates. After the riots, in a series of speeches, he tried to justify the cuts by pointing to the profits that bakers and clothing makers had made by illegally using subsidized goods.[52] However, he gave no indication that he wanted to bolster *infitah* through a democratic bargain.

On the contrary, a month after the January riots, Sadat issued an 11 point decree that gave him almost unlimited powers to crack down on his opponents. In June the parliament passed a Parties Law, which gave the regime indirect control over the legalization of parties. A year later the parliament passed a "political isolation" law that banned prerevolution politicians from the political arena. This action was directed at the recently proclaimed "New Wafd." In protest, the party abolished itself in June 1978.

Why did Sadat turn against the Wafd, a party that spoke for the capitalist sectors that would have made natural supporters of economic reform? Sadat's assault was especially surprising given the events that preceded them: in April Economy Minister Qaisouni resigned in protest of resistance in the cabinet to reducing subsidies. His departure fed speculation that Sadat might form a coalition with the Wafd in order to overcome resistance to reforms in his own party. Why did he shoot himself in the foot?[53]

While part of the answer lies in continued hostility from the opposition parties toward his peace initiative with Israel, the more fundamental root of Sadat's authoritarianism lies in the paradoxical effects of his dualist approach;[54] *infitah* alienated not only potential losers in the reform process but also *potential winners*. It offered its most lucrative opportunities to regime cronies who used clientalist ties to gain a foot-hold in speculative enterprises. The Wafd's hostility to such "parasitic" capitalism became clear when it launched a campaign against the regime's proposal to sell land around the Great Pyramid of Giza for a joint-venture project.[55] Its actions reflected the extent to which *infitah* had become a "lose-lose" game for the regime.

Lacking allies and trapped by the dilemmas created by dualism, the regime pursued its strategy of survival to its "logical" conclusion. On the political plane it struck at its opponents in June 1979 by holding a contrived election in which Sadat's National Democratic Party (NDP) took nearly all the seats.[56] Recalcitrant syndicates such as the Lawyers Syndicate were repressed, while the labor federations were contained by the co-optation of a new cadre of leaders.[57]

On the economic plane, the few reforms that took place did little to stem the tide of economic decline. The regime's reluctance to either lower the subsidy bill, which reached $2.254 billion in 1980 (18 percent higher than 1979),[58] or float the pound contributed to the periodic breakdown of talks between Cairo and the IMF regarding a promised $720 million standby facility.[59]

Unwilling to bend to the IMF's demands, Egypt increased its external debt. Following the January riots, the Gulf oil-producing states promised Egypt some $1.5 billion in aid, most of which had been spent by the summer of 1978. After the Gulf states cut off further aid to punish Egypt for signing of the Egyptian-Israeli peace treaty, the United States increased its economic aid from $900 million in 1978 to $1.2 billion in 1979. Of the latter figure, nearly half ($585 million) was in loans. As a result, Egypt's total *civilian* external debt jumped from $10.5 billion in 1976 to $17 billion in 1981.[60] Debt service in 1979 consumed 51 percent of all export earnings and 96 percent of visible exports earnings.[61]

Survival and the Politics of Accommodation Under Mubarak

The strategy of survival took a significant turn under Mubarak's administration. In the wake of Sadat's assassination and the subsequent campaign directed at his economic policies by opposition politicians, Mubarak tried to forge a compromise with a variety of groups and institutions regarding the limits of economic reform.

It would be an exaggeration to refer to this process as the "negotiation of austerity," much less a democratic bargain.[62] While Mubarak consulted a number of economic bodies that advocated a more "productive" *infitah,* he did not pursue a policy of economic reform through a coherent system of "pact-making."

On the contrary, beginning in 1984 Mubarak promoted a system of "pluralistic accommodation" which instead of advancing economic reform, tended to block it. This system, by shielding workers, managers, and government employees from the costs of substantive economic reform, adhered to the logic of the strategy of survival.

Pluralist accommodation took two forms: in the early eighties, it rested on a system of "inter-elite" bargaining and consultation; after the 1984 elections, it ensued from a fragile balance of power between the regime and its opponents.

Segmented Inter-elite Bargaining

In spring 1982 Mubarak warned that, "economic reform . . . cannot be achieved overnight . . . We know that there is no magic wand that can turn dreams into . . . tangible facts without hard work."[63] But he also promised, some time later, not to impose onerous reforms on the people: "The method of the electric shock is past now. If I applied it, there would never be stability in the country."[64] In his desire to attain a measure of legitimacy for limited economic reforms without unduly opening up the political arena or provoking social unrest, Mubarak consulted with a variety of affected groups.

This approach at first took dramatic shape in early 1982, when the regime held a summit conference at which the leaders of the professional associations and labor unions, in concert with some 200 economists, critically appraised Sadat's *infitah*. The participants recommended that Mubarak hold a series of conferences with the leaders of the parties and occupational associations in order to set the parameters for a new economic-reform policy.[65]

While Mubarak initially endorsed this idea, he soon came under pressure from "Sadatists" within the NDP who opposed providing a public forum for the critics of *infitah*. The latter were invited to either address the regime and the NDP directly, or to take their "chances in the competitive atmosphere of the electoral arena."[66]

The Chambers of Commerce and Industry, the Federation of Egyptian Industries, and the Egyptian Businessmen's Association took up this offer to address the regime directly. The first three groups represented the interests of domestic public and private firms; the fourth was linked to international capital. It emerged with the formation of American-Egyptian committees that met to promote foreign investment and deregulation of the economy.[67]

During the early and mid-eighties, periodic consultations between the above groups and the regime provided a context through which the regime initiated several changes in *infitah*. Pressure from the Egyptian Federation of Industries helped give birth to Law 159 of 1981, which secured for the private sector most of the privileges extended to joint ventures by Law 43. Four years later, Minister of the Economy Mustafa Kamel El-Sayyid, with the backing of the business groups, adopted new measures to draw remittances into official channels and limit imports. These measures included a partial float of the pound, a clamp down on the black-currency market, a requirement that importers pay for letters of credit in Egyptian pounds, and most importantly, the abolition of the "own-exchange" system. Although they did not fully succeed—Sayyid's initiatives led to a reduction in foreign remittances inflows and a foreign exchange crisis—these steps reflected the resolve of government and business to promote a more "productive" *infitah*.[68]

Despite this limited progress, the regime left unattended a host of deeper structural problems. It did not aggressively pursue privatization, given the persistent opposition within labor federations to government proposals to increase private subscription in the public sector.[69] On May Day 1983, Mubarak himself promised workers that would be no "diminution in and no sale of the public sector."[70] This cautious approach was evident in the 1982 Five-Year Plan, which avoided thorny issues such as reducing subsidies.

Egypt's position would have plummeted further had it not been for foreign remittances, which helped reduce the 1983/84 current account deficit by some 40 percent. Still, by fiscal 1984/1985, the current account deficit had grown by half a billion dollars and the gross budget deficit had reached $5.4 billion—pushed by a $5 billion a year subsidy bill.[71] As a result Egypt's foreign debt reached $32 billion in 1984, 24 percent of GDP.

The 1984 Parliamentary Elections: The Old Ruling Bargain?

Against this background of economic crisis, elections were held in May 1984. The Wafd's return to the political arena offered the regime an ally for economic reform. Its alliance with the Muslim Brethren, although controversial, could also be viewed as supportive of economic reform. By the mid-eighties, the Brethren had developed close ties to the "Islamic bourgeoisie," a new social actor that controlled an array of middle-size, private-sector businesses and powerful "Islamic Investment Firms."

However, the 1984 elections did not fulfill their potential role as facilitator of a democratic bargain for two reasons. First, the regime retained the restrictive Parties Law and the Elections Law (amended in July 1983), as well as the 1981 Emergency Laws. These laws undermined the opposition parties by forbidding appeals to a mass audience along either class or religious lines and by limiting the right of public assembly.

Yet while these laws, as well as vote fraud, hindered the opposition, they were not the primary reason for its poor showing in the 1984 elections.[72] The central issue was the persistent belief among the popular classes in the

Nasserist idea that the masses should refrain from politics in return for socioeconomic support. The opposition lacked the means to overcome this institutionalized apathy, preferring instead to adhere to the logic of the old ruling bargain: not one party proposed using the election as a forum for negotiating the boundaries of economic reform. Instead, every party, including the NDP, called for maintaining public sector industries and state subsidies.[73]

Hemmed in by the social and ideological legacies of Nasser's state, the opposition parties made only made limited gains. The Wafd-Brethren alliance won 58 of a total of 488 seats, or 15 percent. In conjunction with independent deputies, the opposition took a quarter of the Assembly seats.[74]

"Pluralist Accommodation": An Inverted Democratic Bargain?

Lacking adequate access to parliament, opposition groups were obliged to speak to the regime through surrogate political institutions such as professional associations and the opposition press. But because these institutions provided the intelligentsia with insulated arenas for dissent without imposing the burdens and responsibilities of representation, they tended to promote ideological maximalism: through them, the opposition "shouted" at the regime, as SLP leader Ibrahim Shukri put it.[75]

For the opposition and the regime alike, this imperfect solution had advantages. By shouting, the former could exercise indirect influence over the regime, while avoiding the duties of a formal role in the Peoples Assembly. The latter, meanwhile, could promote a degree of accommodation by letting the opposition shout, while retaining its formal authoritarian powers in reserve, to use against its opponents when it deemed fit.

Out of this logic the system of "pluralist accommodation" emerged in full form. This system rested on implicit "rules of the game,"[76] the most basic of which was that no side would impose its most valued interests on another. For the opposition, this meant that it could not directly assail the president or the military; nor could it demand a change in the electoral system since its underrepresentation in the Assembly was compensated by its freedom to shout in the press and professional syndicates.

As for the regime, it could not forcefully impose on the opposition policies that undermined the latter's basic interests. Nor could it use the formal authoritarian prerogatives inherited from the Sadat period to repress opposition parties and syndicates, *so long as they observed the implicit bounds of legitimate dissent*. These prerogatives would remain *de jure*, while the political arena would remain, in a *de facto* sense, pluralistic so long as both sides observed the rules of the accommodation game.

While this game provided political stability in the ensuing three years, it secured this stability at the cost of economic reform. Because the opposition parties insisted that subsidies were a fundamental interest that the regime could not threaten, the regime could not reduce subsidies without violating the rules of the game. Pluralist accommodation thus worked like an inverted democratic bargain, premising political peace on the regime's avoidance of tough economic decisions.

The regime was reminded of the costs of unpopular economic decisions in the fall of 1984, when its attempt to enact subsidy cuts provoked a violent response from textile workers in Kafr al-Dawwar. Cairo then canceled the cuts; henceforth, it adopted only limited economic measures. In January 1985 it permitted a controlled float of the investment exchange rate. In April, the appointment of Sultan Abu Ali as minister of the economy broke another logjam in the cabinet. But his cabinet took only modest steps. Bread subsidies in 1985 remained at $2.4 billion; when added to energy supports, the subsidy bill was over $5 billion. By the end of 1985, Egypt's external debt reached $33 billion; servicing this debt consumed 35 percent of annual current account receipts.[77]

Quasi-Rentier Financing and System Breakdown

Egypt sustained the costs of pluralist accommodation by depending on external rents to prop up the economy. By the early eighties, revenues from oil, expatriate workers, and the Suez Canal accounted for 40 percent of GDP, as compared to 15 percent in 1975.[78] In addition, Egypt took in a nearly $1 billion in American economic aid.

However, this "quasi-rentier" system began to run out of steam in the mid-eighties. By then, the oil glut and the sluggish international economy undercut Cairo's rents; remittances fell from $4.4 billion in 1985 to $2.2 billion in 1986, oil revenues from $2.6 billion to $1.2 billion, Suez Canal receipts from $1 billion to $900 million, and tourism from $600 million to $300 million.[79] To make matters worse, in March 1986 Washington indicated that it would delay $265 million in aid until Cairo adopted IMF-demanded reforms.[80]

As external sources of support declined, the entire system of pluralistic accommodation began to fall apart. Having little alternative, Cairo began to negotiate seriously with the IMF. By late spring press reports suggested that

Egypt was about to agree to a package of economic reforms in return for an IMF standby credit of $1 billion and the rescheduling of Egypt's debts.

Such a move would almost certainly provoke a move by the opposition to transgress the rules of the game, since these rules held that the regime could not assail subsidies—a basic interest of the opposition—and reduction of subsidies was likely to be a part of the IMF plan. To avoid a breakdown of the system, Mubarak had his prime minister consult opposition leaders. However, the ensuing talks soon fell apart, while Cairo pursued negotiations with the IMF throughout the summer of 1986.[81]

At this point the opposition, sensing that the regime was about to break the rules of the game, began to directly attack the regime. The Wafd's leader, Fuad Serrag Eddin, demanded that Mubarak abandon his chairmanship of the NDP. NDP spokesmen responded by attacking Eddin. In turn, Mustafa Sherdi, editor of The Wafd, retorted that "if this dog of the government . . . does not stop (these) attacks . . . we will be free to attack the president."[82] This was followed by verbal assaults on the military.

Although stung by these attacks, Mubarak insisted that he would support democracy, "despite . . . [the opposition's] use of uncivilized words in reference to the head of state."[83] The opposition responded by proposing a national dialogue to define more explicit rules for democracy. The administration then held a conference with opposition leaders, during which the two sides discussed the terms for a new "social contract."[84] Towards this end opposition leaders proposed a national unity government, but the regime rejected this idea and continued talks with the IMF.

Reacting to the regime's actions, the opposition stepped up its assaults by challenging the Election Law. The High Constitutional Court responded with a preliminary ruling that implied that the 1984 Assembly had been elected unconstitutionally because the Election Law had excluded independent candidates. Since the Assembly was due to nominate Mubarak for a second term, the regime was obliged to amend the law and hold new elections to create a constitutionally elected Peoples Assembly.

THE 1987 ELECTIONS AND REFORM: TOWARD A DEMOCRATIC BARGAIN?

While the April 1987 elections did not provide an arena for forging a democratic bargain, the link between the elections and the regime's subsequent agreement with the IMF was an issue that, at least obliquely, drew the attention of the opposition parties.

Khalid Muhi Eddin, leader of the leftist National Progressive Union Grouping (NPUG), stated that the "public sector is the most important factor in industry," and called for "reforming the public sector . . . if industrial progress is to be made." Yet he added reforms would fail unless "based on democracy. Democratic reform is our means of achieving economic reform."[85] The Wafd held that the state should "encourage the creative efforts of the private sector" and confine subsidies "to the deserving segments of society."[86] But it added, "economic prosperity depends on political stability, which turn is based on democracy."[87]

The most powerful opposition bloc, the Islamic Alliance, also raised reform issues. While the Alliance rested on a coalition of the Socialist Labor Party (SLP), the Liberal Socialist Party, and the Muslim Brethren, it drew its core support from the Islamic bourgeoisie. Speaking indirectly to these interests, the SLP called upon the regime to "free up Arab and national (*watani*) capital investment," to promote "new means of investment in keeping with the conditions of society's various social sectors."[88]

However, the SLP made only one oblique reference to reform, stating that "reform of the situation," cannot be earned through a "democratic grant," but only by individual action.[89] This hesitation to directly address the economic situation reflected the persistent weakness of the opposition parties. Only the Islamic Alliance made a dent in the chasm of political apathy: its access to mosques helped it win 56 seats. Combined with the New Wafd's 35 seats, the opposition won 91 seats, 31 more than in the 1984 elections. Still, the NDP retained 68 percent of the Assembly seats.

In the wake of the NDP's electoral victory, Mubarak tried to draw a more explicit connection between the ballot and economic reform. Anticipating the agreement with the IMF, he told the newly elected Peoples Assembly:

> You are in the vanguard of those dealing with (economic) problems . . . We must use a variety of opinions . . . in arriving at sound decisions that serve the interests of the workers and those with low incomes . . . We are about to conclude an agreement with the IMF that will open the door to rescheduling our debts.[90]

Two weeks later, the administration announced its IMF agreement. This package reflected the cautious approach that Mubarak had outlined to the parliament after the elections. It included a staged, 18-month unification of the multiple exchange-rate system; a floating of the pound; a 2 percent rise in interests rates, and energy price increases. However, it left direct foods subsidies untouched, interest rates far below annual inflation, and energy costs at 20 percent of world prices.

These shortcomings displeased the IMF, which had pushed for a more radical set of reforms. Nevertheless, IMF officials argued that if the agreement's modest reforms were followed by more substantive measures in the future, it would reschedule $12 billion of Egypt's $40 billion external debt and issue a $328 million standby credit, to be drawn in tranches over a period of 18 months.[91]

The Politics of Piecemeal Reforms

Subsequent events demonstrated that the modest attempts by both the regime and its opponents to link the 1987 elections to economic reforms had failed. The regime had not secured support from a coherent block of potential "winners." On the contrary, it encountered persistent resistance from within its own ranks, as well as from opposition circles.

Opposition to reform from within the NDP manifested itself in July 1988, when Tourism Minister Fuad Sultan stormed out of the Peoples Assembly in protest to an Assembly committee's decision to block his plans to sell Alexandria's state-owned San Stefano Hotel.[92] In the end, however, it was not these dramatic clashes that hindered progress but the regime's failure to follow through on commitments to the IMF. Fearing the response of some 3.2 million state employees, it refused to comply with the IMF's demands to lower energy costs and other subsidies.[93]

Unable to meet its obligations, Cairo tried to negotiate a new 12 month extension of rescheduling to cover $4 billion in payments due between July 1988 and June 1989.[94] By spring 1989, with arrears nearing $2 billion, the May 1987 reform agreement was dead, as was the IMF's promised standby credit.[95]

Feeling the pinch, Cairo finally adopted a number of measures designed to win IMF approval. In addition to a 30 percent reduction of electricity prices and a 3 percent increase in interest rates, the regime began to enforce a 1988 law to regulate the "Islamic Investment Companies." These companies had amassed some $4.2 billion in funds by the mid-eighties through a dangerously unregulated system of "dividends" that effectively offered interest rates of 20 percent.[96]

These measures, combined with a devaluation of the pound, encouraged the IMF to reach a preliminary agreement with Egypt that provided for the rescheduling of $10 billion in debt payments, along with $500 million in standby credits.[97] But the agreement soon fell apart, to be followed by a new round of negotiations.

Between Authoritarianism and a Democratic Bargain

Although these negotiations dragged on into 1990, Cairo indicated that it would pursue reforms. During the first eight months of 1990, the regime increased prices for various commodities by 30 percent, raised electricity by 35 percent, further devalued the pound, and increased interest rates. Moreover, it began to push for privatization of smaller assets such as hotels and candy factories.[98]

The regime presented these steps with unprecedented frankness. Mubarak told an audience of workers on May Day:

> We are in a critical stage in the history of the human race . . . One feature of this new phase is the erosion of ideological polarization. . . We must . . . contribute (to this change) . . . with intellectual openness . . . Brothers, to make myself clear, I want to tell you that with every increase in population and consumption subsidies will increase . . . A time will come when we will have absolutely no funds for anything. We must embark on reforms.[99]

How then did the regime intend to legitimate such reforms? The Peoples Assembly had not distinguished itself since its election in April 1987. None of the opposition parties, including the Muslim Brethren, had won public confidence. As for the NDP, its popularity was at its lowest. Its universally disliked speaker of the assembly, Rifat Mahgoub, was implicated in financial scandals, while Mubarak was seen by many as an honest but ineffectual leader.

Against this background, opposition politicians stepped up their attacks on the legitimacy of the Assembly and the NDP. In the summer of 1990, opposition lawyers succeeded again in compelling the courts to strike down the Election Law, thus forcing the regime to dissolve the Assembly and hold new elections.

This development was accompanied by an unparalleled debate in both opposition and NDP circles about the link between economic and political reform. At a party rally in March 1990, Wafdists insisted that "only a legitimate parliament, rather than an illegitimate one, can get us out of these (economic) crises."[100]

This call was taken up by economist and former dean of Zagaziq University Dr. Saqi Affi. Writing in the semi-official *Al-Ahram Al-Duwali,* he asserted that only "honest elections" will produce "true representatives of the people's will (who) will take on the role expected of the Peoples Assembly following the IMF accord."[101]

Unfortunately, this explicit call for a democratic bargain was not heeded by the regime, despite Mubarak's own attempts to galvanize support for reform. Nor did the opposition parties give it much sustained attention. Instead, they were soon embroiled in a dispute over election procedures with the regime.

The dispute ensued from the decision by the regime to enact a new Election Law without consulting the opposition. All the opposition parties, and nearly all the professional associations, denounced the new law, insisting it did not provide legal and institutional safeguards for a fair and free election.[102]

The opposition's complaints were not unjustified.[103] In the wake of the Gulf crisis, the assassination of Speaker of the House Mahgoub on October 12, and the growing saliency of the army, the NDP may have feared the outcome of an open poll.

However, it is not clear that the Election Law was the only reason why all the opposition parties except the NPUG boycotted the November 29 elections. Having failed to muster grass-roots support, the opposition had an incentive to sit the elections out, rather than to lose a contest designed to bless the NDP's hegemony.

With the opposition out of the picture, the NDP won a crushing 85 percent of the Assembly seats. It then accelerated its negotiations with the IMF, with which it signed an agreement in May 1991.

The May 1991 Agreement: Towards An Exclusionary Political System?

The new agreement was the most ambitious reform ever acceded to by Cairo. In return for the forgiving of $10 billion in debts and the rescheduling of another $10 billion, a $372 million standby credit, and $400 million for job retraining, Cairo agreed to liberalize interest rates, introduce full convertibility of the pound, enact a new sales tax, and substantially raise energy prices.[104]

These measures were expected to take a hard toll on average Egyptians. Household incomes—which fell 13 percent in 1990-91—were to fall further;

overall prices were to rise some 30 percent, and Egypt's unemployment rate was to climb substantially from its level of 15 percent in 1990.[105]

Supporters of the agreement argued that once the reforms took hold and the hemorrhaging of the economy stopped, economic growth would ensue, to the benefit of all Egyptians. The problem was that the regime had not created any political framework to see Egypt through this arduous and protracted period. In the absence of a democratic bargain that could sustain public support, the regime faced two choices. It could resume its policy of pluralistic accommodation; or it could use its control over parliament and security apparatus to impose by force what had not been negotiated by compromise and accommodation.

It is too early to affirm that the regime is moving towards exclusionary authoritarianism. The increase in reported cases of civil and human right abuses in 1990 may reflect the security apparatus's response to the assassination of Mahgoub rather than a pattern of repression induced by a resolve to quell opposition to economic reform.[106] Moreover, there is still a high level of pluralism, despite the absence of competitive democracy. Whether the burdens of economic reform will compel the state to resolve this contradiction remains to be seen.[107]

CONCLUSION: DEMOCRATIZING THE STATE, RECONSTITUTING CIVIL SOCIETY

> We have been burdened with . . . grave legacies from the past. We have been compelled to study them very carefully. We have consulted with many people on them. We are partners in this homeland.[108]
>
> —President Mubarak, April 1987

Since 1970, Egypt's leaders have wrestled with the social, institutional, and ideological legacies of Nasser's populist authoritarian state. Neither Sadat nor Mubarak completely undid the "ruling bargain" that had legitimated this state, nor the institutions and alliances that sustained this authoritarian compact.

In grappling with the legacies of Nasser's state, these two leaders employed different "survival strategies." Sadat, unwilling to alienate popular groups, pursued a dualistic approach that, when coupled with limits on democratic expression, alienated potential allies and opponents of reform. Mubarak fashioned a system of pluralist accommodation to sustain incremental economic reforms. When this system began to unravel with the depletion of external financial resources, he flirted with a democratic bargain. Having failed to secure this bargain, it appears that his regime is now trying to advance economic reform by authoritarian means, or at least without a coherent political foundation for this project.

It is tempting to blame Mubarak for this turn of events. But he must contend with at least two imposing obstacles that are not of his own making. The first obstacle is continued resistance within the NDP to economic reform. To overcome this, Mubarak must compel the NDP to undertake its own "perestroika." Mubarak has referred to the need to reform the NDP, but apparently fears that the NDP's reform would lead to the party's disintegration. This fear is not unfounded, but in the absence of any attempt to "democratize the state,"[109] it will be hard to establish a democratic basis for economic reform.

The other task facing reformists is to "reconstitute" civil society; this involves not so much a strengthening of civic institutions as their transformation. Nasser's most enduring and troublesome legacy was the promotion of associational groups that viewed their relationship with the state in patron-client terms. The leaders of these groups obtained rents from the state in return for their political quiescence. Now, some thirty years later, the professional syndicates, and most importantly, the moribund political parties, must redirect their energies toward society by building "organic" constituencies on the basis a frank assessment of the sacrifices entailed in economic reform.

Ironically, it may be easier to advance reforms in states that lack the legacy of clientalist pluralism typical of Egypt. In Zambia, for example, democratic forces secured a democratic bargain by building new civic institutions from the ground up. In November 1991, workers allied with the intelligentsia to elect the leader of the labor movement, Frederick Chiluba, president.[110] After his victory, Chiluba told his followers that Zambia's economic crisis requires "discipline . . . clean government, and a determination to look at our problems squarely in the face."[111]

In Egypt, the emergence of a "Chiluba" will require a profound transformation of the relationship between workers and the state. Barring such a change, forging a "democratic bargain" will prove extremely difficult.

NOTES

1. The author would like to express his gratitude to Steven Heydemann and Henri Barkey for their comments on the original draft of this paper.
2. Dr. Sadiq Afifi, "Economic Reform Via the Polls," *Al-Ahram al-Duwali* (October 26, 1991), 6 in Joint Publication Research Service, JPRS-NEA-91-005 (January 14, 1991), 9.
3. Samuel Huntington, *Political Order in Changing Societies* (New Haven: Yale University Press, 1968).
4. Guillermo O'Donnell, *Modernization and Bureaucratic Authoritarianism* (Berkeley: Institute of International Studies, University of California, 1979).
5. Stephan Haggard and Robert Kaufman, "Economic Adjustment in New Democracies," in *Economic Crisis and Policy Choice: The Politics of Adjustment in the Third World,* ed. Joan M. Nelson (Princeton: Princeton University Press, 1990), 57-77. Laurence Whitehead, "Democratization and Disinflation: A Comparative Approach," in *Fragile Coalitions: The Politics of Economic Adjustment,* ed. Joan M. Nelson et al. (Washington, DC: Overseas Development Council, 1989), 79-93.
6. Stephan Haggard and Robert Kaufman, "Economic Adjustment in New Democracies," in *Fragile Coalitions,* 58.
7. Karen Remmer, "The Politics of Economic Stabilization: IMF Standby Programs in Latin America, 1954-1984, *Comparative Politics* 19, no. 1 (October 1986), 20.
8. For a rational choice explanation of dictatorship, see Ronald Wintrobe, "The Tinpot and the Totalitarian: An Economic Theory of Dictatorship," *American Political Science Review* 84, no. 3, (September 1990), 849-72.
9. For a discussion of the rise and fall of this authoritarian bargain in the Soviet Union, see Janine Ludlam, "Reform and the Redefinition of the Social Contract Under Gorbachev," *World Politics* 43 (January 1991), 284-312; on Egypt, see John Waterbury, "The Soft State and the Open Door: Egypt's Experience with Economic Liberalization, 1974-1984," *Comparative Politics* 12, no. 1 (October 1985), 65-84.
10. See Robert Bates, ed., *Towards a Political Economy of Development: A Rational Choice Perspective* (Berkeley: University of California Press, 1988).
11. Adam Przeworski, "Some Problems in the Transition from Authoritarianism, " Vol. 3, *Transitions from Authoritarian Rule, Volumes 1-4,* Guillermo O'Donnell, Philippe Schmitter, and Lawrence Whitehead, eds. (Baltimore: Johns Hopkins Press, 1986). Guillermo O'Donnell, "Tensions in the Bureaucratic-Authoritarian State and the Question of Democracy," in *The New Authoritarianism in Latin America,* ed. David Collier (Princeton: Princeton University Press, 1979), 285-318. Nelson, *Economic Crisis and Policy Choice,* 3-32.

12. Joan M. Nelson, "The Politics of Long-Haul Economic Reform" in *Fragile Coalitions,* 3-26.
13. See Robert Kaufman, "Stabilization and Adjustment in Argentina, Brazil and Mexico," in Nelson, *Economic Crisis and Policy Choice,* 89.
14. See John Waterbury, "The Political Management of Economic Adjustment and Reform," in Alan Roe, et. al., "Economic Adjustment in Algeria, Egypt, Jordan, Morocco, Pakistan, Tunisia and Turkey," *Economic Development Institute of the World Bank Seminar Report Number 15* (Washington DC: World Bank, 1989), 55-65.
15. On Mexico, see Pablo Gonzalez Casonava, *Democracy in Mexico* (New York: Oxford University Press, 1970).
16. See Kevin Middlebrook, "The Sounds of Silence: Organized Labor's Response to Economic Crisis in Mexico," paper delivered at the annual meeting of the American Political Science Association, Washington, DC (September 1-4, 1988). On Egypt, see below.
17. See Steven Heydemann's contribution in this volume.
18. See Robert Bianchi, *Unruly Corporatism: Associational Life in Twentieth Century Egypt* (New York: Oxford University Press, 1989); Clement Henry Moore, "Money and Power: The Dilemma of the Egyptian Infitah," *Middle East Journal* 40, no. 4 (Autumn 1986), 634-57.
19. Robert Kaufman, "Stabilization and Adjustment in Argentina, Brazil and Mexico," in Nelson, *Economic Crisis and Policy Choice,* 76-79.
20. Bianchi, *Unruly Corporatism,* 37.
21. I place a "?" next to Jordan because, in contrast to the other cases, Jordan more approximates a "rentier" state than a populist authoritarian state. In the latter case there is an attempt to bring about some change in social relations as a means of effecting economic development. In "rentier" states there is a reliance on external sources of income and little reordering of domestic social relations. Yet as discussed below, aspects of "rentierism" played a part in sustaining survival strategies in Egypt.
22. See Bianchi, *Unruly Corporatism.*
23. John Waterbury, *The Egypt of Nasser and Sadat: The Political Economy of Two Regimes* (Princeton: Princeton University Press, 1988). Waterbury notes on p. 161 that while the foreign-linked bourgeoisie was decapitated between 1956 and 1961, the private sector "maintained its share of total industrial production" between 1962 and 1967, and enlarged its share starting in 1968.
24. See Clement Henry Moore, "Money and Power," 636-38.
25. See the "Charter" in Nissim Rejwan, *Nasserist Ideology: Its Exponents and Its Critics* (New York: John Wiley, 1974).
26. Waterbury, *Egypt of Nasser and Sadat,* 192-95, 210-11.
27. Waterbury, *Egypt of Nasser and Sadat,* 90-91.
28. Waterbury, *Egypt of Nasser and Sadat,* 90.
29. Waterbury, *Egypt of Nasser and Sadat,* 31. Because Nasser was reluctant to "sweat" savings from the Egyptian citizenry, his industrial drive relied,

almost from the very beginning, on external loans. About a third of the total planned investments for the 1960-1965 Five Year Plan was to come from foreign loans, mostly from the Soviets. Soviet loans totalled $496 million by 1964, not including $325 million for the Aswan High Dam. From 1967 to 1973, nonmilitary aid from the Western bloc to Egypt totalled more than $1.2 billion. Total economic and military aid from the socialist bloc between 1955 and 1975 reached $10.5 billion. See Waterbury, *Egypt of Nasser and Sadat,* 85-6, 398; Hamied Ansari, *Egypt: The Stalled Society* (Albany: State University Of New York Press, 1986), 177.

30. Waterbury, *Egypt of Nasser and Sadat,* 330-31. Waterbury quotes from Nasser's speech as reprinted in *Le Monde,* March 5, 1968.
31. See Gouda Abdel-Khalek, "Looking Outside, Or Turning Northwest? The Meaning and External Dimension of Egypt's Infitah 1971-1980," *Social Problems* 28, no. 4 (April 1981), 394-409; Raymond A. Hinnebush, *Egyptian Politics Under Nasser: The Post-Populist Development of An Authoritarian-Modernizing State* (Boulder, CO: Lynne Rienner, 1988).
32. See Marsha Pripstein Posusney, "Labor as an Obstacle to Privatization: The Case of Egypt 1974-1987," paper delivered at the 1989 annual meeting of the Middle East Studies Association, Toronto Canada (November 15-18, 1989), 7-8.
33. The fact that the corporatized labor federations acquiesced to this "dualist approach" does not prove that they brought about this policy. The labor unions were encapsulated in corporatist federations designed to execute rather than originate regime policy. Still, if the regime undertook actions that jeopardized the fundamental interests of labor, even Sadat's most trusted allies might mobilize the federations against him.
34. Bianchi, *Unruly Corporatism,* 162.
35. See the author's "The University Intelligentsia and the Struggle for Democracy in Contemporary Egypt" (doctoral dissertation, The University of Chicago, June 1991), 177. Under Nasser, 85 percent of secondary students were from middle-class families, while only 11.5 percent came from peasant or worker families. The role of the universities in helping to create a new middle class is emphasized in Ahmed Abdalla's *The Student Movement and National Politics in Egypt* (London: Al Saqi Books, 1985).
36. Ansari, *Egypt: The Stalled Society,* 197.
37. Muhammad Anwar el-Sadat, *Waraqat Uktubar* (Cairo: Hay'at al-Isti'malat, Jumhouriya Misr al-'Arabiya, 1974).
38. el-Sadat, *Waraqat Uktubar,* 34-47.
39. Waterbury, *The Egypt of Nasser and Sadat,* 131.
40. Waterbury, *The Egypt of Nasser and Sadat,* 176.
41. Posusney, "Labor as an Obstacle to Privatization," 14.
42. Waterbury, *The Egypt of Nasser and Sadat,* 142-43.
43. Moore, "Money and Power," 639.
44. Waterbury, *The Egypt of Nasser and Sadat,* 178.

45. Waterbury, *The Egypt of Nasser and Sadat,* 149, and Moore, "Money and Power," 641.
46. *Middle East Economic Digest* (*MEED*), December 17, 1976.
47. See *MEED,* June 18, 1976 and July 15, 1977.
48. See Alan Mackie, "Debts weigh down on attempts at social and economic reform," *MEED,* December 31, 1976, 19.
49. Alan Mackie, "IMF approval gives weight to new economic package," *MEED,* January 14, 1991, 3-4.
50. See *MEED,* January 21 and 28, 1977; Nicholas Damiani, "Riots Highlight Egypt's Economic Difficulties," *The Arab Economist* 89 (February 1977), 20-23.
51. *MEED,* January 28, 1977. The regime expected to gain $51.2 million from petrol rises and $43.6 million from cigarette price rises.
52. See *Al-Ahram,* February 1, 1977, "Speech before the Higher Council of the Universities."
53. Alan Mackie, "Cabinet reshuffle does little to encourage confidence," *MEED,* May 12, 1978, 3-5.
54. I would not reduce the explanation to economic or even rational factors. On a personal or psychological plane, Sadat demonstrated an irrational intolerance of dissent that compelled him to escalate his attacks on the opposition. This factor, however, meshed extremely well with the "objective" conditions of *infitah,* which tended to unite disparate social groups in opposition to Sadat.
55. Alan Mackie, "Revival of Wafd party reflects pressures on open-door policy," *MEED,* February 24, 1978, 3.
56. The NDP took 330 seats, while the only opposition party, the Socialist Labor Party (SLP), took 29 seats. Sadat himself had created the SLP a year earlier in an attempt to promote a "responsible" opposition.
57. Bianchi, *Unruly Corporatism,* 138-9.
58. Alan Mackie, "Abdel Majid Rides a Storm," *MEED,* August 8, 1980, 6.
59. Egypt drew the first tranche of the $720 million credit facility in the summer of 1978, but the second was not provided because Egypt did not fulfill the requirements of the IMF.
60. See William Quandt, *The United States and Egypt* (Washington DC: Brookings Institute, 1990), 76; Gad Gilbar, "The Economics of Interdependence: the United States and the Arab World 1973-1977" in *The Middle East and the United States,* ed. Haim Shaked and Itamar Rabinovich (New Brunswick: Transaction Books, 1990), 233. U.S. economic aid to Egypt climbed by $21 million in 1974 and $371 million in 1975, to reach $1.03 billion in 1976. See Gilbar, "The Economics," 233.
61. Waterbury, *The Egypt of Nasser and Sadat,* 411.
62. Bianchi, *Unruly Corporatism,* 89.
63. These statements were made on March 10 and April 26, 1982. See Ami Ayalon, "The Arab Republic of Egypt," *Middle East Contemporary Survey* (*MECS*) 7 (1982-1983), 414.

64. Mubarak's statement on January 22, 1983. See Ami Ayalon, "The Arab Republic of Egypt," 444.
65. Bianchi, *Unruly Corporatism*, 87-8.
66. Bianchi, *Unruly Corporatism*, 88.
67. Bianchi, *Unruly Corporatism*, 174-5.
68. *MEED Annual Survey*, December 21, 1985.
69. Posusney, "Labor as an Obstacle," 20-21.
70. Posusney, "Labor as an Obstacle," 21.
71. *MEED*, December 14, 1985 and July 6, 1985.
72. A correspondent reporting for *Middle East Report* (*MERIP*) during the elections wrote that the opposition parties' "disappointing results reflect more the lack of political groundwork in preceding years than the oppressive scrutiny of the regime and the electoral fraud of the NDP." See Bertus Hendriks's article in *MERIP* 15, no. 129, (January 1985).
73. See party platforms in *Intikhabat Majles Al-Sh'ab 1984*, ed. Ali Hillal Dessouki (Cairo: Al-Ahram Center for Political and Strategic Studies, 1986).
74. An estimated 45 percent of those registered were reported to have voted, but since the potential electorate is twice the number of those registered, it is likely that no more than 22 percent of the electorate participated. See Dessouki, *Intikhabat*, 223.
75. Shukri also added that if the government would listen to the opposition the opposition would become "very polite." See *Middle East Times*, December 7, 1986.
76. These rules can be detected by observing the political dialogue between the opposition and the regime over time. These "implicit" rules became explicit occasionally, when both opposition and regime leaders would refer to the limits of the democratic "ethic."
77. *MEED*, February 8, 1986.
78. Waterbury, "The Soft State," 74.
79. *Middle East Times*, September 21, 1986.
80. *MEED*, March 1, 1986.
81. The opposition charged that the regime was only using the talks as a cover to legitimize what were in fact unilateral negotiations with the IMF. There was some truth to these claims.
82. *Middle East Times*, June 28, 1986.
83. *Middle East Times*, July 19, 1986; Foreign Broadcast Information Service (FBIS), October 10, 1986.
84. *Middle East Times*, December 7, 1986.
85. See party platforms, FBIS, Near East and South Asia, March 27, 1987.
86. FBIS, April 1, 1987.
87. FBIS, March 27, 1987.
88. FBIS, March 27, 1987.
89. See the Alliance platform in *Al-Sh'ab*, March 18, 1987.

90. FBIS, April 24, 1987.
91. See David Butter, "Egypt's IMF Breakthrough," *MEED,* May 23, 1987, p. 8.
92. David Butter, "Egypt's Reformers Under Siege," *MEED,* July 15, 1988, pp. 2-3.
93. See David Butter, "Mubarak runs out of breathing space," *MEED,* October 14, 1988, pp. 39-40.
94. *MEED,* December 1988.
95. David Butter, "Private Sector in Egypt Faces Battle," *MEED,* June 9, 1989, pp. 4-5.
96. See David Butter, *MEED Special Report: Egypt,* October 14, 1988, 44.
97. David Butter, "IMF deal gives Egypt new lease of life," *MEED,* July 14, 1989.
98. David Butter, *MEED Special Report: Egypt,* June 8, 1990, 9-18.
99. See President Mubarak's speech, FBIS, May 3, 1990.
100. See article by Ahmad Fuad et al., "Public Demands Political Reform to Confront Our Difficult Problems," in *Al-Wafd,* March 25, 1990, in JPRS NEA 90-025, May 2, 1990. The article is based on interviews with more than 42 young Wafdists.
101. See "Economic Reform Via the Polls," *Al-Ahram Al-Duwali,* October 26, 1990, in JPRS NEA 91-005, January 14, 1991.
102. See Majdi Hilmi, "Law Professors and National Forces Representatives on Podium and New Electoral Law in Dock," *Al-Wafd,* October 19, 1990, in JPRS NEA 91-005, January 14, 1991.
103. See copy of the Draft Law, "Al-Wafd Publishes . . . Text of New Draft Election Law," in JPRS NEA 062, October 24, 1990.
104. David Butter, "MEED Special Report: Egypt," *MEED,* June 7, 1991, 9-19. In addition, the United States in January 1991 forgave some $7 billion in military debt, while the Gulf states also canceled an equal amount.
105. Tony Walker, "Life Raft for the Economy," *Financial Times,* June 14, 1991, 11.
106. See *Lawyers Committee for Human Rights,* "Freedom of Opinion and Expression in Egypt: A Report by the Egyptian Organization for Human Rights" (August 1990); *Amnesty International,* "Egypt: Ten Years of Torture" (October 1991).
107. The dissolution of Dr. Nawal El-Saadawi's Arab Women's Solidarity Association (AWSA) is a particularly alarming indication that the regime may be unwilling to tolerate the further pluralization of Egypt's civil society. By suppressing this organization, the regime silenced another potential advocate of economic reform. See "Egyptian Government Moves to Dissolve Prominent Arab Women's Organization," *Middle East Watch* (September 1991).
108. Interview with Husni Mubarak, *Al-Ray al-'Amm,* April, 1987, FBIS, April 7, 1987.
109. I am grateful to my friend Gehad Auda for this concept of "democratizing the state."

110. See *Africa News* 35, nos. 7-8 (Nov. 18-Dec. 2, 1991).
111. John Battersby, "Zambian Election Marks Africa's Democratic Shift," Christian Science Monitor, November 4, 1991, 4.

5

Ben Ali's New Era: Pluralism and Economic Privatization in Tunisia

Dirk Vandewalle

Since assuming power in November 1987, Tunisia's president Zine el-Abidine Ben Ali has attempted to implement a number of political reforms while extending the most recent economic liberalization and privatization strategies started under his predecessor Habib Bourguiba, the country's first postindependence leader.[1] Although the attempts to reform the economy—in essence liberalization or, perhaps more accurate in Tunisia's case, reliberalization—have so far been modestly successful, Ben Ali's political honeymoon has ended.[2] After an initial two-year period marked by accommodation, the confrontation with the Islamists that was the raison d'être for Bourguiba's removal has come to dominate the policy agenda of his successor.

In Tunisia, where elite movement and political pluralism had been held in abeyance for an extended period of time under Bourguiba, the replacement of the supreme commander was watched with particular interest by a society that clearly hoped that the preliminary reforms of state institutions sponsored by Ben Ali during his first two years in office would lead to a more profound restructuring of Bourguiba's rational-legal state. The renewed liberalization of Tunisia's economy since the mid-1980s added a new and important dimension to the projected changes; both the government and the various opposition groups judged the combination of development and equity an important consideration and publicly expressed these concerns in the National Pact of November 1988. This pact represented a new "social contract" for the country and was, in contrast to the liberal economic policies of the government, expressed in language that closely approximated that of a welfare state.[3]

Once considered a model of development for much of Africa, Tunisia's reputation as an economic and political *pays pilote* had slipped dangerously during Bourguiba's twilight years. Ben Ali's assumption of power—symbolically called the New Era—was viewed as a shining example of how political decay could be halted and how socioeconomic reform could successfully take place despite the deleterious impact of Bourguiba's last years in power. Ben Ali described one of his main tasks as bringing democracy back to Tunisia.[4]

His assumption of power was undoubtedly fortuitous in light of the escalating tensions inside the country since the mid-1980s—tensions that had started to dissolve many of the underpinnings of the rational-legal state his predecessor had helped to create. The confrontation with the Islamists—whom Bourguiba had intermittently accused since independence of not sharing the underlying philosophical precepts of the state—and with the country's most important union throughout the 1980s focused on and dramatized the conflict between the Tunisian state and its civil society.

The lingering, increasingly public contestation demonstrated that civil society had remained much more differentiated than Bourguiba—and modernization theorists—had predicted and had changed to an extent that even Ben Ali had seemingly underestimated. The new president assumed office 30 years after independence in a Tunisian society that had been irrevocably altered: high urbanization rates, educational opportunities that emerged as the prime vehicle for social stratification, the decline of the country's party system, and the disillusionment with the country's economic performance had all contributed to this profound change. The confrontation with the Islamists that ultimately led to the removal of Bourguiba also illustrated that the state as a modernizing force had not been able to eradicate what it once considered to be vestiges of an outdated religious traditionalism, and it brought home the disconcerting message to many Tunisians that the state was willing to violate—using intimidation and physical force if necessary—the rules it had once created and nurtured.

Bourguiba's inability to comprehend the lingering power and the diversification of civil society, Ben Ali's difficulties in moving beyond the promises of the National Pact, and the country's future political and economic liberalization efforts are all intricately linked to postindependence political statecraft. The Tunisian state emerged in 1956 as an overdeveloped state, showing the impact of "consistent and continuous state formation" during the colonialist period.[5] An early crisis on the eve of independence over who would govern the state had been settled with French aid.[6] It left control over the country's elaborate bureaucratic state apparatus firmly in the hands of Bourguiba's Neo-Destour Party. The Neo-Destour—"Destour" meaning "constitution"—represented an extremely effective one-party system, concentrating its organizational power through an elaborate system of formal rules and institutional procedures, interwoven with a less formal network of personalized, clientalist relationships. At the same time, Tunisia is a small country with a relatively concentrated population along the littoral and with a good infrastructure that makes both communication and control easy. The crucial role of the Neo-Destour in attaining independence and the charisma of the supreme commander added to the party's standing among Tunisians.[7] Party discipline was high—until it started to erode in the mid-1970s. Membership in the Neo-Destour (renamed the *Parti Socialiste Destourien* (PSD) in 1964) showed little flux until that time and had grown steadily since independence.[8]

This powerful party-state combination—what was known in Tunisia as the New State—was capable of "dominating all indigenous social forces."[9] It successfully prevented any serious challenge to its power until the mid-1980s. The party elites monopolized all social and political expression in Tunisia, gathering under the umbrella of the Neo-Destour all representatives of the country's professional and nonprofessional organizations. Those that could not be fully incorporated—such as the *Union Général des Travailleurs Tunisiens* (UGTT) and, later, the Islamic movement—were forcibly suppressed.

So complete was the political and ideological hegemony[10] of the party-state that even when some political parties emerged in the 1970s and early 1980s, they acted safely within the confines and rules of the political game Bourguiba controlled, never challenging the parameters of the political system itself. To add further testimony to the lingering strength of the Tunisian state, when the country's Islamic Tendency Movement (*harakat al-ittijah al-islami*) emerged a decade later as the most important full-blown challenge to the state, its leaders too would *initially* adopt stipulations to play within the rules of the political game—although they proceeded to abandon them when accommodation with the government, on mutually agreeable terms, proved impossible.

Although governability had ebbed somewhat at the end of the Bourguiba era, it was quickly restored under Ben Ali. This can be explained in part by the fact that an overwhelming share of the contestation in Tunisia had focused on Bourguiba himself; his removal was judged by all sides as making real progress toward pluralism possible. A second reason was that despite its authoritarian nature, the Tunisian political system had been an inclusionary one that recruited a relatively broad range of participants. Finally, this rapid—although perhaps not complete—recuperation must be explained by another characteristic of the strong state: the high level of institutionalization in Tunisia. The Ben Ali takeover, for example, demonstrated that in one of its crucial tests—accession—the political system's institutional guidelines were respected. Indeed, it is a telling commentary on Bourguiba's political legacy that both the intransigence of the party in power and the initial reckless disregard of the Islamic movement for acceptable sociopolitical norms within Tunisia's political culture were in the end contained. Bourguibism—the sociopolitical legacy of the first president, codified in the country's legal system—survived despite the abuses to which its creator eventually put it.

Ben Ali's challenge as he elaborated in his earliest speeches, was twofold: to move toward greater political pluralism that would prevent further conflict with civil society, and to promote the extension of the country's economic liberalization and privatization strategy. The reforms of the country's political system instituted during his first two years in office were daring and far-reaching—even if most of those reforms were imposed on society rather than negotiated with it and only a few of Ben Ali's immediate advisors were involved in the decisions. These reforms, including greater freedom of the press, the release of political prisoners, the abolishing of the State Security Court, which had been resurrected to judge Islamists, the legalization of several opposition parties, and a modest reform of the *Rassemblement Constitutionnel Démocratique* (RCD)—relieved the pressure on the new government and garnered a strong measure of support among broad sectors of society, including the intellectuals who had traditionally remained suspicious of Bourguiba's Neo-Destour. But as the events described below indicate, the initial reforms gave no clear indications of how social justice and equity—the issues that had propelled the Islamist movement to prominence—would be achieved.

Power and legitimacy in the Tunisian state have traditionally relied upon a powerful combination of at least two factors: the ideology of nationalism—linked symbiotically to the single party and to independence—and the government's ability to support wide-ranging networks of patronage. Both factors had been irreparably harmed by the beginning of the 1980s. First, the party in Tunisia gradually lost its highly symbolic link to the struggle of independence. Despite Bourguiba's rhetoric that the Neo-Destour and, later, the PSD were the embodiment of that struggle, the party had gradually become valued for what it could deliver, and less for its ideological message. The political exclusion, the lingering succession issue, Bourguiba's increasing authoritarianism, and the growing violence used by the state made the traditional claims of the party—that it alone represented progress and modernity and formed a defense against outside and local agitators against the state—look tarnished and hollow.

Second, by the early 1980s the state could also no longer deliver the goods that had maintained and strengthened its role as patron in the quarter century since independence. The growth of Tunisia's economy during those first 25 years had been remarkable, fueled by a mixture of tourist receipts, foreign investment, and the export of phosphates. By 1980 per capita income had quadrupled, despite a burgeoning population. But the success story masked a number of inefficiencies and inequities—state enterprises and consumers that relied on substantial subsidies; outdated finance, pricing, and tax structures; low productivity in the agricultural sector—that only structural change could hope to address. For almost six years after 1980 the government agonized over the shape of possible reforms, its decisions slowed down by the different constituencies that profited from the earlier strategy, and by indecision and outright neglect as the country's political elites remained mesmerized by the struggle over the succession to Bourguiba.[11] The subtle but growing impact of transnational capital and rapid population growth combined with declining growth rates limited the extent to which patronage could continue to play its traditional role in the country's one-party system.

This did not mean that the RCD[12] left to Ben Ali was no longer an instrument of patronage—only that its network of influence had slowly been penetrated by a larger number of competing national and international actors. Tunisia after 1980 was, from an economic point of view, very different from the années heureuses that had prevailed during the socialist experiment in the 1960s and the timid attempt at liberalization in the 1970s that had maintained patronage—or at least held in abeyance any serious challenge to it.

An important ideological convergence also occurred while political and economic stagnation set in. The rethinking of what is now considered the development orthodoxy of the 1950s and 1960s has taken place in all North African countries except Libya, where generous oil revenues and a small population allow the Qadhafi government to further indulge in spending without development. As in other countries studied in this volume, in Tunisia the turn toward market-oriented economic reform was brought about by local economic failures and at the behest of international bilateral and multilateral lending institutions. Elites and economic decision-makers in Tunisia were thinking differently in the 1980s about the role of the state in a development strategy. This changed perception has perhaps best been exemplified by the role and the policies of Tunisia's former Central Bank director, M. Ismail Khelil.[13] As many of his counterparts in the Maghreb and the Machrek, Khelil is reconceptualizing what nationally planned and centrally controlled development should look like. This rethinking is in some ways a recognition of the fact that, among other factors, the state can no longer perform—or is no longer willing to shoulder—some of its distributive functions. It is for example no coincidence that Private Voluntary Organizations, particularly among Islamic groups, have been a rapidly growing phenomenon in countries ranging from Morocco and Tunisia to Egypt, Algeria, and Syria. Economic liberalization and privatization are the most powerful expressions of this now well-entrenched trend in North Africa to hand over economic activities to nonstate actors.

But what is ultimately at stake in all countries, and particularly difficult in Tunisia in light of its political and economic history, is the larger issue of reshaping the role of the state—and by implication of how different groups within civil society will be accommodated while maintaining, or rekindling, economic growth. Since assuming power four years ago, the Ben Ali government has suggested some tentative answers to this conundrum. The remainder of this chapter focuses on Ben Ali's initial attempts to negotiate political change between the party-state and different social groups in Tunisia, the likely success or failure of reforming his successor's authoritarian single-party system into a political regime generating and sustaining genuine participation, and the prospects and possible contribution of the country's economic liberalization and privatization in fostering political change.

My argument is that Ben Ali's major challenge in redefining the role of the state has embodied a number of contradictions that so far he has not resolved. Most important among these is the dilemma that in restoring its legitimacy among society at large, he must divorce the state from the two pillars that have traditionally preserved its strength: its intimate connection to the single party and its tutelary and clientalistic relation to the remainder of civil society.

REDEFINING THE ROLE OF THE STATE: THE POLITICAL DIMENSION

The November 7 takeover came after a prolonged crisis of legitimacy and regulation that marked a profound economic and social crisis as well.[14] Ben Ali's first round of reforms after his takeover was meant to restore a measure of confidence in a political system whose capriciousness had surprised even its supporters. In his first year in office, in a series of sweeping reforms that enjoyed widespread popular support, he adopted a liberal new press law, provided amnesty for several thousand prisoners, abolished the presidency-for-life, and forced the National Assembly to adopt a new law that allowed opposition parties to function more freely.[15] He corrected long-standing grievances about freedom of expression—while keeping intact a well-organized and highly efficient police apparatus he helped organize when Bourguiba was in power. At the same time, two ministerial reshuffles in April and July 1988 brought a number of technocrats, who had proven their worth in public companies and in the administration, into the top elite. Most of them were of a generation that had not been intimately involved with the decolonization and independence struggles. At the same time they were no longer allowed to combine governmental and nongovernmental posts. Similarly, ministers, ambassadors, and chief executives of public companies could no longer be deputies in the National Assembly.

These initial measures allowed the new president to consolidate his own authority and that of the personnel around him, and to draw a clear blueprint for his policies. With public and elite support seemingly intact after one year he then moved on to a second and more ambitious stage: an attempt to create a wide-ranging national coalition to deal with Tunisia's economic and political problems, representing a return to the inclusionary politics of the early independence period.[16] The result was the National Pact, signed, symbolically, exactly one year after the Ben Ali government had taken over the leadership of the country.

The National Pact

Negotiated since July 1988, Tunisia's National Pact came at a crucial juncture in Tunisian politics. Initial enthusiasm for the new regime had started to wane. The first complaints about political conformity and the appearance of "Benalisme"—replacing "Bourguibisme"—were made by opposition figures and publications.[17] Ben Ali's four main aims for the National Pact were clearly spelled out in a letter the president had published in Tunisia's newspapers a few weeks before its actual signing. In the letter he had argued for a renewed cultural identity, for democracy, and for a redefinition of the role of society and of economic development in the country's political and economic life. The general purpose of the pact was "to define a common denominator and a minimum of principles on which all Tunisians can agree and that can be adopted as a basis for political action and development."[18]

Clearly Ben Ali and those he wanted to include in the Pact—RCD party officials and opposition groups within society—differed on its precise meaning. The president considered the National Pact a "social contract," binding upon all signatories, that would allow him to move forward unimpeded with his reforms.[19] Fearing a retrenchment of the RCD's prerogatives, several party officials objected to it from the start. Opposition figures in private complained that in the wake of the Pact's signing, any criticism of government policies was now rejected as unpatriotic and as detracting from the spirit of the November 7 movement. As one former labor leader shrewdly observed on the day of the signing of the pact, it represented an agreement "that no one would have signed a few months ago, and no one will sign a few months from now."[20]

The initial reactions to the pact pointed to the difficulties ahead. In Ben Ali's search for a more pluralist society, the reform of the one-party system constituted a crucial part of his strategy. His efforts centered on removing old-line party supporters at the top who opposed many of his economic and political liberalization policies. Despite his personal appointment of more than half of the reshuffled Central Committee at the July 1988 RCD Congress and the fact that 80 percent of all delegates were new and substantially younger than those they replaced, he was dealt several setbacks. The democratization of the party proved a much slower process than Ben Ali seemed to expect and remains incomplete at the time of writing. Resentment remains strong among some National Assembly members, governors, and party committee members who have succeeded in obstructing several important pieces of legislation.

The April 1989 Legislative Elections

If Ben Ali could claim only modest success in reforming the RCD, the party's overwhelming victories in the parliamentary by-elections of 1988 and the legislative elections of April 1989 confirmed the lingering power bestowed on it under the single-party system. Ben Ali's suggestion for a national front during the legislative elections—a so-called presidential coalition—which would have guaranteed some seats to the opposition, backfired. His suggestion had been as much an attempt to restrict the RCD as to make sure that the opposition would have access to the political system. It was an attempt to demonstrate that the new democracy in Tunisia could work and to encourage further opposition participation in the government. Events proved that the Tunisian president was outpacing both his own party and the opposition. Not only did the RCD balk at the idea of a common front during the presidential/legislative elections, the leader of the country's largest (legal) opposition party also voiced his reservations. Ahmed Mestiri, head of the *Mouvement des Démocrates Socialistes* (MDS), pointedly noted that real democracy could only be served if real opposition took place. But because of the majority voting system that overwhelmingly favored the RCD, no opposition party managed to obtain any of the 141 seats in the National Assembly, leaving a rather embarrassed Ben Ali to afterward assure that all "tendencies" would nonetheless have a chance to express themselves.

In another important respect, the April 2, 1989, elections resulted in a setback for Ben Ali. They indicated for the first time, and with reasonable clarity, the strength of the Islamist movement in Tunisia. The *Mouvement de Tendence Islamiste* (MTI)—renamed the *Hizb al-Nahdha* (Renaissance Party)—had not yet been issued its permit to operate as a recognized party. Its representatives therefore appeared on so-called independent lists. The Islamist "party" received 14 percent of the votes nationwide, and as many as one third in some cities. Were it not for Tunisia's majority voting system, the Islamists would have obtained at least 24 out of 141 deputies in the National Assembly. In eight of the country's governorates the *Hizb al-Nahdha* received more than 25 percent of the vote. To avoid that the Islamists monopolized religious expression, the RCD had raised much the same issues in its campaign and suffused its program with numerous references to *suras* from the Quran. Telling of the shift in Tunisian politics is the fact that every party—with the exception of the communists—claimed to be "the guarantor of religion" in the country.

While the elections left some doubt as to the real strength of the Islamic movement—a doubt that in some ways adds to the mystique of those who represent the Renaissance Party—it was obvious from the results that the other opposition parties in Tunisia were squeezed out. This evisceration is a heavy legacy of the Bourguiba era that has now come to haunt his successor. Ben Ali's proposal for a national front was specifically meant to ensure that the elections would not end up as a contest between the ruling party and the Islamists. With a keen sense of political reality, Ben Ali realized the danger of the RCD winning all the seats, thus perpetuating its traditional power by electoral means.

As a result of the frustration among the opposition with the continued lack of access, the inability of the RCD to reform itself sufficiently to meet the spirit of the National Pact, distrust of Ben Ali's tactics among the opposition,[21] and the growing visibility of the Islamist movement politics, Tunisia after the 1989 elections was much as it had been in the last of the Bourguiba years. Four years after the November 7 takeover—and despite a number of important real and symbolic changes—Tunisia's political system remains governed by the RCD, with Ben Ali as the party leader as well as head of the Tunisian government. The explicit condemnation of single-party politics in the National Pact and its insistence on political tolerance—it included a specific reference to "the legitimate right to disagree . . . without [this being labeled] sedition"—was lost in the renewed battle with the Islamists, reinforcing Ben Ali's concern to put security concerns above those of political pluralism.

REDEFINING THE ROLE OF THE STATE: ECONOMIC ASPECTS

As in most developing countries, the Tunisian state assumed control over the country's economy in the wake of independence in March 1956. The nationalization of the public service companies—transport, mining, and energy—was not only meant to prevent further chaos as the French withdrew, but also to fill the void of local capital and entrepreneurship and to provide greater participation to certain powerful groups within the country, particularly the UGTT. By the end of 1961, virtually all of the country's major economic enterprises, including a number of newly created financial institutions and all commercial companies, belonged to the state. Centralized economic planning introduced that year expanded the state's purview and was even further enhanced in 1962 and 1964, when collectivization and nationalization policies, aimed at reducing the power of local private producers, were extended to the agricultural sector, the retail and wholesale trade, handicrafts and manufacturing.[22] Although the economic aspects of Tunisian socialism were abandoned in September 1969 for a number of political and economic reasons, the growth and regulatory power of the state continued to increase: after a temporary halt in the creation of new state enterprises, more than 100 new ones were created in the decade following the 1973 oil crisis.[23] The windfall from Tunisia's modest oil exports and the easy availability of capital during that decade led the Tunisian government to add new state enterprises, or put inefficient ones under state control, and to increase subsidies to the public sector and consumers alike in an effort to maintain its social policies. Furthermore, the state enterprises created after 1973 needed much larger infusions of capital than the original ones nationalized by the state.[24] In all, the 1970s in Tunisia represented a victory of internal political concerns over economic considerations, despite the liberal leanings of the Hedi Nouira government (1970-1980).

In terms of employment, contribution to the Gross Domestic Product (GDP), and investment, the state enterprises in Tunisia had grown rapidly, both absolutely and in relation to the rest of the economy. The high investment rate had been particularly useful at a time when national savings were low and private capital was virtually nonexistent. It increased production and allowed the government to create unprecedented levels of job opportunities throughout the 1970s and to manipulate income distribution. Public expectations were satisfied through artificially low prices on basic goods and services. At the same time the public companies became highly inefficient. The differing positive and negative aspects of the national enterprises can be gleaned from the following table tracing the contours of state enterprise involvement in the Tunisian economy between 1970 and 1980.

Until the 1980s, in all Tunisian state enterprises, profit considerations had yielded to a number of objectives that had strong noneconomic components including, but not limited to, the pursuit of a "social contract" that included the creation of employment, subsidies, and regional development projects that favored areas traditionally supportive of the Destour. At the enterprise level the centrally planned decisions—concerning wage policy, pricing, targeting of specific markets, employment levels, physical location of the enterprise, and levels of investment—had an equally deleterious impact. Judging from reports published by the country's National Institute of Statistics and the Central Bank of Tunisia, the overwhelming share of state enterprises by 1980 showed no profit while state capital transfers had skyrocketed from approximately 12 million dinars when the socialist experiment was abandoned to almost 200 million dinars in 1980; state financing of state enterprises as a percentage of total state expenditure rose from 6 percent in 1969 to 20 percent in 1980.[25] High management costs, fixed prices, inefficient capitalization, and underutilization of production were singled out as the most important factors in the deteriorating financial situation of the public companies—despite rising subsidies and substantial public investment.

By 1980 Tunisia's public enterprises had become highly inefficient, for a combination of structural (economic) reasons and political expediency,

Table 5.1: Role of State Enterprises in the Tunisian Economy (%)

	1970	1980
Share in GDP	26.0	25.0
Share in gross investment	31.0	34.0
Share in nonagricultural salaries	20.0	30.0
Share of merchandise exports	80.0	70.0

Source: Abdessatar Grissa, "The Tunisian State Enterprises and Privatization Policy," in *Tunisia: The Political Economy of Reform,* ed. I. William Zartman (Boulder, CO: Lynne Reinner, 1991).

while a parallel private sector selectively benefitted from the exemptions granted by the state. Most worrisome to the Mzali government that took office in 1980 was the fact that, despite growing international economic restraints, in only a handful of cases did public capital transfers contribute to gross capital formation within state enterprises. Although it was clear that the increasing financial deficits needed to be addressed, it was not until 1986, for reasons explained above, that Tunisia moved decisively toward restructuring and toward reassigning to the private sector a more important role in the development of the country.[26] By that time the Tunisian government and the state enterprises, with government guarantees, had borrowed extensively: in 1986, when the IMF-administered restructuring effort was formally adopted, the country's total debt represented half of its GDP (compared to less than 30 percent in 1969) and the ratio of debt servicing amounted to a third of the value of exports. In addition, state enterprises consumed an estimated one third of available domestic credit.

The *plan de redressement économique* was formally put into action on August 19, 1986.[27] Following a particularly severe financial crisis in 1985 when Tunisia's external current account deficit made further borrowing on the international market virtually impossible, the country turned, for the first time since 1967, toward the IMF. As part of an austerity plan, the Tunisian government committed itself not only to privatizing certain state enterprises—wholly or in part—but also to eliminating import restrictions, liberalizing pricing mechanisms for agricultural, manufacturing, and industrial products, reducing the massive public deficit, devaluing the dinar, and creating real interest rates that were realistic and no longer deliberately kept negative.[28]

The scope of the plan—a mixture of privatization and liberalization measures that threatened to affect either the political or economic interests of virtually all clients or interest groups in Tunisian society—raised many questions beyond those of pure economic efficiency. If fully implemented the plan meant a retreat from the welfare state comparable only in scope to the abandonment of socialism in 1969, an event that had triggered a profound crisis from which the state had never fully recovered.[29] Immediately the Tunisian opposition and the Islamists, in particular, raised the issue of equity—a concern heightened by the absence of legal norms regulating the process of privatization at the enterprise level.

In its pursuit of privatization, Tunisia has followed what amounts to well-accepted procedures: clarifying and changing the legal statutes of the public enterprises; allowing private competition for economic activities previously monopolized by the state enterprise; the leasing or outright sale of state enterprises; swapping shares in public companies for debt owed to private entrepreneurs.[30] The legal framework of July 20, 1985, which stated that state enterprises were those in which the state owned 10 percent or more of the paid-up capital, was amended in 1987 and again on February 1, 1989, raising this level to 50 percent. The new law instantly removed one third of the state enterprises from the public sector.[31] They were subsequently either eliminated altogether or found new private owners, or were leased under debt-equity arrangements. The latter were particularly successful in the hotel business.[32] By mid-1989, 22 state enterprises had been privatized. The new legislation on liberalization of the mid-1980s closely dovetailed the structural adjustment plan advocated by the IMF. It provided for further denationalization and more flexible rules on foreign exchange, investments, and imports. These measures—further extended under the Ben Ali government—resulted in (relatively small) private investments in the textiles and garments sector where relatively low capitalization, inexpensive labor, and high returns made infusions of private capital attractive. Private investment in commodities was equally selective, concentrating in areas where prices had been decontrolled, for example, food processing and building materials.

Despite their relative success in these particular areas, both privatization and liberalization strategies have been hindered by the heavy debt of most of the public companies and the tight credit policies in Tunisia. The former has resulted in making many of the public companies unattractive to local and foreign investors alike.[33] To ease the credit problem the government embarked on a restructuring of the banking system. On January 1, 1987, the first restrictions on interest rates were abolished. Within a few days, however, one of Tunisia's banks, the *Societé Tunisienne de Banque* (STB), "informally" proposed rates to be charged for money deposited or borrowed. The other state banks adopted STB's suggestions soon after, in effect sidestepping official recommendations. Besides this circumvention of the rules, there was an additional difficulty. In the past bank directors in Tunisia had virtually no discretion in deciding upon the creditworthiness of public companies. It is difficult to expect them to disengage themselves from clients that have close links to the State—even if these clients' companies are in the red. It seems clear that a hurdle still has to be jumped, although there is some evidence that by mid-1991 private banks in Tunisia have begun to refuse clients, thus setting a trend for state banks to follow. In general, the restructuring of the banking system in Tunisia—as in all North African countries—has been much slower than predicted. But it is also clear that if Tunisian banks want to maintain their credit ratings in the international market, they will have little choice but to pass on some of these efficiency considerations to their clients—no matter how close former links may have been.

In the summer and fall of 1991, the revenue losses resulting from the Gulf crisis prompted the Tunisian government to attempt a further expansion of its privatization drive.[34] The previous privatization effort had generally been limited to smaller enterprises or those—such as the hotel industry—that proved attractive to Tunisian and other Arab investors. The total value of state assets sold was approximately $120 million, a figure both local and World Bank economists considered too low to have a real impact.[35] The current second phase of Tunisian privatization is substantially more ambitious and will involve several of the "strategic state enterprises" the government was unwilling to sell until now. These include parts of the state-owned shipyards, internal transportation that remains a virtual state monopoly, and a share of the country's cement industry. Included in this second phase is an attempt to upgrade the role of the Tunis stock exchange, to further attract foreign investment and, as a palliative to local labor, to provide incentives for employee share-ownership programs in the privatized enterprises.

STATE AND SOCIETY, ECONOMIC LIBERALIZATION AND DEMOCRACY

Tunisia's current economic strategy aims to go far beyond the lackluster liberalization policies that followed Ben Salah's socialist experiment in the 1960s. If the current combination of readjustment, privatization, and liberalization is fully implemented, Tunisia will not only have shed a sizable number of its public enterprises, but will also have put into place export-oriented measures for whose sake prices, interest rates, credit, and import duties will be drastically relaxed while subsidies are phased out. This would in effect disengage the Tunisian state more fully from the daily management of the country's economy than at any point in its postindependence history.

As the Tunisian state removes itself from its distribution and investment functions, the market becomes an important arbiter and the arena for greater conflicts among groups within society. Deregulating the banking sector, for example, means in effect that the state is giving up the control and provision of credit, one of the most powerful means of patronage. Further financial deregulation will give political intermediaries even more autonomy in a sector the state once considered vital to economic policy and to its ability to extend patronage. The issue of autonomy in what has been a clientalist system until now forces the state to make several difficult choices. It must hand over its former pricing and market-allocation responsibilities without losing the confidence of either its international creditors or that of the clans and clienteles upon which it has traditionally relied.

In addition, the country's long history of state-directed economic development and close political tutelage now forces the state to face the even more acute problem raised by Ben Ali in the National Pact: that of redistribution and equity. Who does the state negotiate with on these issues? Showing clear analogies to the inclusionary authoritarian politics of his predecessor, the Tunisian president initially answered the question forcefully and unequivocally: the state's attempt to reinvigorate the country's political life while attempting economic growth, adjustment, and a greater reliance on market-oriented growth must include every organized group within civil society. In his speech that preceded the signing of the National Pact, Ben Ali clearly indicated that the structural adjustment policies could only be successful if some sort of political liberalization—what he consistently referred to as democracy—was instituted as well. Tunisia, he argued, could not afford sustained opposition from the organized and unorganized groups within its society; their cooperation in the productive process was essential to the efficient operation of its economy. His initial strategy therefore was to accommodate the differing groups to the largest extent possible—but on terms that proved unacceptable not only to his opposition but, on several occasions, to a part of the RCD as well. In every case, significant changes were suggested, implemented, and supervised by the president who argued that political reform and democracy in Tunisia must come about gradually: pluralism without limits can lead to demagogy.[36]

This unilateral intervention, however, hints at some of the continuing difficulties Tunisia faces in its quest for true pluralism. The first is that in

Tunisia the central state apparatus is able to make virtually all major decisions unencumbered by pressures from society. The temptation for unilateral action is heightened by the lingering presence of a hegemonic party system where opposition parties are legal but do not have a real chance to compete against the dominant party.[37] This autonomy is further enhanced by this system's outcome: the absence of an opposition with clearly articulated programs. The Tunisian syndicalist movement remains fractured after its internal disagreements and the altercations with the government of the last decade. Of the opposition parties, only the MDS has belatedly (in 1987) drawn up an economic blueprint for Tunisia's future. The Islamists' program, beyond a general call for a gradual return to Islamic principles described in its *bayan,* has few concrete guidelines to offer—even though its calls for social justice are seen by many of its adherents as a program.

All these contributed to the exceedingly difficult and increasingly frustrating first two years of Ben Ali's tenure. At a time when his country had become too differentiated to be ruled by a single person, he initially outpaced the ability to reform of both his own party and of the opposition. The result, clearly visible since then, has been the creation of what Youssef Cohen, writing about Brazil in the early 1960s, has called "democracy from above"—where a small circle of powerful state elites shapes internal political representation to meet both its own criteria of participation and democracy and those of its international supporters. As in Brazil, where this "imposed democracy" eventually paved the way for "political polarization and radicalization of the democratic regime,"[38] the danger in increasing radicalization in Tunisia clearly exists, as events of the last two years indicate: the authoritarian but (historically) inclusionary regime seems poised to become an exclusionary type now that one of the major players clearly no longer accepts the rules of the game once contained within Bourguiba's rational-legal state.

The obstacle course the government created for dealing with the Islamists outlived its practical value. The state, once so successful that the country's main Islamic thinker explicitly renounced violence and proposed an accommodation that programmatically fell within the norms of the National Pact, has reverted to open confrontation.[39] Not even Ben Ali's attempt to mute the militant secularism of his predecessor can obfuscate the different perceptions of justice and equity and solutions to them the state and the Islamists have.

Beyond the Islamists there is society at large. If, as David Marquand observes, "the undistorted market automatically rewards those who have the wit and the will to adjust, while punishing those who lack them," a substantial part of Tunisia's poor and urbanized population have little to expect in the short run from the economic liberalization.[40] They include those who have no stake in Tunisia's growth or future, a group Serge Adda has called "the second country," marginalized by the country's "*développement à deux vitesses.*" This group, estimated to encompass as much as 40 percent of the active, nonagricultural population and 30 percent of total population, has little to gain or lose by what is decided between the state and the opposing forces in society.[41]

The winnowing process that has reduced the political struggle to the representatives of the state and the Islamists makes Ben Ali's tightrope act even more difficult as his attempts at democratization and economic liberalization proceed. In these attempts as well as on issues involving equity and redistribution, the Islamists accuse the government of acting too slowly. They argue that Ben Ali is not really concerned with the redistribution of power and wealth, as a real democracy would imply. If privatization and liberalization lead to greater economic differentiation in the country—as it has in most Middle Eastern countries that have attempted similar strategies—the Islamists and the unions may seize upon this development as an indication of the government's bad faith. And no matter how rational the reduction of social security provisions and subsidies may appear in a *plan de redressement,* the impact is bound to reverberate most strongly among the poor that make up a substantial part of the Islamist membership.

On the other hand, the country's political elite and its *bourgeoisie d'affaires* may well view any attempt to tinker with the privatization strategy as a way of subverting existing arrangements, claiming that Ben Ali's real motive is a redistribution that would meet some of the demands of the Islamists. Affected already by the current stabilization program, these elites have shown little stomach for the kind of social giveaway clamored for by their opponents. Since mid-1989, the end result increasingly appears to be one of an escalating crisis between the two sides, heightened by the perception that the state is no longer interested in mediating.

For all of these reasons, one wonders whether Ben Ali's democracy is not, as Cohen has observed in Latin America, a "gift" from a small number of powerful state elites to a rather powerless society.[42] *La Presse,* with perhaps unintentional accuracy, wrote on the day of the April 2, 1989, elections that "the presidential election in many aspects looks like a referendum on the project for society proposed by the candidate Ben Ali."[43]

Tunisian elites have shown a growing concern with economic rationality, stimulated by internal and international factors and considerations. At the same time the resistance of the RCD to serious political reform remains a fact. It is hard to escape the conclusion that in Tunisia the political interests of the local elite do not substantially coincide with those of general economic development. The government has seemingly been intent on combining what Clifford Geertz, writing about developing countries in general, has called "a Smithean idea of how to get rich with a Hobbesian idea of how to govern."[44]

It is almost ironic that the man who during his first two years in office tried to create a new social contract has now returned to this Hobbesian pursuit. Although Ben Ali can perhaps no longer say, as his predecessor once did, that he *is* the Tunisian political system, it is clear that he is the most significant actor in that system and that the democratic rights he has bestowed upon Tunisia can be removed with almost the same ease with which they were granted. This descent toward political exclusion seems to have marked the Tunisian president's term in office since 1989, the result in part of frustration, fueled by what Carl Brown once termed the "Pygmalion Syndrome": a situation in which reform-minded elites are unable to reform civil society to their liking and ultimately became paternalistic and authoritarian, making the necessary reforms increasingly unlikely.[45] At least twice in the last century Tunisian rulers have fallen prey to this self-defeating circle of imposed reforms that find their origin in international as well as local pressures. The question is whether Ben Ali can resist this drift toward increased authoritarianism under the difficult circumstances and prospects his country now faces. The tentative answer, so far, seems negative.

NOTES

1. A mainstream definition of economic liberalization and privatization is used throughout this chapter. The former refers to the adoption of a number of measures—most notably the reduction of subsidies and the provision of a wide range of incentives—that allow prices of goods and commodities in a country to more accurately reflect their real cost of production. Privatization refers to the actual divestiture—in part or wholly—of state assets in favor of the private sector.
2. Tunisia partially abandoned its original socialist experiment in the agricultural sector in 1969, but retained state control over the country's approximately 300 national enterprises.
3. "Le Pacte Nationale" (Tunis: Ministry of Information, 1988, Mimeographed).
4. See for example his speech to the Tunisian parliament on the occasion of the National Pact, "Discours de Monsieur le Président de la République à la Chambre des Deputés a l'occasion de l'anniversaire du 7 Novembre 1988" (Tunis: Ministry of Information, November 7, 1988, Mimeographed), 3-4; also "Le Pacte National," 6.

5. Lisa Anderson, *The State and Social Transformation in Tunisia and Libya, 1830-1980* (Princeton: Princeton University Press, 1986), 231.
6. This is the so-called Salah Ben Youssef crisis. Ben Youssef had been party leader while Bourguiba was in exile prior to independence. Although both men represented different constituencies within the country, the catalyst for Ben Youssef's ouster from power was his objection to the autonomy agreements with France that Bourguiba supported. Ben Youssef was forced into exile and later assassinated in Frankfurt. For a recent Tunisian appraisal of the Ben Youssef affair, consult Ali Hamdi, "Regard sur le mouvement Youssefiste," *Realités,* February 21, 1988, 47-49.
7. On charismatic leadership in Tunisia, see the author's "Bourguiba, Charismatic Leadership and the Tunisian One-Party System," *Middle East Journal* 34, no. 2 (1980).
8. A good account of the first decade of single-party politics in Tunisia can be found in Clement Henry Moore, *Tunisia since Independence: The Dynamics of One-Party Government* (Berkeley: University of California Press, 1965).
9. Hamza Alavi, "The State in Post-Colonial Societies: Pakistan and Bangladesh," *New Left Review* 74 (July-August 1972), 61. For an elaboration and a criticism of the notion of an overdeveloped state, see Colin Leys, "The 'Overdeveloped' Post-Colonial State: A Re-evaluation," *Review of African Political Economy* 5 (January-April 1976). According to Leys, in an overdeveloped state "the inherited state apparatus is larger, its coercive or administrative powers weightier or more ramified, than they would be if the colonial state had not had to subordinate all the domestic classes." (p. 41).
10. What Ahmed Ben Salah, the architect of the country's socialist experiment that ran from 1961 until 1969, once called "a temporary and inevitable tutelage," quoted in *La Tunisie au présent: Une modernité au-dessus de tout soupçon?* ed. Michel Camau (Paris: Editions du C.N.R.S., 1987), 31.
11. For an overview of the period, see Lisa Anderson, "Democracy Frustrated: The Mzali Years in Tunisia," in *The Middle East and North Africa,* ed. Reeva Simon (New York: Columbia University Press, 1990).
12. The new name of the PSD was adopted by Ben Ali in February 1988. It hints at both continuity and discontinuity. As the PSD it qualified as a "constitutional" party, a reference to Bourguiba's rational-legal state. But the new party is now called a *rassemblement* rather than a single party, an obvious attempt to establish a broader base of support within Tunisia. Equally significant, it is now termed *démocratique*—a notion particularly important in Ben Ali's attempt to rally support to his government.
13. See the letter from Khelil to Ben Ali, "Lettre de Ismail Khelil au Président de la République," reproduced in *Realités,* September 16, 1988, 12-14; also his interview in *Le Renouveau,* August 5, 1988 in which he reiterates and defends the economic liberalization and restructuration principles adopted earlier.

14. See Serge Adda, "Enjeux: Le possible et le probable . . ." in *La Tunisie au présent,* ed. Michel Camau, 403.
15. Law No. 88-32, announced on May 3.
16. In contrast for example to the Algerian National Charter of 1976—and its updated version of 1986—that was primarily meant to consolidate consensus behind the one-party system.
17. Personal interviews by the author with Brahim Khayder of the *Mouvement d'Unité Populaire,* Najib Chabbi of the *Rassemblement Démocratique Socialiste* and Tayib Baccouche of the *Union Générale des Travailleurs Tunisiens,* November 2 and 3, 1988, Tunis.
18. Letter from Ben Ali addressed to all Tunisian national organizations and personalities, published by *Le Renouveau,* August 5, 1988.
19. *Le Renouveau,* the RCD newspaper, referred in its November 8, 1988 issue to the National Pact as "The Contract." *La Presse* described the purpose of the National Pact as the establishment of "a democratic state obtaining its legitimacy from the people."
20. Comment by Habib Achour to the author at the Carthage palace, November 7, 1988. Mr. Achour is the former leader of the UGTT who confronted the Bourguiba regime on several occasions. He was imprisoned several times for his activities. He resigned from all UGTT activities a few weeks before the signing of the National Pact, at the request of Ben Ali.
21. Opposition members pointed out that in some ways, Ben Ali was also reaping the fruits of his own policies. They argue that since assuming power, he has skillfully adopted several aspects of opposition parties' programs, in effect weakening them further by incorporating their demands into his own platform. He even went so far as to co-opt opposition figures into his government, or to send them off on diplomatic missions, much to their dismay. Ben Ali has described these actions as evidence of his desire to incorporate opposition figures in his policies.
22. The changing of the the Destour's name to *Parti Socialiste Destourien* in 1964 closely reflected this new orientation.
23. For details on the expansion of the public enterprises in the 1970s, consult Mohamed Midoun, "Entreprises publiques et développement économique" in *Administration at Développement en Tunisie* (Tunis: Institut International des Sciences Administratives, 1985).
24. The number of public enterprises had also grown rapidly and had increased to 560 by 1986.
25. Figures from annual Central Bank reports and Institute of Statistics quarterly reports, 1968-1988. For greater details of the deteriorating financial situation of the state enterprises, see the annexes in Abdessatar Grissa, "The Tunisian State Enterprises and Privatization Policy," in *Tunisia: The Political Economy of Reform,* ed. I. William Zartman (Boulder, CO: Lynne Rienner, 1991).
26. This was despite a number of studies that indicated the severity of the problems in the public sector. See for example the *Commission d'Etude, chargée de l'examen du fonctionnement des Entreprises publiques et de*

leurs relations avec l'Etat (Tunis: Ministry of National Economy, 1973). A National Commission in 1979 again investigated the problems; some of its recommendations were briefly considered after October 1979. In 1983 the Central Bank, after a revaluation of the Tunisian dinar, provided 90 million dinar toward a public company consolidation fund, which proved only a stopgap measure.

27. For more details, see especially the five-part review by Chadli Ayari, "L'application des Programmes d'Ajustement Structurel (PAS) en Tunisie (1986-1989); Un bilan critique," *Le Maghreb* (February 16 and 23, 1990; March 2, 9, and 16, 1990) and Mohammed Bouaouaja, "Privatization in Tunisia: Objectives and Limits," in *Privatization and Structural Adjustment in the Arab Countries,* ed. Said El-Naggar (Washington, DC: International Monetary Fund, 1989). The plan had been worked out in great part before Prime Minister Mzali's departure in July 1986 and was incorporated into the 1987-1991 Five-Year Plan, presented in July 1987. It was put into action on August 19, 1986 and closely resembled the earlier recommendations of the World Bank and the IMF.
28. Perhaps because of its sensitivity to the connotations associated with the word "privatization" the Tunisian government has not used it in its official documents, preferring instead to use the French words for "stabilization" and "readjustment." For a critique of privatization in the Tunisian context, see Azzam Mahjoub, "Etat, secteur publique et privatisation en Tunisie," *Annuaire de l'Afrique du Nord 1987* (Paris: Editions du C.N.R.S., 1989), 299-315.
29. For greater details on the symbolic aspect of that earlier abandonment, consult Elbaki Hermassi and Dirk Vandewalle, "The Second Stage of State-building in the Maghreb," in *State and Society in Contemporary North Africa,* ed. I. William Zartman (Boulder, CO: Westview, forthcoming).
30. The actual sale of shares in public companies has been discussed but not yet implemented, largely because the Tunis stock exchange remains very weak at this point.
31. One indirect early victim was the *Société Tunisienne d'Industrie Automobile* (STIA) in Sousse, a car assembly plant that was closed in 1988.
32. The public hotel industry in Tunisia (the *Société Hotelière et Touristique de Tunisie*—SHTT) is in many ways exceptional. Created in 1959 at the time when tourism was still unknown in Tunisia, it built most of the infrastructure that would fuel the tourist industry of the 1960s. Compared to many other public entities it was little burdened with debt and promised investors relatively quick and sizeable profits. Several of the hotels were handed over to *Société Tunisienne de Banque* to settle debts SHTT had incurred at that bank.
33. The first example of active foreign involvement in a public enterprise was the participation of *Dominion Textiles de Canada* in SITEX, a small subsidiary of the restructured *Société Générale des Industries Textiles* (SOGITEX), the country's public textile concern that had been created in 1960.

34. An important aspect of this renewed attention to privatization concerned the return to normalcy of tourist receipts that had brought an unexpected windfall to Tunisia in 1988 and 1989 after neighboring Libya opened its borders, allowing its citizens to travel. They spent an estimated $1.5-2 billion in the country. Losses directly related to the Gulf crisis—a downturn of regular tourism, lost expatriate and export earnings, lost Arab aid—are estimated at $1.5 billion for 1990-91 alone.
35. *Mideast Report* 24, no. 16 (September 15, 1991), 7.
36. See for example his interview to *Le Monde* of September 10, 1988, reprinted as "Interview accordée par le President Zine el Abidine Ben Ali au Journal *Le Monde*" (Tunis: Ministry of Information, 1988), and a collection of statements and decisions in *Le Processus Démocratique* (Tunis: Ministry of Information, May 1988). This theme was repeated at the RCD Congress in July 1988. Consult Ben Ali's *Discours d'ouverture du Congrès du Salut* (Tunis: Ministry of Information, 1988).
37. For notions of the hegemonic party system consult Larry Diamond, Seymour Martin Lipset and Juan Linz, "Building and Sustaining Democratic Government in Developing Countries: Some Tentative Findings," *World Affairs* (Summer 1987).
38. Youssef Cohen, "Democracy from Above: The Political Origins of Military Dictatorship in Brazil," *World Politics* 40 (October 1987), 30-54.
39. See my discussion of Rachid al-Ghanouchi's changing ideas about violence and other concepts in "From the New State to the New Era: Toward a Second Republic in Tunisia," *Middle East Journal* 42, no. 4 (Autumn 1988).
40. David Marquand, *The Unprincipled Society: New Demands and Old Policies* (London: Jonathan Cape, 1988), 2.
41. Serge Adda, "Enjeux: le possible et le probable . . ." in *La Tunisie au présent,* ed. Michel Camau, 404.
42. Cohen, "Democracy From Above," 46.
43. *La Presse,* April 2, 1989.
44. Clifford Geertz, comment in Plenary Session in *Daedalus* (Winter 1989), 238-239.
45. L. Carl Brown, *The Tunisia of Ahmad Bey, 1837-1855* (Princeton: Princeton University Press, 1974), 363.

Part III

Economic Reform and the Politics of Regime Transformation

6

Jordan's Great Gamble: Economic Crisis and Political Reform

Robert Satloff

The 1980s ended on a particularly ominous and jarring note for the Hashemite Kingdom of Jordan. In April 1989, thousands of Jordanians took to the streets to vent their anger against price hikes announced as part of an economic adjustment plan agreed to by the central government and the International Monetary Fund (IMF). For five days, protests spread throughout the country, claiming at least 12 lives and causing millions of dollars in property damage. That the demonstrations originated in the south of the Kingdom and included almost exclusively Transjordanians, long considered the bedrock of the Hashemite family's popular support, came as a rude shock to Jordan's political firmament.

Six months later, East Bankers delivered a second shock to the ruling establishment with the results of elections to choose a new parliament for the first time in more than two decades. Of the 80 deputies elected on November 8, 32 were affiliated with Islamic opposition political groups inside the Kingdom and another ten were leftist critics of the regime. At year's end, the Jordanian government found itself trying to strike an elusive balance between living up to the terms of the IMF agreement on the one hand and satisfying the demands of an increasingly obstreperous parliament and public opinion on the other.

Those two events—violence and voting—formed a trying and troublesome ending to a decade that had opened with promise and optimism. Jordan ended the 1970s with one of the world's fastest-growing economies.

Between 1972 and 1983, for example, the Kingdom was able to boast real annual growth rates (GNP) averaging almost 10 percent.[1] Business boomed; construction, banking, and trade all flourished and unemployment was practically nonexistent. It was a heady time for a country whose main exports were people—a highly educated labor force that built, serviced, and maintained the Gulf economies and the moderate political image of its king, Hussein bin Talal.

Jordan owed its phenomenal growth—and its subsequent economic decline—to its position as a non-oil-exporting oil economy.[2] The three main components of Jordan's post-1973 economic prosperity were all derivatives of the oil boom and the massive transfer of wealth to OPEC countries following the October 1973 Middle East war. These components were Arab aid, export growth, and workers' remittances. Inter-Arab government-to-government transfers (Arab aid) to Jordan, formalized by the 1978 post-Camp David Baghdad Arab League summit resolution to provide assistance to "front-line" states, rose from $71.8 million in 1973 to $1.179 billion in 1981 (current dollars). Jordan's commodity exports, most of which found their way to Gulf oil producers, increased in the same period from $57.6 to $734.9 million. And the net gain from the remittances of the more than 350,000 Jordanians (mainly of Palestinian origin) employed outside the Kingdom—about 40 percent of Jordan's workforce—jumped from $15 million in 1970 to $900 million in 1981. Together, these three sources of revenue amounted to 84 percent of the Kingdom's 1981 GDP.[3]

In some ways, the pattern of Jordan's economy remained true to historical form. Lacking in natural resources (its only commodity exports of note are phosphates, fertilizer, and cement) and burdened with the demographic dislocations of war and a rapidly growing population (one of the fastest growing in the world), Jordan has never been able to stand on its own economic feet. From its inception in 1921, first as the Amirate of Transjordan and then as the Hashemite Kingdom, Jordan's economic health has been precarious. The Kingdom has always relied for its survival upon injections of capital from outside donors. Throughout the first five decades of its history, those patrons were Britain, the United States, and the UN Relief and Works Agency for Palestine Refugees (UNRWA), and their contributions to Jordan's economic existence were no less critical than the aid offered by Arab states in the 1970s and 1980s.[4]

But there are two key differences between Jordan's experience with predominantly Western aid pre-1970 and Arab aid since then. First, whereas Western aid was normally only adequate to stave off economic privation and maintain a certain controlled level of development, Arab aid was of a completely different magnitude. It was mammoth enough to permit the Kingdom to embark upon far-reaching development and infrastructure projects, large-scale armament purchases and unprecedented consumer purchasing. In short, it was large enough for the Kingdom to "get hooked" on a standard of living it could not possibly enjoy through its own or any other means.[5] Second, there were fundamentally different rationales behind Western and Arab aid. The offer of Western aid grew out of a political determination on the part of the major donors to assist a moderate, anti-Communist regime; it was not, for the most part, a function of the economic health of the donor countries. In contrast, Arab aid rose and fell with the region's changing economic circumstances; the price of crude oil, not "Arab solidarity," was the main factor governing economic relations within the Arab world. This distinction grew in significance with the onset of a depressed oil market in the mid-1980s, when the economic self-interest of most Gulf oil exporters outweighed their protestations of "Arab solidarity" and Jordan's petro-windfall disappeared. During the era of Western aid, a realignment of Jordan's foreign policy could satisfy its patrons and elicit more economic assistance, but the era of oil-based aid left Jordan with very little control over the source of its financial support. That Jordan's political leaders failed to recognize the distinction between the two types of aid early on proved to be a painful and costly error.

Beginning in 1983, the reverberations of the global glut in oil began to be felt inside the Kingdom. From a high of $1.2 billion, Arab aid fell to well under $400 million in 1988, with only Saudi Arabia fulfilling (more or less) its Arab League commitments.[6] As construction, teaching, and engineering jobs grew scarce in the Gulf, workers' remittances were cut in half, from $1.237 billion in 1984 to little more than $600 million in 1989.[7] Only Aqaba's pivotal role as Iraq's main transit point for supplies of food and matériel in its war with Iran kept Jordan's export and re-export earnings relatively sound, but even they came upon hard times with the end of the Iran-Iraq War.

In most countries, an economic turnaround of such proportions would have monopolized the time and interest of political leaders. But not so in Jordan. Given its reliance on outside benefactors and its peculiar role in the Arab-Israeli conflict, Jordan's political firmament has long focused a disproportionate amount of its energy and attention on inter-Arab and international relations rather than on domestic and financial matters. This has been anecdotedly reported by one historian who wrote of a foreign diplomat close to Hussein who told him of the "glassy look" that came over the King's eyes "the moment the conversation turned to details of finance, however important."[8] More recently, a paper outlining Jordan's strategic imperatives written by a top political advisor to King Hussein in 1986 had virtually nothing to say about finance, trade, debt, or economics.[9] Therefore, even though the signs of imminent decline in the Kingdom's principal sources of hard currency—remittances from workers abroad, Arab financial assistance, and other spin-off benefits from the Gulf oil boom—were clear by 1984, the Kingdom failed to respond with tight fiscal policy, prudent borrowing, and closely managed importing of goods and foodstuffs.[10] On the contrary, Jordanian political leaders (and none of Jordan's prime ministers in the 1980s—Mudar Badran, Ahmad Obeidat and Zayd al-Rifa'i—escape guilt) chose one of three paths: to ignore the glaring structural weaknesses in the economy, to hide them under the rug of further borrowing at commercial rates, or to exacerbate them with expansionary policies that only shrank the Kingdom's finite foreign currency reserves.

From the beginning of the oil recession to the end of the 1980s, Jordan took on billions of dollars in commercial debt, signed weapons contracts (including deals for French and British airplanes and Soviet missiles and air defense systems) worth billions more, and continued to commit hundreds of millions of dollars to questionable development projects (such as the expansion of the telephone network and the unification of electric grids with neighboring Arab states). In the early recession years between 1984 to 1986, government spending actually increased as a percentage of GDP by nearly 10 percent. To correct the trade deficit, which has exceeded $1.5 billion every year since 1980, the government's preferred policy was to institute costly subsidies and export supports. The Kingdom drew down its foreign exchange reserves held abroad to finance its recurring budget deficits, which resulted in a drop in investment income from $205 million in 1982 to $58 million in 1987. By the end of that year, the Kingdom's real GNP growth was -2.4 percent, and the ratio of debt to GNP a decidedly unhealthy 70 percent. By 1988, the Kingdom's annual debt service amounted to about $900 million on debt that, after the 1989 deluge, was found to total more than $8 billion.[11]

To be sure, Jordan was let down by wealthier Arab states, all of which (except Saudi Arabia) failed to live up to their 1979 aid commitments. And the Kingdom's very successful educational program—Jordan has one of the highest student populations per capita in the world—produces far more skilled laborers and professionals than the country can absorb. Moreover, the roller-coaster nature of U.S. security and economic assistance over the past decade could only have complicated the job of Jordan's economic planners.[12]

But when the fat years turned lean in the mid-1980s, Jordan took few steps to rein in public and consumer spending to enable the Kingdom to live within its own means. Government policy in those years did not improve the deteriorating situation, but worsened it. Economic decisions of momentous political importance were taken throughout the 1980s, but they were rarely the subject of debate within the political leadership, let alone among the public at large. Finally, in 1988, a series of events combined to alter the typical pattern of Jordanian politics with the result that the Kingdom's leaders—and its people—turned inward for the first time since the 1970 civil war. What they found was an economy in disarray.

Jordan's principal foreign policy objectives in the mid-1980s were threefold: subordination of the Palestine Liberation Organization (PLO) to Jordan's peace-process policy; Arab solidarity with Iraq in its battle with non-Arab Iran; and restoration of good-neighbor relations with Jordan's potentially most bellicose neighbor, Syria.[13] By 1988, all three of these goals were either met or moot. A series of Jordanian initiatives to repair ties with Syria, including a commitment not to flout Damascus's interests in the peace process, had proven successful, and on the inter-Arab level, the King's strategy of championing Iraq was working as well. As host of the Arab League summit in Amman, November 1987, the King capped his diplomatic success by engineering unanimous approval for a strongly worded condemnation of Iran and by gaining Syria's acquiescence in the restoration of bilateral ties between other Arab states and Egypt, ostracized by much of the Arab world since the signing of its peace treaty with Israel. In clearly establishing the Iran-Iraq War as a higher Arab priority than the Palestine conflict, the Amman summit was a personal victory for King Hussein and a stunning and humiliating defeat for his longtime rival, PLO leader Yasir Arafat.

But with the approval of a ceasefire in the Gulf in 1988, the importance of the Iran-Iraq War in inter-Arab politics receded and with it went Jordan's peculiar role as a small state rallying larger and more powerful states to action. The Palestinian uprising against Israeli rule in the West Bank and Gaza supplanted the Iran-Iraq War on the inter-Arab agenda and the Arab world once again turned its attention toward the politics of Palestine. There, Jordan found itself at a distinct disadvantage.

Traditionally, that politics is defined by Jordan's state of perpetual tension with the PLO, the Kingdom's historic rival for the allegiance of Palestinians and for the territory of Palestine. Since its inception in 1964, the PLO has clashed with Jordan in messy and often violent competition for the loyalty of—and control over—the Palestinians.[14] The coincidence of the *intifada* and the winding down of the Iran-Iraq War offered Arafat a chance to reclaim his spot on the Arab stage with a vengeance. Hussein's own commitment to the Palestine cause was called into question by the thousands of Palestinian demonstrators whose slogans seemed to target him almost as much as the Israeli occupation. As a result, Jordan, with its own huge Palestinian population, was forced into a defensive and vulnerable role virtually overnight. When the PLO succeeded in scuttling the Jordan-focused peace plan tabled by U.S. Secretary of State George Shultz, Hussein knew that the tide of Arab politics, which he had ridden so high the previous November, had now turned against him. At an extraordinary Arab League summit in Algiers in June 1988, Arafat sought not only to reestablish his imprimatur on all matters relating to Palestine but to avenge his humiliation at the Amman summit meeting eight months earlier. King Hussein stood his ground in a combative but statesmanlike defense of his country's contribution to the Palestine cause, but to salvage both his personal stature and his country's own security, he decided that drastic measures were needed.

Those measures reached their climax with the dramatic decision, announced by the King on July 31, to sever all "legal and administrative ties" to the West Bank and to relinquish any Hashemite claims to the territory lost in the June 1967 war.[15] Hussein's moves shocked both the American and the Israeli diplomatic establishments, in whose conventional wisdom had long ago been enshrined a place for Jordan as the principal Arab partner for peace. For the time being, at least, the "Jordanian option" for Arab-Israeli peace, in all of its various permutations, was no longer in the cards.

Jordan's disengagement from the West Bank brought to a close an era of fast-paced, high-profile political and diplomatic activity in the international arena. The end of the Iran-Iraq War and the onset of the *intifada* together deprived the Kingdom of the environmental conditions that had allowed it to assume such an extroverted identity in the mid-1980s. Instead, the Kingdom turned inward, and a series of domestic problems that had been percolating beneath the surface inside the East Bank came to brew with the divorce from the West Bank. The economy topped the list.

An IMF team that visited Jordan in March 1988 for its periodic consultation discussions was presented with a rosy appraisal of the Kingdom's medium-term financial prospects. Imports, they were told by Jordanian representatives, would be kept to their 1987 level; higher levels of Arab aid, they said, were assured. Indeed, the Jordanians expressed hope that the regional "economic recession"—i.e., the price of oil—and the "current political strains"—i.e., the *intifada*—might soon ease. At the time, the IMF team urged the Jordanians to abandon their piecemeal response to the regional recession and to deal head-on with the structural deficiencies in the local economy. The Jordanians demurred, and because the country's problems "still appeared to be manageable," the IMF team did not press too forcefully for the "drastic measures" it thought would be needed at a later stage. The Jordanians evidently believed they would be able to find the capital to service their commercial debt and thereby avoid having to turn to the IMF. They were wrong on both counts.[16]

Even before the disengagement announcement, Jordan faced serious economic difficulties that had nothing to do with the *intifada*. For example, a crisis in trading relations with the Kingdom's largest trading partner had broken out in May 1988, when the Jordanian government froze letters of credit to Jordanian exporters to Iraq because the Iraqis had run up $240 million more in orders than was allotted for in the bilateral trade protocol. By the end of 1988, overall Iraqi debt to Jordan reach nearly $600 million, an enormous "accounts receivable" on the Kingdom's already fragile balance sheet.[17] Then, in May and June 1988, as Jordan's political fortunes in the Arab world worsened, there were two small but worrisome runs on the normally stable Jordanian dinar, each resulting in a 5 percent depreciation of the currency. By the end of June, foreign currency reserves had dropped to an all-time low of $18.7 million, a 92 percent drop in one year and not enough to cover two weeks of imports.[18] Timely aid from Saudi Arabia and the United Arab Emirates averted bankruptcy in July but the disengagement decision at the end of the month unleashed forces that sent the dinar, and the economy, into a tailspin.

The politics of the *intifada* and the West Bank disengagement decision turned a numbing economic decline into an immediate crisis. Cutting ties to the West Bank placed new restrictions on Palestinian travel, study, and commerce in Jordan, but, more importantly, it reopened old wounds about the role Palestinians play—and are allowed to play—in the Kingdom itself. When, in his July 31 speech, Hussein underscored the need for a society in which "order and discipline prevail," many longtime Palestinian residents of the East Bank took it to mean that their status as Jordanian citizens was now in jeopardy. The removal of one of the Kingdom's leading Palestinians from the upper house of parliament, the imposition of tight restrictions on several prominent Palestinian journalists, and the replacement of regular five-year passports with special two-year travel permits for West Bankers lent credence to these fears.

Palestinians control the bulk of the wealth in Jordan's banking, trade, and commercial sectors and their political fears were soon translated into economic jitters. In August and September, the lack of Palestinian confidence and security in their position inside the Kingdom turned the trickle of Palestinians selling dinars for dollars into a flood.[19] Though Jordan saved $60 million by cutting spending on West Bank salaries and development projects, that gain was more than offset by the post-disengagement run on the dinar. This was especially so on the West Bank itself, where the currency's black-market rate plummeted to nearly par with the dollar.[20] Despite government measures to shore up the dinar, another 15 percent of the currency's value was lost in mid-October. The slide was halted by the imposition of new government regulations, amounting to the first flotation of the dinar in the Kingdom's history, but not before the dinar had lost about one-third of its value within six months.

In early November 1988, the government unveiled its first major austerity program, freezing spending on development projects, banning the import of many luxury goods, and sharply raising fees for foreign worker permits, customs duties, and taxes on hotels and restaurants. In announcing the measures, Finance Minister Hanna Odeh boldly claimed austerity would save the Kingdom $200 million in foreign currency by the end of 1989 and "shift [Jordan] from a consuming to a producing society." But as Prime Minister Zayd al-Rifa'i noted at the time, the government had no stomach to cut current expenditures, nearly two-thirds of which, he said, were committed to defense outlays and government salaries. Nevertheless, al-Rifa'i ruled out any suggestion of resorting to international lending agencies to help relieve Jordan's debt-service burden of $900 million per year. "We honor all our debts," he said. (In fact, as of the end of September 1988, Jordan was 90 days in arrears on more than $58 million owed to the United States.)[21]

Despite the heady rhetoric, the austerity program proved too little too late. Within days, speculative trading pushed the dinar even lower. This had the effect of reinforcing the disincentive for expatriates to remit their salaries back home while it took a further bite out of the purchasing power of the many Jordanians who live on fixed public-sector incomes. King Hussein tried to put the best possible face on the depressed dinar in a December 1988 interview with the Kuwaiti daily *al-Siyasah*. "We are very happy with the decline in the exchange rate," he said, "because this will lead to an increase in exports and will assure the foreign investor that there will not be any future decrease [in the value of the dinar]."[22] Again, this was optimistic.

The crisis of confidence in the dinar and in the overall wisdom of the government's economic policies came to a head in late January 1989. The Jordanian government was forced to withdraw a seven-year, $150 million loan just a few days after it was opened for syndication in Europe because it had virtually no subscribers. This highly public repudiation of the Kingdom's creditworthiness was a sobering shock to the government, which had almost casually run up billions in debt in recent years, as well as to local bankers and speculators. News of the loan withdrawal generated a further run on the dinar. On February 8 the government reacted with some measure of determination, invoking martial law to close down the 70-odd moneychangers that operated on the fringes of the Kingdom's banking regulations.[23] But speculation was a symptom, not a cause, of the Kingdom's financial woes. When several of Jordan's lenders refused to agree to a three-month rollover of $16.5 million in interest payments on a five-year-old commercial Euroloan, it was clear that Jordan's earlier unbridled optimism was unfounded. On February 28 Central Bank Deputy Governor Mahir Shukri announced that Jordan intended to request standby credit from the IMF to help the Kingdom weather its financial crisis. Only three weeks earlier, Prime Minister al-Rifa'i had told an interviewer that "Generally speaking, the economic situation in Jordan is good and suffers no problems."[24]

An IMF team arrived in Amman March 17; negotiations with the government began ten days later.[25] By that time, Jordan was already $185 million in arrears on external debt payments, $77 million of which was on interest. Perhaps as a way to impress upon the IMF officials its fiscal seriousness, during the talks the government announced the indefinite postponement of its $875 million purchase of British Tornado strike-fighter aircraft.[26]

The IMF team remained in Amman nearly a month, working out the details of a structural adjustment plan with the Jordanian team, chaired by Finance Minister Odeh. On April 13 Odeh and Central Bank governor Hussein Qasim formally requested an IMF standby credit arrangement and approved an adjustment plan that, as the staff report on the Jordan-IMF talks noted, was designed to "promote private savings, reduce the budget deficit, improve resource allocation, contain monetary expansion, promote exports, remittances, and tourism, and limit contraction of new nonconcessional external debt." The medium-term macroeconomic objectives of the plan called for the recovery of economic growth to 4 percent per year by 1991; a 50 percent drop in the inflation rate from 15 percent in 1989 to 7 percent in 1993; and the elimination of the external current account deficit (including foreign grants) by 1993.

The formula for reaching these goals was simple—cut spending and imports and raise revenue and exports. The government committed itself to reducing total expenditure from 54 percent of GDP in 1988 to 46 percent in 1993 and to increasing revenue during the same period from 32 percent of GDP to 36 percent. Similarly, it agreed to limit import growth to just 4 percent per year while pursuing export-promotion policies to boost exports by 11 percent annually.

The "core" of the structural adjustment effort, the IMF staff report explained, "lies in raising revenues and containing expenditures so as to reduce the budget deficit." Because the austerity plan Jordan had implemented in late 1988—freezing government spending and subsidies and imposing several new duties and taxes—would have only a relatively insignificant impact on the deficit, it would need to be augmented by "additional measures." These measures, implemented by the Jordanian government on April 16, included price increases on a wide range of goods: petroleum products (11-33 percent); alcoholic beverages (40-50 percent); cigarettes (25 percent); soft drinks and mineral water (18 percent); detergents (25 percent); and steel bars (67 percent). Water charges in the Jordan Valley were doubled; automobile registration and licensing fees were raised and a "royalty tax" was placed on phosphate and potash production. In tandem with these price increases, the government agreed to reduce its subsidies on barley, bran, olive oil, and powdered milk by raising their domestic retail prices. Moreover, the government agreed to reduce or eliminate all subsidies for production and exports. All told, these measures were supposed to contribute to a decline in the budget deficit (excluding grants) from 23.7 percent of GDP in 1988 to 19.6 percent in 1989. In return for implementing and maintaining this strategy, Jordan earned the right to obtain up to $275 million in loans and credits over the subsequent 18 months, opening the door to rescheduling with the Paris Club (government-to-government debt) and the London Club (commercial debt) thereafter.[27]

To most Jordanians, announcement of the price hikes and subsidy cuts came as a complete shock. To be sure, the presence of the IMF team was widely noted in the local press and the need for stiff austerity measures widely recognized by local economists, businessmen, and bankers. But the al-Rifa'i government did virtually nothing to prepare the populace for the swiftness of the plan's implementation and the breadth of its scope. In fact, the prime minister had played down the effects of the anticipated adjustment plan in an interview with the national news agency PETRA just a few days before its implementation. "We did not discuss with representatives of the IMF the issue of changing the rate of exchange, nor the devaluation of the Jordanian currency," Rifa'i said on April 10. "Nor has there been any talk of lifting government subsidies on basic foodstuffs." Indeed, throughout the recession, subsidies and prices on staple goods were considered virtually sacrosanct—despite the fact that prices on some goods were permitted to rise as a result of the decision not to increase subsidies in line with the devaluation of the dinar. "The crisis," al-Rifa'i was fond of saying, "is financial, not economic."[28] In the midst of the holy months of Ramadan and with King Hussein on a state visit to Washington, few Jordanians expected an announcement from the government of the sort made over state-run television and radio the morning of April 16.

The popular response was swift and sure. In a matter of hours, Jordan's southern cities erupted in protest. In Ma'an, Kerak, Tafileh, and later, Madaba and even Salt, local townspeople threw rocks, looted, and chanted slogans against the al-Rifa'i government's alleged mismanagement of the economy. They charged high officials with wanton corruption and an uncaring "let-them-eat-cake" attitude toward the average Jordanian worker. The four days of protest that were to follow were only quelled by the despatch of Jordanian security forces. Embarrassingly, the King was forced to cut short his trip to Washington and London to return home and take control of the situation.

Economically, the adjustment plan was sound. It was not premised on any Pollyannaish notions of a resurgence in official Arab aid[29] or an abrupt turnaround in the prices of Jordan's export commodities, nor did it demand the immediate curtailment of subsidies on basic goods or the dismissal of large numbers of civil servants from the state bureaucracy. But whereas the Jordanians implemented the plan immediately after reaching agreement with the IMF team, they postponed discussion of specific "policies to protect the poor" for future IMF and World Bank missions. In doing so, the government failed to anticipate the extent to which the adjustment plan would touch a raw nerve among the body politic and unleash a popular backlash. The burden of the plan—whether real or perceived, it matters little—fell too heavily on low-wage Jordanian workers and laborers, mainly East Bankers from the south of the Kingdom, who had already benefitted least from the Kingdom's boom years in the early 1980s. According to Crown Prince Hassan, who visited the riot-torn southern cities soon after the outbreak of violence, "These [IMF] measures will be more than we can bear unless we can secure Arab aid."[30] Moreover, coinciding with Ramadan, the plan's implementation played into the hands of Muslim fundamentalists who, in several areas, were able to exploit and exacerbate the rioting for their own political purposes.

Especially notable about the rioting was that Transjordanians, not Palestinians, had risen in protest. Indeed, in Amman and Irbid, home to the lion's share of Jordan's Palestinian population, the days after the announcement passed almost without incident. Palestinians, along with Jordan's liberal and left-leaning professional organizations, did little more than send petitions to the Palace urging it to reconsider the austerity measures and to sack the prime minister, who was personally vilified as the man responsible for the Kingdom's economic morass. PLO officials liked to note that in Jordan's refugee camps, quiet was maintained on formal instructions from Arafat in Tunis. In fact, though, it was the realization among most Palestinians that participation in rioting might rip apart the carefully woven web of coexistence inside the Kingdom that kept them off the streets. Their quiescence proved that any fear about the possible spread of the Palestinian uprising from the West Bank eastward was clearly unfounded.

Of potentially greater gravity was the extent of disaffection among Transjordanians, the traditional mainstay of the Hashemite regime. Though the rioters' slogans were targeted against the al-Rifa'i government and not against the King,[31] the monarchy could not help but realize the depth of the dissatisfaction with the country's political and economic management. Almost immediately, the regime took steps to accommodate all the rioters' demands—save one. From the very beginning, the regime was resolved not to step back from the adjustment plan that sparked the riots in the first place.

First, on April 24, the King dismissed al-Rifa'i. Only four months earlier, Hussein had given his premier and boyhood friend a ringing vote of confidence—"[He] has achieved much and it is unfair to burden him with the government's negative responsibilities," Hussein said of al-Rifa'i. "[He] was able to carry out his duties the way we wanted him to."[32] But in Jordan's monarchical system, the prime minster must bear the burden for governmental errors even if they are shared by the Palace.[33] In al-Rifa'i's place the King appointed Chief of the Royal Court Sherif Zayd bin Shakir. A former armed forces commander and distant cousin of the King, Bin Shakir had a firm reputation for honesty and, given his role as military commander during the 1970 war against the PLO, was seen as sympathetic to the "East Bank first" partisans inside the Kingdom.

Second, the government took steps to restore confidence in the dinar. Foremost among these was the reappointment, after several years out of office, of Dr. Muhammad Sa'id al-Nabulsi as bank governor and the naming of Basil Jardaneh as minister of finance. Together, they decided to "come clean" with the Jordanian people regarding the true magnitude of the country's indebtedness and overall economic situation. In May 1989, a month after the riots, it was revealed that the al-Rifa'i government had sold more than 25 percent of the Kingdom's gold reserves to service its debt burden, which was in fact about $8.3 billion, nearly $2 billion more than had been previously reported.[34] Nabulsi and Jardaneh issued a series of sound reform measures aimed at stabilizing the dinar, bolstering the central bank's currency reserves, and rationalizing the use of foreign exchange.[35] They not only had to deal with the economic aftershocks of the price riots but also with the concerns of international credit and lending agencies. In the uncertainty that surrounded the riots and al-Rifa'i's resignation, the export-import banks of Japan, Britain, and West Germany all suspended or curtailed planned loans or medium- to long-term credits until the successful conclusion of debt rescheduling talks with the Paris Club. Jardaneh, therefore, proceeded apace with the Paris Club talks, and agreement was reached in mid-July on the rescheduling of principal and most of the interest on all payments falling due until the end of 1990, thereby opening the way for bilateral negotiations with each of the governments holding Jordanian debt. Moreover, Amman opened formal rescheduling talks with the Soviet Union, its largest creditor outside the Paris Club, in August and with the London Club of commercial banks in September. Eventually, agreements were reached covering all government and commercial debt.[36]

Third, King Hussein solicited millions of dollars in emergency aid, which was critical to the short-term stability of the dinar, from Saudi Arabia and other Gulf states throughout the spring and summer. But the generosity of Jordan's longtime patrons was not quite what Amman had thought to expect. About a month before the price riots, the Kuwait Fund for Arab Economic Development had suspended disbursements to Jordan because of Jordan's difficulties in meeting payments on its more than $200 million debt. (Indeed, Kuwaiti bankers have long proved to be among Jordan's most difficult and parsimonious creditors.) Following the riots, Gulf donors did provide Jordan with about $350 million in emergency aid (some of it in the form of crude oil) but there was no sign of any multiyear aid commitments that might have brightened Jordan's medium-term financial prospects. Moreover, a plan floated by Amman whereby Gulf states would deposit a total of about $1 billion in currency reserves in the Jordan Central Bank for Jordan's use languished for months and was only implemented in skeletal form.[37] By autumn, however, the dinar had recovered some of its lost value and Jordan's foreign exchange picture, if not bright, was certainly not as dark as it had been six months earlier.[38]

The riskiest and most uncertain aspect of the Kingdom's response to the April 1989 price riots was its strategic decision to temper the repercussions of the IMF adjustment plan with unprecedented domestic political reform. This was an especially important move given the al-Rifa'i government's reputation for restricting civil liberties and political rights. Over the previous two years, as Jordan's regional political and economic position took a turn for the worst, the government's limitations on constitutionally protected freedom of the press, movement, association, and speech grew more restrictive.[39] One member of the government went so far as to bemoan—on the pages of the *Washington Post*—the King's "isolation," the government's "rampant corruption," and the "official intolerance and growing power of the security services."[40] As part of his follow-up to the 1988 West Bank disengagement, King Hussein had suspended parliament because half its members represented communities on the West Bank, ostensibly no longer an area of Jordanian authority. Although Jordan's parliament lacked the power to influence government policy in any appreciable way, Hussein had long promised to revitalize it as an institution answerable to the concerns of the people. His objective was to reshape parliament into an East Bank-only assembly, thereby giving substance to his divorce from the West Bank. But the same week as the IMF riots broke out, the Interior Ministry announced plans for a new voting procedure and postponement of the election of a new parliament until 1990 at the earliest.

Almost immediately upon Bin Shakir's taking office, he and Hussein undertook to break the link between economic and political privation by embarking on a process of reform and liberalization. That process was highlighted by the restoration of parliamentary life as an outlet for political discontent; the King announced that long-promised parliamentary elections would definitely be held before year's end. In addition, days after the rioting, the King released all those detained for their role in the violence and authorized a partial amnesty for other prisoners, including political detainees. In the following weeks, Bin Shakir reinstated several prominent journalists who had been proscribed under the previous government and allowed local media to comment with some freedom on the internal economic and political situation.

Underpinning these efforts was a keen desire on the part of the regime to return to its East Bank roots and to reaffirm its ties to its most important domestic constituencies. Time and time again, the King addressed delegations of notables from the East Bank cities and towns that had been the scene of the April riots. His message often amounted to an apology for having spent too much time in the international arena and too little supervising domestic developments. "I believe I personally was probably not as involved as I might have otherwise been in the affairs of Jordan internally," said the King. "I had focused my attention on the Arab world and the world scene."[41]

The parliamentary elections of November 1989 were the climax of Jordan's internal drama. Elections were supposed to fulfill three objectives. First, their very occurrence was itself the fulfillment of the King's standing promise for the broadening of democracy, what former Foreign Minister

Taher al-Masri called "Jordanian glasnost."[42] Second, their restriction to the East Bank was meant to confirm to America, Israel, and the PLO that the King was serious when he severed ties to the West Bank, in effect relinquishing any claims to Palestine. And third, the regime hoped that the restoration of parliament would provide Jordan's growing middle class and technocracy with enough of an outlet for pent-up political frustration to gain tacit support for the next stage of its economic austerity plan.

The campaign process turned out to be more open and free-wheeling than most observers had expected. More than 640 candidates vied for the revamped parliament's 80 seats. (Among the candidates were 12 women, running in the first national election in which women were allowed to vote. However, no women won.) Since political parties have been banned since the imposition of martial law in 1957, all ran as independents. Nevertheless, the regime turned a blind eye to the formation of electoral blocs and political groupings, ranging from Communists to Ba'thists to centrists to Islamic fundamentalists. Moreover, although access to television, radio, and much of the press was denied to all candidates, a large number of public debates and campaign gatherings were held throughout the country.[43]

The election's clear winner was Jordan's Islamic bloc.[44] The Muslim Brotherhood and its sympathizers crushed all opposition in garnering almost half of parliament. Of its slate of 26 candidates, 20 won, and the Brotherhood could count on the support of at least a dozen other fundamentalists who campaigned as independents. The fundamentalists' victory was particularly great in the cities. In Amman, for example, fundamentalists took at least 13 of 17 slots reserved for Muslim candidates. If Jordan's electoral districts had not been drawn to exaggerate minorities and rural areas and discriminate against the urban vote, the fundamentalists might have gained an outright majority.

For their part, regime loyalists fared very poorly. At least a dozen former cabinet ministers, senior officials, governors, mayors, ambassadors, bedouin chiefs, and ex-army officers failed in their parliamentary bids. Two of the most prominent loyalist politicians in the campaign, former Foreign Minister Masri and former Chief of the Royal Court Dhuqan al-Hindawi, only squeaked into parliament by bare margins. Given the seats won by leftists and Arab nationalists, the "King's men" could not even count on a razor-thin majority without at least the tacit support of some opposition deputies.

Fundamentalists won for three reasons. First, as the only quasi-political organization allowed to function in Jordan for the past three decades, they were able to capitalize on their comparative advantage in organization. Second, of all the candidates, the fundamentalists' rhetoric appealed most to the hopes and fears of Jordan's poor, unemployed, and undereducated. Their platform called for the prosecution of former government officials who allegedly mishandled the economy into bankruptcy and for the abrogation of the Kingdom's agreement with the IMF. Third, and perhaps most important, the fundamentalists main opposition—the PLO—stood on the sidelines. As a result of King Hussein's support for the PLO's declaration of statehood, most mainstream local Palestinian leaders took no part in the elections, on the grounds that it would be inappropriate to seek office in one state after having "established" their own west of the Jordan River. That left the field open for fundamentalists, whose platform rejects the West Bank disengagement and calls for a holy war against Israel, to win electoral districts carved out of the most hard-bitten and irredentist Palestinian refugee camps. The fundamentalists' solid showing was clearly not the outcome the regime hoped for. Though the King professed satisfaction with the election results, he had warned the electorate against mixing religion and politics, and the fundamentalists' victory must, in some sense, be taken as a personal affront.[45]

Given its results, the election only fulfilled two of its three intended objectives. On the positive side, the election proved that the King was a man of his word when he promised to hold a free and fair vote, and it gave a flavor of irreversibility to his disengagement from the West Bank. But on the crucial issue of opening up the political process to the middle class and the forward-looking technocrats, the elections were not a smashing success. Indeed, if the idea behind elections was for government to gain a parliamentary partner with which to share the burden of responsibility for continued austerity and retrenchment, the elections may even have been a step backward. In their aftermath, with the opposition (combining right and left) having won a potential majority, the regime faced an existential challenge almost on par with the 1970 civil war: to rebuild a governing coalition in disarray while still holding fast to the agreement with the IMF.

To engineer that balancing act, King Hussein appointed Mudar Badran, a former prime minister and intelligence chief, to succeed Bin Shakir. Badran had a reputation of close relations with the Muslim Brotherhood. Not only is he related by marriage to prominent Brotherhood leader Ishaq al-Farhan, but he came to office with a view that the Islamists were not to be treated as an opposition to be countered, but rather as an important interest group to be courted. In anticipation of the parliamentary vote of confidence in his government, Badran announced a wide-ranging political liberalization policy, which included a declaration of amnesty for most political prisoners, the return of all confiscated passports, the lifting of state control on daily newspapers, and the freezing of martial law. He tried hard to chip away at the Brotherhood's internal cohesion through the time-honored method of co-optation. He held out the prospect of ministerial positions and a few MPs linked to the Brotherhood grabbed the opportunity.[46] Despite often vicious criticism of the government's continued reliance on the structural adjustment plan, the Brotherhood lent its support to Badran after he agreed to demands for new laws to limit the sale of alcoholic beverages to Muslims. In early January the government won the confidence vote by the surprisingly wide margin of 65-9, with six abstentions. One month later, a smaller but still clear majority of 52 deputies gave parliamentary approval to the government's proposed budget.

Over the following six months, the initial conciliatory attitude between government and opposition began to wear thin. This was the result of two main developments: the radicalization of Jordan's Islamic movement and the reemergence of the PLO in internal politics, with the government's tacit blessing, as a potential counterweight to the fundamentalists. Through it all, the regime maintained its commitment to the IMF program, despite the domestic dislocations it continued to cause.

Jordan's Islamic movement has never been a unified, cohesive organization, nor has its relationship with the government been consistent over time. For decades, there have been competing trends within the Islamic movement, arguing on the one hand for an evolutionary approach to political change and on the other hand for a revolutionary—or, as they prefer to call it, a "purist"—approach to government and politics. These divisions have at times fostered ambivalence in the relationship between the movement and the government and continue to do so.[47]

In the second quarter of 1990, this competition worsened. Specifically, "Young Turks" within the Brotherhood, including a handful of parliamentary deputies, grew frustrated with the accommodating posture of the traditional leadership and pressed for a more activist political agenda. Within the murky politics of Jordan's Islamic groups, it is now known that radical Brotherhood members have repeatedly urged the leadership to consolidate the "Palestinization" of the Brotherhood and have goaded the leadership into heightening the role that jihad against Israel has in the pantheon of Brotherhood political priorities. In a secret internal leadership vote, the radicals reportedly made a strong showing against the more conservative leadership, virtually ensuring a more confrontational approach in the Brotherhood's relationship toward the Palace and the government.[48] Early manifestations of that more activist policy included Brotherhood demands for violent strikes at American and Soviet interests to protest Soviet Jewish immigration to Israel in March; the inflammatory role Islamic groups played in rioting inside Palestinian refugee camps in May; and signs throughout the summer that the Brotherhood was considering withdrawing confidence in the government.[49]

It was the prospect of that change in Brotherhood policy that prompted the regime to change its own conciliatory stance. In response to the radicalization/Palestinization of the Brotherhood, the regime has tacitly supported the creation of a political coalition of secular and leftist political groups, mainly Palestinian in orientation, one of whose chief goals is to combat the growing influence of the Islamists.[50] Most significantly, this has included the return of Fatah wing of the PLO to domestic politics—with the regime's blessing, no less. In mid-July, the Jordanian Communist Party, Nayif Hawatimeh's Jordanian People's Democratic Party, George Habash's Popular Front for the Liberation of Palestine, and Fatah joined together to form the "Jordanian Arab National Democratic Coalition," a political movement aimed at winning back the Palestinian support that had been ceded to the Islamists over the previous year. Exactly two years after the disengagement from the West Bank, Jordan is now permitting intra-Palestinian politics—the battle between secular and religious nationalists that is at the heart of the *intifada*—to be played out on the streets of Amman. At the end of July 1990, it looked as though the next phase of Jordan's domestic politics would be termed "*intifada*-ization."

To engineer competition between the opposite ends of the political spectrum is a high-risk/high-gain strategy. It was evidently born out of a realization on the part of the regime that it lacks sufficient political appeal on its own to draw support away from the fundamentalist groups. Indeed, one other fallout from the November elections has been the growing realization among Palace loyalists of the costs of the regime's historical failure to build and foster a moderate, centrist political party. While the extremes have always been represented in Jordanian politics, there has never been a serious attempt to form a party of the center akin to Egypt's ruling National Democratic Party. There is evidence that the regime is convinced of the need to go this route, and the political posturing of Independent Deputy 'Abdullah Nsour and the formation of a National Charter commission may be the germ of just such an effort.[51] But the key ingredient—royal imprimatur—is still missing.

Throughout these political twists and turns, Jordan's economic management team has held fast to the IMF accord. In April 1990, an IMF team completed a review of Jordan's progress and a second year of standby credits was approved three months later. In July, the Central Bank announced the country's first current account surplus in more than a decade, underscoring the government's success in holding down imports and boosting exports by devaluation of the dinar. The real drop in the value of imports in 1989 was reported to be around 12 percent and exports were reported to have increased by the same amount.[52]

Nevertheless, the Kingdom's financial situation remained decidedly shaky. Thanks to poor management and financial scandal, the Central Bank was forced to pump more than 250 million scarce dollars into two of the country's largest commercial enterprises—Royal Jordanian (Alia) Airlines and Petra Bank, the country's second largest. Indeed, the bilking of Petra Bank by its chairman, Ahmad Chalabi, is a financial debacle whose relative impact on the Jordanian economy dwarfs the savings and loan controversy in the United States and which has threatened to undermine confidence in the Kingdom's entire banking system.[53] King Hussein's plaintive, almost melancholy appeal to Arab leaders for financial assistance at the May 28 emergency Arab League summit meeting in Baghdad—"Abandoning Jordan," he said, "is abandoning Palestine"—went largely unheeded. The only state to make a formal public pledge at the time was Iraq, still deeply indebted to Jordan, which promised $50 million.[54] By the end of May 1990, Jordan's real foreign currency reserves hovered around $40 million.[55] Internally, the dinar remained weak and unemployment continued to rise.[56] The unease of Jordan's economic situation was summed up in a headline that London's *Economist* magazine ran over an editorial highly critical of the King's erratic (i.e., pro-Iraqi) regional diplomacy. "Don't Bank on Jordan," it counseled.[57]

As of the end of July 1990, therefore, Jordan was engaged in a great gamble. After two decades of authoritarian and relatively uneventful domestic rule by King Hussein and his chosen lieutenants, the Kingdom found itself in mid-1990 absorbed in a fundamental reordering of both its economic and its political priorities. Either alone would have been a difficult task for even the most well-anchored regime, but Jordan, whose political leadership was repudiated at the polls just nine months earlier, had to deal with both at the same time. The tensions among the regime and its people—both economic (including unemployment and a massive drop in quality of life occasioned by the devaluation of the dinar) and political (mainly the East Bank/West Bank and Islamic/secular divisions that polarize domestic politics)—remained great; virtually the only point of agreement among all Jordanians was that the near future held little promise of economic recovery and political stability. Yet as the anniversary of the adjustment plan passed with neither popular disturbances nor backtracking from the plan itself, there was at least a glimmer of hope that Jordan's gamble might pay off.

But on August 2, Iraq's invasion of Kuwait turned Jordan's economic and political world upside-down. The loss of the Kingdom's largest trading partner (Iraq), the split with its largest financial donor (Saudi Arabia), the slump in the kingdom's largest export market (the Gulf), and the burden of a totally unexpected flood of refugees was nothing short of an economic catastrophe. Similarly, the radicalization of Jordan's domestic politics, based on the common ground found by leftist and Islamists in opposing the buildup of Western forces in the Gulf, created a volatile political tinderbox. Never before was Jordan faced with such isolation from both its main Arab neighbors and its potential superpower patrons. Only time will tell whether Saddam Hussein dealt the chances for survival of his only sure and lasting ally an irreversible blow.

NOTES

1. Eliyahu Kanovsky, "Jordan's Economy: From Prosperity to Crisis," Dayan Center Occasional Papers, no. 106, May 1989, 1. This concise paper offers a sectoral analysis of the Jordanian economy and provides perhaps the most exhaustive study of its rise and fall over the past decade.
2. Indeed, as late as 1986, Jordan was still advertising itself in promotional inserts in media outlets such as *Institutional Investor* as a "'shadow' oil economy."
3. The net impact of remittances is gained after deducting the salaries of foreign workers (who numbered about 125,000 in 1981) in low-paying jobs inside Jordan. For details, see the chapter on "Oil and the Economy" in my *Troubles on the East Bank: Challenges to the Domestic Stability of Jordan* (Washington, DC: Center for Strategic and International Studies, 1986).
4. For details, see the doctoral dissertation by Bassam Khalil Saket, *Foreign Aid to Jordan, 1924/25-1972/73: Its Magnitude, Composition and Effect,* University of Keele, 1976.
5. By 1981, the total value of imported goods had grown to 10 times its 1973 level. In just two years (1978-1980), the government's spending increased 57 percent on development and 47 percent on defense and police. Satloff, *Troubles on the East Bank,* 9-19.
6. And even then, Saudi Arabia never made good on promises to make up to Jordan what other Arab states failed to pay.
7. *Middle East Economic Digest(MEED)*, August 4, 1989.
8. Uriel Dann, *King Hussein and the Challenge of Arab Radicalism, Jordan 1955-1967* (New York: Oxford University Press, 1989), 190, note 1.
9. Adnan Abu 'Awdah, "Jordan's Foreign Policy in its Regional and International Dimensions," unpublished paper, 1986.
10. Kanovsky, "Jordan's Economy," 70.
11. See *MEED,* February 24, 1989, and Kanovsky, "Jordan's Economy," 39-42.

12. From a high of $210.3 million in 1990, total U.S. assistance plummeted to just $26.75 million in 1989. During that time, though, it fluctuated wildly. Aid during the three fiscal years 1981-83 totalled slightly less than $200 million; for the three subsequent years, it was more than $500 million. Statistics provided by US Department of State. For details and background on U.S. assistance to Jordan, see Agency for International Development, *USAID to Jordan: 35 Years of Commitment* (Washington, DC, 1988).
13. This section is drawn from my article "Jordan Looks Inward," *Current History* (February 1990).
14. A useful rule of thumb is that about one-third of the world's Palestinian population lives west of the Jordan River, one-third east of the river and the remaining third scattered throughout the Middle East and the rest of the world.
15. See Amman Domestic Service, July 31, 1988; cited in Foreign Broadcast Information Service (FBIS), August 2, 1988. These statements were followed by a series of practical measures that included moving the work of the Ministry of Occupied Territory Affairs to a department inside the foreign ministry; canceling the West Bank development plan; and stopping the payment of salaries to West Bank bureaucrats and teachers. The only official ties left between the two banks consist of Jordan's continued maintenance of Palestinian mosques and religious establishments.
16. International Monetary Fund, "Jordan—Staff Report for the 1988 Article IV Consultation" (Washington, DC), May 19, 1988, confidential.
17. *MEED*, May 13, 1988.
18. *MEED*, October 21, 1988.
19. For more than a year after the disengagement, the Jordanian authorities refused to recognize publicly any linkage between the King's decision and the dinar's tumble. For an admission by Crown Prince Hassan of the "*intifada*'s" deleterious impact on the Jordanian economy, see the *Wall Street Journal*, May 25, 1990.
20. Indeed, speculation among West Bankers and even some Israelis was furious and Jordan's Central Bank went as far as to accuse Israel of undermining confidence in the Jordanian currency. During the IMF adjustment talks in April 1989, the Jordanian side argued that Israeli government "restrictions" on dealing in dinars were "having an adverse effect on the stability of the exchange rate and may interfere with the achievement of their economic objectives." The IMF team had no comment in response. IMF, "Jordan—Staff Report for the 1989 Article IV Consultation and Request for Stand-by Arrangement" (Washington, DC), June 2, 1989.
21. Jordan refinanced its FMS (foreign military sales) debt in in December 1988. See US General Accounting Office, *Report on Security Assistance: Foreign Military Sales Debt Refinancing* (Washington, DC, August 1989). Also, for the quotations, see *New York Times*, November 7, 1988 and *MEED*, November 11 and November 18, 1988.
22. Quoted in *MEED*, December 23, 1988.

23. See Amman Domestic Service, February 8, 1989; cited in FBIS, February 9, 1989.
24. *al-Ra'y* (Amman), February 6, 1989; cited in FBIS, February 7, 1989.
25. In fact, two IMF observers held talks with the Jordanian government in Amman in late February 1989 as part of a joint mission with the World Bank.
26. For details, see "Deficit Woes Prompt Jordan to Postpone Tornado Purchase," *Aviation Week & Space Technology*, April 5, 1989.
27. This included $100 million-$125 million in IMF standby credits and a $100 million-$150 million sectoral adjustment loan for industry from the World Bank.
28. See, for example, an interview in *al-Sharq al-Awsat* (London), March 3, 1989; cited in FBIS, March 7, 1989.
29. Importantly, there are signs that Jordan's financial managers have weaned themselves away from the illusion of expected increases in Arab aid. The adjustment plan was based on the anticipated receipt of only $296 million in official bilateral grants from Saudi Arabia, Kuwait, the UAE, Oman and the United States in 1989 and even less—$260 million—in 1990. Nevertheless, as evidenced by repeated statements of King Hussein, Crown Prince Hassan and Prime Minister Badran, Jordan's political echelon still views Arab aid as an essential element of the Kingdom's economic future.
30. Interview in *al-Sharq al-Awsat*, London, April 23, 1989; cited in FBIS, April 26, 1989.
31. For the first time, however, there were palpable murmurings of criticism targeted against members of the Royal Family, specifically Hussein's American-born wife, Queen Noor.
32. Interview in *al-Siyasah*, quoted in *MEED*, January 13, 1989.
33. Indeed, it is ludicrous to suggest that the Palace had neither knowledge of nor responsibility for the Kingdom's major economic decisions.
34. *MEED*, June 2 and 9, 1989.
35. See Amman Domestic Service, May 29, 1989; cited in FBIS, May 31, 1989; and *al-Dustur*, July 28, 1989; cited in FBIS, July 28, 1989.
36. Talks with the Soviet Union were especially thorny. Debt totaled about $230 million, almost all of which was for weapons purchased in the mid-1980s. Final agreement on the rescheduling terms was not reached until early 1990.
37. On August 18, Prime Minister Bin Shakir announced on Jordanian television that Arab states would make interest-free deposits with Jordan's Central Bank, which would then place money with local banks, which could then earn money on the interest. But months passed with no action on the plan. Finally, Reuters reported on November 30 that five Gulf states agreed to deposit $300 million for Amman's use with the Dubai-based Arab Monetary Fund. The Jordanian government would pay interest 2 percent below market rates and then deposit an equivalent amount in local currency in blocked accounts at its Central Bank as collateral for each contributing country. The end result was far different, and far less attractive, than

Amman's original hopes for an interest-free deposit of $1 billion for its general use. See *MEED*, September 1 and December 15, 1989.

38. Central Bank holdings of foreign exchange were reported to have risen from $140 million in May to more than $500 million in September. These included grants and assistance amounting to $200 million from Saudi Arabia; $80 million from Kuwait; $70 million from the United Arab Emirates; $20 million from Oman, and at least $40 million from Iraq, which still owed Jordan about $600 million left over from the Iran-Iraq War. *Jordan Times*, September 28, 1989; cited in FBIS, October 5, 1989.
39. Jordan's minister of information justified his confiscating the passport of a local journalist, thereby preventing her from taking up an appointment as an associate of Harvard's Center for International Affairs, by saying that he "could not accept someone who insults me and my country." *Wall Street Journal*, November 15, 1988.
40. *Washington Post*, November 7, 1988.
41. *Jordan Times*, July 17, 1989; cited in FBIS, July 17, 1989.
42. *Washington Post*, October 3, 1989.
43. *New York Times*, October 26, 1989.
44. Election-day turnout was officially estimated at 62 percent of registered voters, with about 540,000 people going to the polls. *New York Times*, November 10, 1989.
45. See King Hussein's nationwide television address warning of the politicization of religion, October 7, 1989; cited in FBIS, October 10, 1989.
46. Because Badran refused to name a Brotherhood member to the key post of education minister, which would have given the Islamists control of patronage throughout the Kingdom's school system, the Brotherhood as a bloc refused to join the government. See the *New York Times*, December 7, 1989.
47. For example, in 1957 Jordan's Muslim Brothers sided with the King in his battle against leftists. One year later, many of the Brotherhood's leaders found themselves in jail for their own insurrectionary activity.
48. The Brotherhood's traditional leadership, including Comptroller General Muhammad 'Abdul Rahman al-Khalifa, is predominantly Transjordanian. A moderate Palestinian wing of the Brotherhood is led by a former cabinet minister, Ishaq al-Farhan. The more radical group goes by the name "Qu'ran al-Thawri" (Revolutionary Qu'ran), and includes Deputies Hammam as-Said, 'Abdul Aziz Jabr and Muhammad Abu Faris.
49. Regarding the Brotherhood's violent policy toward Soviet Jewish immigration, see *al-Rayah al-Islamiyah* (Amman), March 30, 1990, cited in FBIS, April 2, 1990; regarding the Islamists' role in the May riots, see Agence French Presse, May 22, 1990; regarding the Brotherhood's growing animosity toward the Badran government, see *Jordan Times*, June 28-29, 1990, cited in FBIS, June 29, 1990 and *Mideast Mirror*, June 22 and 28, 1990.
50. Indeed, the King himself met with leaders of the long-banned Jordan Communist Party for the first time in 15 years. See *Jordan Times*, April 17, 1990, cited in FBIS, April 19, 1990.

51. For the membership of the 60-member National Charter commissions, chaired by former prime minister Ahmad Obeidat, see *Jordan Times,* April 10, 1990, cited in FBIS, April 12, 1990.
52. Finance Minister Jardaneh's interview with Amman Television, reported in *Jordan Times,* April 9, 1990, cited in FBIS, April 10, 1990.
53. I am thankful to Patrick Clawson for putting the Petra Bank scandal into its proper perspective. For details of the financial troubles of Alia, which had amassed more than $1 billion in debt by the end of 1989, see *Mideast Mirror,* June 4, 1990.
54. Iraqi debt repayments probably do not include the 40 cars that Saddam Hussein presented to his hosts when he visited Jordan in February 1990, including a Rolls-Royce for the King and Porsches for his two eldest sons. *Wall Street Journal,* March 6, 1990.
55. This figure excludes gold, compulsory reserves of commercial banks, and bank-to-bank deposits from other Arab central banks. *MEED,* June 8, 1990.
56. Joblessness has been a serious domestic problem since the mid-1980s, when employment prospects in the Gulf began to run dry. Not only are there few jobs for the tens of thousands of Jordanian doctors, engineers, architects, and other college and university graduates, but thousands of Jordanians who had been working in the Gulf have begun to return home in search of new employment. Since the *intifada,* this trend has been worsened by the net influx of Palestinians from the West to the East Bank, said to have reached 70,000 by July 1990. Most estimates place Jordan's unemployment rate at about 20 percent, with the rate among professionals significantly higher. *MEED,* August 3, 1990.
57. *The Economist,* June 2, 1990.

7

Algeria's Implicit Stabilization Program

Karen Pfeifer

The *Economist Intelligence Unit*'s summary assessment of the status of the Algerian economy as of July 31, 1989, read: "The IMF stand-by and contingency credits have been formally approved. GDP declined in 1988 but the prospects are brighter for 1989."[1] This turn to the IMF (International Monetary Fund) is a step the government of Algeria had repeatedly and publicly declared it would not take, choosing instead to send shock waves of strict austerity to rein in the economy during the 1980s and in effect inflict on itself a "stabilization" program not unlike what the IMF would have imposed had it been invited to do so.

What happened to Algeria, a model of economic success and political independence in the 1970s, to bring it to this critical situation? Is Algeria finally turning in desperation, as have so many other countries in Asia, Africa, and Latin America, to the International Monetary Fund for debt relief, or, as critics of the IMF might see it, finally succumbing to pressures for full integration into the world capitalist system?

HISTORIC CONTEXT

Worldwide economic development in the 1945-80 era was characterized by two seemingly contradictory tendencies. On the one hand, there was a long period of international economic expansion, governed by the institutions of the Bretton Woods system and its complements, the IMF and the World

Bank. This expansion was led at first by industrial and financial capital based in the United States, and preserved by U.S.-led military organizations and interventions.[2] An important impetus to the expansion in the 1940s and 1950s was the surfeit of exportable goods and investment capital in the United States, the economy of which, in contrast to other capitalist countries, had been strengthened rather than damaged by World War II. Many of these goods and much of this capital flowed to other advanced capitalist countries, but some also went to the Third World. As the expansion quickened in the 1960s, capital based in other advanced capitalist countries, now defined by membership in the Organization for Economic Cooperation and Development (OECD), augmented the flow of exported goods, services, and investment to the Third World.

On the other hand, there was a long series of successful national liberation movements in the Third World. In many of the newly established countries, such as Algeria, nationalist economic policy simultaneously stressed rapid development and put severe restraints on the role that foreign private capital could play in direct investment. The two remaining ways, then, in which OECD-based capital could continue to play a profitable role in these controlled economies were through direct sales of commodities and services and, indirectly, through international commercial-bank lending to Third World governments or government-backed groups. Countries such as Algeria thus came to play a new role in the turnover and expansion of OECD-based capital as purchasers of OECD exports and as debtors, though they were not under foreign direct authority with regard to investment decisions.

By the mid-1970s, while simultaneous stagnation and price inflation set in in the OECD economies (the U.S. in particular), the Third World debtor countries experienced a unique combination of sustained demand for their exports, devaluation of their dollar-denominated debt, and a decline in real interest rates, which meant a decline in real debt-service obligations. These circumstances encouraged them to maintain their own economic growth through augmentation of their debt and expansion of both exports and domestic demand for imports. As oil and gas prices rose in real terms, exporters such as Algeria were particularly well favored by these circumstances.

By the early 1980s, the monetarist response to stagflation in the OECD countries, still dominated by the economy of the United States, induced a severe business recession felt worldwide. These recessionary conditions led to decreases in demand for debtor-country exports at the same time that the accompanying tight monetary policy led to higher interest rates. This new combination translated into the beginnings of a crisis in the Third World: export revenues were much harder to come by and debt became more difficult and much more expensive to incur or to renegotiate. Debt-burdened oil exporters like Algeria were especially hard hit. Dealing with the crisis led many Third World countries to become subject to the terms of IMF stabilization programs and their concomitant free-market economic policies. Algeria, however, refused to subject itself to IMF arrangements and instead imposed a stabilization program on itself throughout most of the decade.

ECONOMIC NATIONALISM AND THE USES OF BORROWED CAPITAL

The rising volume of debt incurred in the Third World through the 1970s was to a significant extent put to productive uses in the conscious attempt to build national economies in the recipient countries.[3] While Algeria, like other state-managed economies in the Middle East, has been criticized for the unproductive use and even waste of resources at times, the focus of its economic program was ostensibly to use the nationalization of resources and allocation of public investment to build infrastructure, to promote economic growth and structural change, and to provide for the development of human resources dismally neglected under the previous colonial regime. A much smaller domain was left for private domestic capital in non-capital-intensive industry, in agriculture, and in services.[4]

Economic growth and structural change certainly did take place in the postindependence era in Algeria. These changes are summarized in Table 7.1. The average annual growth rate of the Gross National Product (GNP) per capita was 2.7% from 1965 to 1988. Despite a high rate of population growth, averaging 3.1% per year over this period, Algeria's Gross Domestic Product (GDP) grew at the rate of 6.8% per year from 1965 to 1980, indicating a potentially rising average standard of living. Indeed, while Gross Domestic Investment grew at 15.9% per year from 1965 to 1980, both government and private consumption also rose by over 8% per year on average. We will discuss below the reasons for the sharp deterioration of these figures, to -0.8, 5.1, and 1.4% respectively, in the 1980-88 period.

The most dramatic shift in the distribution of GDP was toward industry, from 34% in 1965 to 43% in 1988 (with a drop in agriculture's share from 15% to 13% and a drop in services from 51 to 44%). However, the manufacturing portion accounts for only a small rise from 11 to 12%, while the

Table 7.1: Basic Macroeconomic Indicators

Population 1988	**23.8 million**	
Average growth rate, 1980-1988	3.1% per year	
GNP per capita 1988	**$2382**	
Average growth rate, 1965-1988	2.7% per year	
Average annual growth rate of real GDP		
	1965-1980	**1980-1988**
	6.8%	3.5%
Distribution of GDP, %	**1965**	**1988**
Agriculture	15	13
Industry	34	43
(Manufacturing)	(11)	(12)
Services	51	44
Components of aggregate demand, average annual growth rates		
	1965-1980	**1980-1988**
Gov't consumption	8.6%	5.1%
Private consumption	8.8	1.4
Gross domestic investment	15.9	-0.8
Price inflation, average annual rate		
	1965-1980	**1980-1988**
	10.5%	4.4%
Monetary holdings, average annual nominal growth rate		
	1965-1980	**1980-1988**
	22.3%	17.5%

Source: *World Development Report,* 1990, Table 1, p. 179, Table 2, p. 181,Table 3, p. 183, Table 8, p. 193, and Table 10, p. 203.

rest of industrial growth was concentrated in mining, construction, and hydrocarbon production.

All indicators of health and education signal signficant improvement in the development of human capital, starting from an extremely low base at the time of independence. These changes are summarized in Table 7.2. Between 1965 and 1988, the infant mortality rate fell by 50% and life

Table 7.2: Health and Education Indicators

	1965	1988
Infant mortality rate (per 1000 live births)	154	72
Life expectancy at birth		
Male	49	63
Female	51	65
	1965	**1986**
Daily calorie supply, per capita	1,681	2,715
	1965	**1984**
Population per physician	8,590	2,340
Population per nursing person	11,770	330
	1965	**1987**
% of age group enrolled		
in primary school	68	96
Female	53	81
in secondary school	7	55
Female	5	46
Pupil-teacher ratio	43	29

Source: *World Development Report,* 1990, Table 28, p. 233, Table 29, p. 235, and Table 32, p. 241.

expectancy rose by 14 years for both men and women. Similarly, the daily average calorie intake rose by 60%, and population per physician fell by almost three-fourths. The pupil-teacher ratio fell from 1:43 in 1965 to 1:29 in 1987, while the percentage of primary-school-age children in school rose from 68% to 96% (females 53% to 81%), and the percentage of secondary-school-age children in school rose from 7% to 55% (females 5% to 46%).

A primary feature in the evolution of the Algerian economy was that, in spite of the stress on national development and on import-substituting

Table 7.3: Value of Merchandise Trade

	($ millions)		Terms of trade
	Exports	Imports	(base=100 in 1980)
1982	12,533	10,937	106
1983	11,158	10,332	102
1984	12,622	10,286	99
1985	13,034	9,061	94
1986	7,875	10,162	44
1987	9,029	7,028	56
1988	7,674	7,432	41

Average annual growth rates of merchandise trade:

	Exports	Imports
1965-80	1.5%	13.0%
1980-88	3.4%	-5.9%

Source: *World Development Report,* volumes for 1982 through 1990, table entitled "Growth of Merchandise Trade," e.g., Table 14, p. 205 in 1990 volume.

industrialization, the development of modern industry and agriculture entailed increased imports, as it did in other nationalist economies in the 1960s and 1970s. Foreign firms served as suppliers of raw materials, intermediate goods, technology, and capital goods for industry, and they provided seeds, tools, machinery, and fertilizer for agriculture. Similarly, rising public and private consumption, in tandem with the rising standard of living and development of human capital, entailed increased imports of food and nonsubstitutable consumer goods, construction equipment, and transportation systems.

A contributing factor to the growth of the import bill was the failure of agriculture to keep pace with the rest of economic growth. The average index of food production had fallen to 81 by 1979-81, from a base of 100 in 1969-71. Cereal imports rose from 1,816 thousand metric tons in 1974 to 3,261 thousand metric tons in 1981.[5]

Given restrictions on direct foreign investment, there are only two means by which a country can finance increased purchases of imported commodities—either by increasing exports of goods and services or by international borrowing. As Table 7.3 indicates, Algeria did increase export revenues in the 1965-1980 period, at the rate of 1.5% per year on average. However, since imports were growing much faster, at the rate of 13% per year, it clearly became necessary to turn toward international borrowing in order to fully finance the domestic investment and consumption program. As Table 7.4 shows, for example, even with workers' remittances of $178 million and net private direct investment of $45 million in 1970, for example, Algeria incurred a current account deficit of $125 million. Algerian planners, like those in many other Third World countries in the 1970s, gambled that world demand for their exports would remain high and that interest rates would remain low for the forseeable future and undertook debt to cover the current nonchronic shortfalls in revenue.

ABSOLUTE AND RELATIVE SIZE OF DEBT OUTSTANDING

Algeria's external public long-term debt grew by a factor of 16 between 1970 and 1980, from the equivalent of 19% of GNP to 39% of GNP, and then declined by 14% from 1980 to 1983, during the recession years. Table 7.5 displays these figures. The actual dollar value of total disbursed debt outstanding in 1983, the low point, was $13.8 billion, yielding a debt/GNP ratio of 28%. Table 7.6 displays the growth of Algeria's debt, along with the sources and terms of the loans and debt-service obligations for the 1972-1982 period.

In contrast to other countries with significant private sector debt, all of the debt held by Algeria was public or publicly guaranteed. However, also unlike many other Third World debtors (including Middle Eastern countries like Turkey and Egypt), most of this was borrowed from commercial lenders on market-determined terms. This combination would come to impose a severe strain on the Algerian economy in the 1980s.

FORMS OF INDEBTEDNESS

During the 1970s, there were two important changes in the way in which international capital flowed into the Third World.[6] First, there was a major shift toward more finance through private commercial banks and away from both concessional forms and direct foreign investment. Second, the private commercial banks began to impose variable interest rate structures on more international loans in order to protect themselves from price inflation. The

Table 7.4: Balance of Payments and Reserves ($ Millions)

	Current account balance[a]	Workers' remittances	Net direct private investment	Gross international reserves	Months of coverage
1970	-125	178	45	352	na
1980	249	406	315	7,050	5.7
1981	85	447	-1	5,915	4.6
1982	na	na	na	na	na
1983	-86	383	-14	4,010	3.5
1984	75	329	-14	3,185	2.8
1985	1,015	313	-2	4,644	4.3
1986	-2,224	309	290	3,843	3.9
1987	-406	434	-20	4,343	4.5
1988	-2,040	279	-48	3,191	4.0

[a] Includes official transfers.
Source: *World Development Report*, volumes for 1982 through 1990, table entitled "Balance of Payments and Reserves," e.g., Table 18 on p. 213 of 1990 volume.

effect of these changes on Third World borrowers was to bind them more tightly to world-market fluctuations in the availability of credit, in interest rates, and in the demand for and prices of the exports they sold to raise revenues for servicing their debt and paying for imports.

Because Algeria is a major exporter of hydrocarbons and a member of OPEC, its credit rating in the international financial arena remained excellent through 1980. Algeria was encouraged to rely heavily on financial markets rather than grant aid. Calculating percentages from Table 7.6, the proportion of Algeria's debt in concessional form fell from 23.5% in 1973 to 6.6% in 1982. While the proportion in the form of variable interest-rate loans fell somewhat from 36.5% to 24.9% in the same period, debt owed to the financial markets rose from 45.1% of total debt in 1973 to 58.9% in 1982, yielding a 22.1% annual rate of growth, slowing down only after 1980. In comparison, the annual rate of growth of debt held by official creditors was but 15.6% in the same period.

Table 7.5: Volume of Debt and Relative Size of Debt and Debt Service

	External debt[a] ($ millions)	Debt as % GNP	Debt service as % Exports[b]
1970	937	19.3	3.2
1980	15,073	38.7	24.9
1981	14,392	35.2	24.6
1982	13,897	31.9	34.0[d]
1983	12,942	28.0	33.1

	Long-term debt	Total debt	Long-term debt as % GNP	Long-term debt service, % exports
1984[c]	12,052	13,811	24.3	33.6
1985	13,664	15,526	24.0	33.3
1986	14,777	17,929	24.8	54.8
1987	19,240	22,881	30.5	49.0
1988	23,229	24,850	46.6	77.0

[a] External public and publicly guaranteed debt, outstanding and disbursed.

[b] Debt service as a percent of goods and services exports.

[c] Beginning in 1984, long-term debt is singled out as the most important form of debt in the statistics cited.

[d] No figure was given for this year in the *World Development Report* for 1983, 1984, or 1985. This figure is obtained by adding together the interest paid on debt and the principal repaid in 1982 and dividing by the value of merchandise exports for that year.

Source: *World Development Report*, volumes for 1982 through 1990, e.g., Tables 21, p. 219, and 23, p. 223, of volume for 1990.

TERMS OF INDEBTEDNESS

Differences among developing countries in the terms of indebtedness reflected how lenders, both official and private, evaluated the ability to repay and creditworthiness of the various countries. The average terms of new commitments of public or publicly guaranteed debt for Algeria are displayed in Table 7.6.

Official creditors charged Algeria among the highest of interest rates and gave it shorter maturity terms and shorter grace periods than they gave to countries such as Egypt. They provided Algeria with a lower grant element. Thus, little concessional aid was provided to Algeria.

Table 7.6: Algeria's Indebtedness, 1972-1982

	1972	1976	1980	1981	1982
Total debt outstanding disbursed (US $ millions)[a]	1488.0	5846.1	15,078.1	14,309.1	13,567.2
Official creditors	584.2	1161.8	2478.7	2546.0	2900.6
Private creditors	903.9	4684.3	12,599.4	11,763.1	10,666.6
Suppliers	603.0	1659.4	3537.9	3043.0	2676.0
Financial markets	300.9	3024.9	9061.4	8720.1	7989.9
Total debt service (US $ millions)	189.1	773.5	3710.4	3850.3	3914.6
Official creditors	54.6	105.5	302.3	448.4	486.3
Private creditors	134.5	668.0	3408.1	3402.0	3428.3
Suppliers	101.3	448.3	1174.3	1084.9	1018.5
Financial markets	33.2	219.7	2233.9	2317.1	2409.7
Average terms: Public debt new commitments					
Official creditors					
Interest (%)	4.2	8.4	8.1	8.3	8.4
Maturity (years)	15.1	11.6	14.2	19.7	19.9
Grace (years)	3.6	3.0	4.3	6.2	6.4
Grant element (%)	32.0	6.7	9.3	10.2	9.7
Private Creditors					
Interest (%)	7.0	8.0	8.5	10.2	9.4
Maturity (years)	7.6	10.6	8.7	8.7	12.4
Grace (years)	3.0	3.4	2.6	3.5	3.5
Grant element (%)	10.8	8.2	4.3	-2.9	1.6
Disbursed outstanding debt as % of GNP	21.2	35.5	38.7	35.0	32.5
Total debt service as % of exported goods and services	11.7	13.0	24.9	24.8	na

[a] All public or publicly guaranteed debt. No private, nonguaranteed debt is recorded for Algeria.

Source: World Bank, *World Debt Tables,* 1983, pp. 216-17; 1984, pp. 224-25.

Private creditors, on the other hand, viewed Algeria from a different angle because of their profit orientation. Apparently seeing Algeria as a good risk, they charged it some of their lowest interest rates, accompanied by moderate maturation periods and long grace periods. In contrast with official creditors, private creditors provided Algeria with a relatively high grant element.

DEBT SERVICE OBLIGATIONS

Algeria ranked fifth on the OECD's list of the 20 developing countries with the largest debt-service payments in 1981-1982. These 20 countries together paid about three-fourths of the developing countries' debt service and were responsible for about two-thirds of total Less Developed Countries (LDC) debt.[7]

Algeria's debt service obligation in 1982, $3.9 billion, was equal to 27% of its total debt. These obligations had grown at the rate of 33% per year from 1973 to 1982. While the service owed to the financial markets (61.6% of all debt service) had grown at the impressive rate of 53.3% per year, even the service owed to official creditors had grown fast at 22.5%. Algeria's debt service burden had grown to about 25% of the value of merchandise exports in 1982.[8]

The buildup of debt and the debt-service obligations tied the fate of the Algerian economy to events in world financial markets and to dependence on continued growth of revenues from exports. Algeria provides an example of the problems that arise when the three conditions for maintaining development with debt are violated; that is, when macroeconomic growth slows, demand for exports decline, and export prices fall in relative terms.

CRISIS YEARS: THE 1980s

Although Algeria's GNP continued to grow in real terms, at about 11% per year, from 1976 through 1980, disputes among Algeria's economic policy-makers led to the stagnation of government-initiated investment in industry and agriculture.[9] Because most of Algeria's borrowing had previously been for industrial investment projects, this period of internal indecision was reflected in a moratorium on the incurrence of new debt. Although the internal disputes were dampened with the victory of the new president, Chadli Benjadid, the onset of the worldwide recession in 1981 and the reduced willingness of creditors to lend encouraged the continuation of this moratorium through 1982.

The decline in world demand for oil and gas products after 1981 and the relative decline in oil and gas prices caused Algeria's terms of trade to deteriorate and made it increasingly difficult to earn the hard currency needed to pay for imports and repay debt. By 1984, Algeria's terms of trade were 99% of what they had been in 1980 (see Table 7.3), down from a high of 116% in 1981, and service on long-term debt alone had risen to 34% of exports (Table 7.5).

There was no imminent threat of default, but, on the advice of the World Bank and its international private commercial creditors, the Algerian government imposed austerity budgets, cut imports, curtailed public investment in industry, and turned in 1983 and 1984 toward freer domestic markets as well as toward a greater role for both foreign and domestic private capital than at any time since independence.[10] These policy changes did not immediately result in an infusion of new capital for productive investment or an effusion of economic growth: Algeria's average rate of real GDP growth from 1980 through 1983 appears to have been under 2%.[11] However, international lenders rewarded the Algerian government for its financial prudence by encouraging Algeria to return to the financial markets for renewed borrowing in 1983 and 1984. Its outstanding debt began to grow again, reaching approximately $14 billion by the end of 1984.

Despite the long recovery in the OECD economies from 1983 to 1988, financial circumstances remained much less favorable to Algeria than they had been in the 1970s. Interest rates rose sharply in the earlier part of the decade and remained higher, in real terms, than they had been in the 1970s. Financial flows from commercial banks to developing countries slowed dramatically, falling by more than 50% (in constant dollars) in the 1986-88 period as compared to the 1980-82 period. When interest payments, as well as principal repayments, are included in flow calculations, middle income developing countries (including Algeria—see Table 7.7) continued to experience a net drain on funds in 1985, 1986, 1987, and 1988. Furthermore, although official flows to low-income developing countries continued in real terms at about the same level through the 1980s, official flows to middle income developing countries declined, standing in 1988 at a level 29% lower in real terms than they had been in 1980.[12]

Algeria continued through the 1980s to be more dependent on commercial than on concessional credit. In 1988, only 24% of Algeria's debt was from official sources, as opposed to 76% from commercial sources, the reverse of other Middle Eastern debtor countries such as Morocco, Tunisia,

Table 7.7: Inflow of Loans and Outflow of Principal and Interest ($ millions)

	Public loans[a] gross inflow	Repayment principal	Interest payments[b]	Net Flow[d]
1970	292	33	10	249
1980	3,401	2,405	1,305	1,891
1981	2,781	2,399	1,481	-1,099
1982	2,238	2,893	1,368	-2,023
1983	2,921	3,292	1,212	-1,583
1984	3,014	3,269	1,291[c]	-1,546
1985	3,354	3,286	1,297	-1,229
1986	3,430	3,905	1,250	-1,725
1987	4,196	3,543	1,377	-724
1988	5,922	4,534	1,809	-421

[a] Public and publicly guaranteed long-term and medium-term loans from abroad. Algeria has no private international loans recorded in these tables.

[b] Interest payments on public debt.

[c] From 1984 on, this column includes interest payments on long-term debt only.

[d] This figure is reached by adding columns 2 and 3 and subtracting the sum from column 1.

Source: *World Development Report*, volumes for 1982 through 1990, e.g., Table 22, p. 221, and Table 23, p. 223, in 1990 volume.

and Egypt. Algeria held 36% of its debt at floating interest rates in 1988, similar to Morocco, but much higher than Tunisia with 17% and Egypt with 1.4%.[13] At the same time, Algeria faced higher average interest rates (7.6% in 1988 versus 5.6% in 1970), lower average maturities (six years in 1988 versus 12 in 1970) and lower average grace periods (two years in 1988 versus three years in 1970).[14]

International trade circumstances continued to deteriorate for Algeria as the 1980s wore on. Revenues from oil exports declined with the rise of increased competition among suppliers and downward pressure on oil prices. In 1986, Algeria's terms of trade were just 44% of what they had been in 1980, and, in spite of the contraction of imports (a decline of 3.1% per year from 1980 to 1986), the value of trade imports exceeded exports by a record $2.287 billion in that year (see Table 7.3).

Algeria's total debt stood at $18 billion in 1986, the long-term portion of which ($15 billion) equalled one quarter of GNP. The debt-service burden tended to increase, as new debt was taken on or old debt was rolled over, as indicated in Table 7.5. Debt service equalled 55% of the value of goods and services exported in 1986.[15] Higher debt-service payments and lower export revenues can easily add up to balance-of-payments problems, especially if a country is trying, as Algeria was until 1986, to keep up purchases of imports for the industrial development program and for basic consumption (food accounted for about one-fourth of the value of Algeria's imports).[16]

Agriculture had recovered slightly in the first half of the 1980s, the average index of food-production-per-capita for 1984-86 stood at 101, as compared to the base of 100 in 1979-81. But cereal imports continued to rise, to 4,664 thousand metric tons in 1986 as compared to 3,261 thousand metric tons in 1981.[17]

STABILIZATION PROGRAMS: STRUCTURE AND FUNCTION

When a country is having difficulty servicing its debt or otherwise paying its outstanding bills to vendors in other countries, international lenders become concerned about being repaid; that is, they worry about the "stability" of the flow and real value of international capital. They expect the debtor country to demonstrate that it is taking measures to stabilize its economy, control inflation, and maintain its ability to repay debt, hence the notion of a "stabilization program."

What options does a country like Algeria have in this difficult situation? It wants to meet its obligation to keep up its debt-service payments and thereby keep up its reputation as a worthy borrower, so as not to foreclose the possibility of future borrowing. However, it needs to do so in a way that will cause the least disruption to the domestic economy, which is bound to feel repercussions from any changes in the flow of trade and payments. One possibility is to ask creditors for a rescheduling of the debt repayment and debt service, stringing it out over more years, perhaps at lower interest rates, and effectively buying time for the economy to recover its lost footing.

Rescheduling is often negotiated through the IMF, one of whose main functions is to help its member nations to cover shortfalls in their annual balance of payments. The instrument used most frequently is the "stand-by" agreement, in which the IMF lends a country the funds to cover its deficit over a period of from one to three years, while the country makes certain adjustments, such as in its export programs and its exchange-rate policy.

The stand-by agreement is useful only as a short-term arrangement for a country expected to solve its deficit problem relatively quickly; it is inadequate to correct long-term and chronic balance-of-payments problems. Hence, in the late 1970s and increasingly in the 1980s, as debt problems loomed larger and more intractable all over the developing world, the IMF turned to extended arrangements of three years or more. For hopelessly indebted countries, these arrangements entailed a commitment to making profound changes in the structure of their economies in exchange for both direct IMF lending and IMF help in negotiating and renegotiating loans from other official and commercial sources. The IMF-sponsored stabilization program grew out of the evolution of these extended arrangements.[18]

At a minimum, a stabilization program aims to restructure the debtor economy so as to provide for increased inflows of the foreign exchange needed to service the debt and a reduction of outflows for other purposes. Tactics such as devaluation of the national currency, deregulation of domestic prices and interest rates, and restricting the rate of growth of the money supply are intended to make the country's exports cheaper, and therefore more attractive on world markets, and to bring inflationary pressures under control, in order to assure potential foreign investors and lenders that the value of their capital will not be eroded.

In the longer run, a stabilization program involves changing domestic investment laws to encourage entry by foreign industrial, commercial, and financial capital, in the hope of increasing the inflow of foreign exchange through these investments and improving the level of technology and efficiency of production. In addition, government programs that are believed to contribute to rigidity and inefficiency in production are constricted or eliminated altogether. These include centrally planned economic programs, particularly those that pump investment funds into state-run enterprises. These enterprises may be broken up into competitive units, or sold to the private sector (domestic or foreign), or required to operate solely on a profit-or-loss basis, without the use-value considerations for final output involved in central planning decisions.

The goal of improving economic efficiency, in the standard orthodox sense, is also served by shifts in employment and income distribution. Efficiency in enterprise is enhanced through the laying off or firing of unnecessary workers and through the suppression of wage demands (to improve productivity, enhance the profitability of the enterprise, and help control inflation). Government subsidies on basic necessities (food, pharmaceuticals, energy, transportation, housing) are to be reduced or eventually eliminated in order to bring the public deficit under control and to help move prices toward "more realistic" (i.e., world market) levels. This package of changes is intended to dampen domestic demand for consumer goods and raise the amount of savings available for investment, and thus generate future economic growth at a higher rate. Out of this future growth, it is argued, expansion of employment opportunities and a rising standard of living will eventually trickle down to all, thus making up for short-term unemployment and income suppression for the working classes.

The Expected Benefits of Such a Program

- Short-run debt-service payments may be strung out over a longer period of time, giving the country's economy a chance to shift its structure of production to accommodate a changing world economy.
- The shift to more profitable export production, decreased regulation of domestic producers of exports, and increased foreign investment may lead to increased inflows of foreign exchange.
- The compression of domestic demand may lead to decreased import costs.
- The realignment of currency rates may lead to reduced capital flight.
- More low-cost foreign aid may be made available by international agencies to replace or augment the high-cost loans.
- Tighter control on the money supply, reductions in government deficits, and reduction in consumer demand may lead to lower rates of inflation.
- The constriction of government intervention in the economy and the liberating of public enterprises toward free-market behavior, along with the laying off of redundant workers and the shift of labor into employment in the more profitable enterprises may lead to more flexible and efficient economic development.
- The stimulation of both industry and agriculture to produce for the world market instead of the restricted domestic market, the deregulation of domestic private capital, and the reduction of government deficits, which tend to drain capital from productive investment, may lead to renewed economic growth.

The Costs of Such a Program

- Imports of technology, raw materials, and other industrial inputs may become more expensive and thus make it harder for domestic firms to compete with foreign capital. As these prices rise, along with the outflow of repatriated profits to foreign capital, there may be a negative effect on the balance of payments.

- Inflationary pressures may appear from new sources as the currency is devalued (domestic prices will have to rise), when previously controlled prices on domestically produced inputs to industry are deregulated, and when government deficits fail to disappear as revenues from formerly public enterprises decline. (Only a thorough tax program could prevent this, but that may induce a recession.)
- Domestic firms' investment in industry may decline due to the decrease in government spending for contracts, the increase in interest rates, and the rise in the prices of imported inputs.
- Aggregate demand may be restructured away from basic needs and toward production for export. Given the structure of the international market, there is no guarantee that the provision of basic needs will be met by the profit motive.
- Domestic consumption may decrease, due to the reduction in government subsidies for food and other necessities, wage compression and rising unemployment, and the decontrol of prices.
- The country's economy may become more tightly tied into the international trading and financial system, allowing debt to become a permanent fixture in the economic structure of the country. The economy may come to require the recurring infusion of foreign private capital in order to avoid future balance-of-payments crises and to depend on foreign aid from the World Bank, AID, and other international agencies as well as from the IMF. With this aid may come political and even military obligations, as well as economic commitments, stretching far into the future.

The debate around the benefits and costs of IMF stabilization programs has been extensive.[19] In an empirical study of 18 Latin American countries over the 1965-81 period, Manuel Pastor[20] found that the most consistent benefit obtained from IMF stabilization programs was an improvement in the balance of payments coming mainly through the capital account—that is, that international lenders and investors are more willing to send investment into an IMF-secured economy. The greatest cost was a consistent shift in the distribution of income, away from labor and toward capital, particularly capital producing for the international market. There was little consistent evidence of sustained improvements in the current account balance or in economic growth (findings which are substantiated in IMF studies also), and increases, not decreases, in inflation rates tended to follow in the wake of IMF programs.[21]

In another comparative study, Andres Solimano examined specifically the income-distribution effects, as well as success in attaining the formal stated objectives, of various stabilization programs, some orthodox and some heterodox. He defines an orthodox stabilization program as one which "combines the correction of fiscal deficits to reduce (or eliminate) inflation with real depreciation of the exchange rate to correct deficits in the current account of the balance of payments."[22] Chile, Argentina, and Uruguay implemented such plans from the mid-1970s to the early 1980s. Although they tried to abandon the orthodox versions in midstream with attempts at direct exchange-rate controls, all three were required to return to them due to disequilibrium in the balance of payments. The end results were "accelerated inflation, reduced economic activity, and lower real wages."[23] Israel and Mexico in the mid-1980s, on the other hand, followed heterodox stabilization plans that combined incomes policies with fiscal-deficit reduction and devaluation of the currency. Partly due to the fact that they also had generous transfers of resources from abroad, these two cases showed that it is possible to reduce inflation without inducing severe recessionary conditions and unpalatable income distribution effects.[24]

NATURE OF THE SELF-IMPOSED STABILIZATION PROGRAM IN ALGERIA

For many a government in former colonial countries in Asia, Africa, and Latin America, the price of IMF intervention is high in political terms, because the nation has to yield part of its sovereignty over economic policy-making to an international agency operating on behalf of international finance capital. The government may be held accountable by its citizens and political opposition for whatever economic costs the domestic economy might suffer in the process of implementing the stabilization program.

Faced with the prospect of a high political price for sovereignty loss during the crisis years of the mid-1980s, the Algerian government repeatedly renewed its refusal to subject the economy to an IMF-determined stabilization program. Instead, it decided to reduce other claims on the country's increasingly scarce foreign-exchange resources in order to keep up debt-service payments, while it publicly reaffirmed the right to maintain its sovereignty over national economic policy. From 1984 to 1989, the Algerian

Table 7.8: Structure of Aggregate Demand Distribution of GDP, in %

	Government consumption	Private consumption investment	Gross domestic savings	Gross domestic nonfactor	Exports goods and services
1960	15	60	42	25	31
1965	15	66	22	19	22
1980	14	44	41	42	35
1981	16	45	37	39	34
1982	15	46	38	39	30
1983	16	46	37	38	28
1984	16	45	38	39	26
1985	15	46	36	38	24
1986	G + C = 69		32	31	16
1987	16	55	29	29	14
1988	16	53	31	31	16

Source: *World Development Report,* volumes for 1982 through 1990, table entitled "Structure of Demand," e.g., Table 9, p. 195, in 1990 volume.

government effectively imposed its own "stabilization program" on its populace.

The consequences were perhaps more drastic than the Chadli government could forsee. The complete lack of economic growth from 1986 to 1988 meant a falling standard of living, especially for the poor and unemployed in the cities, and fed the rising popular discontent with the government and the ruling party. It became clear that the decision to go with the self-imposed stabilization program would entail a high political price of its own and set the stage for further changes in economic policy and challenges to the political system.

The 1986-88 recession in the Algerian economy was brought on partly by external factors, namely the fall in oil and gas export revenues and the fall in the value of the dollar, in which Algeria's exports and debt service are denominated. This led to balance-of-payments problems. In addition, the economy had been suffering from domestic inefficiences. The severity of the problem was made manifest, for example, in declining productivity in industry. Real earnings per employee in manufacturing fell steadily from a base of 100 in 1980 to 73 in 1986, even though employee earnings retained a constant share of 53% of value added in manufacturing, while gross output per employee fell from a base of 100 in 1980 to 81 in 1986.[25]

The clearly discernible trend in the composition of aggregate demand in the 1980s was a shift in favor of government and private consumption at the expense of investment, savings, and exports. From 1980 to 1987, government consumption rose from 14 to 16% of GDP, and private consumption rose from 44 to 55% of GDP, while the shares of gross domestic investment, gross domestic savings, and exports all fell, from 41 to 29%, 42 to 29% and 35 to 14%, respectively (see Table 7.8).

Algeria's self-imposed stabilization program was part of a larger reform strategy that stressed reduction in the influence of the central government in economic decision-making and a turn toward free-market economic principles. It included many features remarkably similar to what an IMF program would have required.

- The Algerian dinar (AD) was gradually devalued. The official rate fell from $0.20 in 1985 to about $0.11 by August of 1990 and was expected to fall another 40% by 1992.[26]
- Prices of domestically produced goods were deregulated and across-the-board subsidies to producers and consumers were reduced in favor of targetted subsidies to exporters and to basic needs for the poorest consumers.
- Interest rates were allowed to rise, for example, on short-term commercial loans, from 5% in 1987 to 7% in 1988 to 8.5% in 1989.[27]
- The rate of growth of the nominal money supply was slowed from an annual average rate of 22.3% before 1980 to 17.5% from 1980 to 1988 (refer to Table 7.1).
- The government pledged to reduce the size of the national budget deficit, which had risen to a record high of 14.5% of GDP (AD 26.8 billion) in 1988, and which then fell dramatically to 4.2% of GDP (AD 6.1 billion) in 1989.[28]
- New legislation governing investment now places fewer constraints on domestic and foreign private capital (for example, liberalizing the holding of overseas bank deposits and repatriation of profits) in order to encourage expansion and diversification of exports.
- The Chadli government vowed to allow unprofitable newly autonomous local companies to go bankrupt. A total of about 300 former state-run companies will have been made autonomous by the end of 1991.[29]

- Changes in the institutions governing the labor market now aim to control the growth of the wage bill and improve productivity. The laws regulating collective bargaining now restrict the authority of the *Union Générale des Travailleurs Algériens* (UGTA), the labor federation, to represent workers in various sectors. New forms of management labor contracts, now made with individual workers rather than groups of workers, tie wage increases directly to an employee's productivity.[30]

BENEFITS OF ALGERIA'S STABILIZATION PROGRAM

The pursuit of this program has provided some of the expected benefits defined above.

- The rate of price inflation was brought down temporarily. The average annual rate in the 1980-1988 period of 4.4% was significantly lower than the 10.5% rate prior to 1980 (see Table 7.1). The consumer price index showed a downward trend from 12.4% in 1986 to under 6% in 1988; however, rises were expected for 1989, up to as high as 10%.[31]
- The pronounced trend in the structure of demand in the 1980s to favor government and private consumption at the expense of investment, savings, and exports, began to show signs of reversal. While government consumption held constant at 16% of GDP from 1987 to 1988, private consumption fell from 55 to 53%, gross domestic investment and gross domestic savings both rose from 29 to 31%, and exports of goods and services rose from 14 to 16% (see Table 7.8). It is noteworthy that these rates of GDI, GDS, and exports relative to GDP are comparable to those of Japan (31%, 33% and 13%, respectively, in 1988) and superior to those of the United States (15%, 13%, and 11%, respectively, in 1988).[32]
- There was some improvement in agriculture. The average index of food production per capita rose to 106 in 1986-88, from a base of 100 in 1979-81.[33]
- Although the terms of trade turned dramatically against Algeria, from a base of 100 in 1980 to 41 in 1988, the dollar value of imports shrank by an average 5.9% per year from 1980 to 1988 (see Table 7.3). The volume of imports in 1988 was only 61% of what it had been in 1980.[34]
- The volume of exports, on the other hand, continued to expand, to 117% in 1988 of the 1980 volume, although the value of exports in 1988, approximately $7.8 billion, was significantly below their value of $14 billion in 1980.[35]

- By 1986, the inflow of capital in the form of foreign loans resumed the level it had attained in 1980, and then surpassed itself in 1987 and again in 1988 (see Table 7.7).
- The current account deficit dropped sharply in 1987, although it rose again in 1988. The sharp drop, plus the continued inflow of credit from abroad allowed gross international reserves to remain at a level providing about four months of import coverage in 1986, 1987, and 1988 (see Table 7.4).
- Growth of real GDP turned positive in 1989, with a 3% increase over 1988.[36]

COSTS OF ALGERIA'S STABILIZATION PROGRAM

Real GDP growth was negative from 1986 to 1988, shrinking by a total of 5.3% in that two-year period.[37] Per capita GDP was $2150 in 1988 as compared to $2555 in 1986, using the official exchange rate (even after accounting for its official devaluation). One source uses the "relative purchasing power parity exchange rate" formula to argue that real per capita GDP in 1988 equalled only $770.[38]

- Growth rates of gross domestic investment, of industry in general, and of manufacturing in particular continued to be negative in 1988 and 1989.[39] It is noteworthy that there is no mention of industrial policy, outside of hydrocarbons, petrochemicals and infrastructure, in the 1990 issues of the *Economist Intelligence Unit* on Algeria, in contrast to as recently as the early 1980s. However, the EIU points out that whereas industrial production overall fell by 2.4% in 1989, the drop is much steeper, 5.5%, if the hydrocarbon sector is excluded, and that the resulting shortage of raw materials and spare parts constrained results in all other sectors, including agriculture.[40]
- Unemployment rose from 18.5% of the labor force in 1987 to 22% in 1988 to an estimated 25% in 1989. Both the EIU and the U.S. Department of State report high levels of labor unrest in 1989 with an average of over 250 strikes per month over issues of wages and working conditions.[41]
- Private consumption declined by about 10% in 1987,[42] and by another 6.2% in 1988, but recovered by 9.6% in 1989.[43]
- Agriculture improved in absolute terms, as we saw above, but fell behind in relative terms. Cereals imports rose to 6,130 thousand metric tons in 1988, with food comprising 30% of imports in that year.[44]

- Exports have yet to be diversified. Crude oil and other hydrocarbon products still comprised 95% of exports in 1988.[45]
- Because Algeria's exports have not been significantly diversified, and because hydrocarbon product prices are denominated in dollars, the devaluation of the dinar has provided little stimulus to the economy. The devaluation has made imports more expensive in the meantime.
- The current account remained $1.255 billion in deficit for 1989, although this was an improvement over 1988.[46] The inflow of direct foreign investment was small or negative throughout the 1980s, as indicated in Table 4.
- As Table 7.7 indicates, the outflow of debt repayments and interest was greater than the inflow of new loans in every year from 1981 to 1988.
- As displayed in Table 7.5, Algeria's external debt, both long-term and total (that is, of all durations), has grown consistently larger since 1983, with a concomitant enlargement in debt expressed as a percentage of GNP and in debt service as a percentage of exports. In 1989, Algeria's total debt reached a record $25.33 billion, of which $23.6 billion was long-term, almost half of the value of GNP. Its debt-service ratio in 1989 continued to be in the 75% range, not significantly different from 1988, and its repayments are scheduled to be more than $7 billion per year for the forseeable future.[47]

Chadli's public declaration in September of 1988 that the country's foreign debt was unmanageable after all, combined with rising popular anger over the rumored corruption and cronyism with the government and the ruling party, the FLN, led to strikes by workers and students. Although there is mixed evidence on how it all started, on October 4, it is clear that by October 5 young men from the poorer and working-class sections of Algiers began attacking and looting first state stores and then private shops. In the days that followed, violent confrontations between the rioters and the army left an estimated 400 dead and hardened popular discontent with government economic policy.[48]

Despite calls by the opposition for a new economic policy to create jobs and meet the pressing need for housing and other mass consumer goods and public services, the government responded with a pledge to "democratize" the political process, meaning a shift toward multiparty parliamentary forms that Chadli backers had long desired, and quietly renewed its efforts to expand the stabilization program under the more formal auspices of the IMF.

A NEW POLICY REGARDING DEBT AND DEBT SERVICE?

It was the debt and debt-service burden of growing scope that finally pushed the Algerian government into the arms of the IMF, even if only in a discreet affair rather than a marriage. In 1989 the IMF provided a nonconditional one-year stand-by agreement of $600 million while the World Bank came forth with development loans for infrastructure projects such as port and irrigation facilities. Algeria's creditors, including the U.S.-based Chase Investment Bank and a consortium of French banks, were so pleased with the country's prudence in imposing a stabilization plan on itself that they too came forth with new loan packages to keep the debt rolling over in 1989 and 1990.

Unlike other IMF/debtor agreements, this one entailed no explicit commitment by the Algerian government to the standard IMF stabilization package so that there were no publically known formal conditionality measures attached to the influx of funds. But, as the EIU puts it:

> It would not have been approved had the IMF not given its blessing to the next round of the government's reform strategy... [Making the public announcement of the IMF stand-by agreement] in the unusual form of an interview published in the two main daily newspapers on June 18 [1989], the IMF's director, Michel Camdessus, said the IMF board had been unanimously in favour of the deal because Algeria had tackled its problems itself.[49]

Meanwhile, the government continued to pursue its informally IMF-approved stabilization program. This involved the usual IMF package of reforms, devaluation of the currency, decontrolling interest rates and prices, inviting the influx of foreign capital on more profitable terms, and at least verbally encouraging diversification of exports and expanded export production. The government continued to dismantle state-run enterprises, breaking them up into competing units and liquidating those that were not profitable, and promoted the growth of the private sector, especially in export production or other industries that might attract foreign exchange or foreign investment, such as tourism and the heralded joint ventures in auto production with Fiat and Peugeot.[50] The government continued to seek less costly means of bringing in external finance by pressing the buyers of its oil and gas to obtain their own external credit and by refinancing short-term debt through the issue of long-term bonds.[51]

The bankers predicted that Algeria's economy would revive, with the influx of funds following on the heels of the IMF seal of approval, the recovery of hydrocarbon prices in international markets, and the expected success of Algeria's economic reforms in stimulating the private sector and attracting foreign investment,[52] although the latter two have yet to prove the durability of their impact. In conformity with Pastor's and Solimano's findings, the most important effects of Algeria's unorthodox stabilization program have been the short-run infusion of international capital and the longer-run shift in the balance of power among economic actors and political forces in Algerian society.

Algeria has reversed the usual sequence of events, first imposing a stabilization program on itself, then experiencing a major economic recession, and then inviting the IMF in for a friendly voluntary arrangement. Algeria had already incurred a large part of the cost of a stabilization program, and then obtained some of the benefits. It is now an open question whether the social groups which have borne the brunt of the costs will continue to cooperate, without having to be forced to do so by a more authoritarian government. The promised democratization of the political process offers them a chance to publicly voice their opinions, but the government and ruling party have yet to prove that they will allow those voices to be raised in opposition to its economic programs.

Algerian ruling circles are grappling with the question of whether the turn in the summer of 1989 toward a stand-by agreement with the IMF is just a pragmatic compromise in the face of the realities of the international trade and finance system or a stepping stone on the road to a full debt rescheduling and IMF-imposed stabilization program, implying a reversal of previously proclaimed policy. The *Economist Intelligence Unit,* published for an audience mainly of bankers and international traders, summed up the situation for its worried subscribers in these reassuring tones:

> *Rescheduling can be avoided.* A centrepiece of economic policy remains Algeria's determination not to reschedule. This is likely to continue. Although there is currently a major debate on debt policy going on within the country, only if the present government is replaced by a very different administration would this change . . . [Or] only if the external situation deteriorates very severely next year will the government have to reconsider the rescheduling option—unless the political situation requires the populist gesture of debt moratorium. This must be recognised as a possible alternative scenario but would represent a major break with past practice . . . Algeria will thus continue to service its debt.[53]

Apparently the creditors may rest assured that they, at least, will continue to get their share of the benefits from the Algerian stabilization program.

NOTES

1. *Economist Intelligence Unit, Country Report: Algeria,* no. 3, 1989, p. 1.
2. Two sources that analyze the institutions of this era and the reasons for its demise are Fred L. Block, *The Origins of the International Economic Disorder* (Berkeley: University of California Press, 1977) and E. A. Brett, *International Money and Capitalist Crisis: The Anatomy of Global Disintegration* (Boulder, CO: Westview Press, 1983).
3. This argument is made for the Third World in general, with reference to Latin America in particular by Jeff Frieden in "International Finance and the Third World," *MERIP Reports* 13 no. 117 (September 1983).
4. Abdellatif Benachenhou, *L'éxperience algérienne de planification et de développement, 1962-1982,* 2nd ed. (Algiers: Office des Publications Universitaires, 1982), and Marc Raffinot and Pierre Jacquemot, *Le capitalisme d'état algérien* (Paris: Maspero, 1977), treat the history of economic nationalism in Algeria. Aissa Bennamane, *The Algerian Development Strategy and Employment Policy,* monograph no. ix (Swansea, Wales: Center for Development Studies, 1980), discusses the specific uses of investment funds.
5. *World Development Report,* (Washington, DC: World Bank, 1983), Table 6, p. 159.
6. See OECD, *World Economic Interdependence and the Evolving North-South Relationship* (Paris: OECD, 1983), especially Table 7, p. 65, which shows a real compound annual growth rate of nonconcessional flows to developing countries of 8.6%, as compared to 4.9% for Official Development Assistance flows, between 1970 and 1981.
7. OECD, *External Debt of Developing Countries* (Paris: OECD, 1984), Tables 21 and 22, pp. 76 and 77. The other countries, in 1983 rank order, were Brazil, Mexico, Argentina, Venezuela, South Korea, Iran, Yugoslavia, Chile, Indonesia, Saudi Arabia, Nigeria, Iraq, Peru, Philippines, Greece, Portugal, and India.
8. OECD, *External Debt of Developing Countries,* shows a debt for Algeria of $16.8 billion at the end of 1982, higher than the figures it offers for Egypt and Turkey. This source explains that the calculation of any country's debt varies by the currencies in which the debt is held and by the exchange rates chosen to convert to United States dollars. The high value of the dollar at the end of 1982 tended to overstate the value of debt held in various alternative currencies.
9. Discussion of the internal problems of the Algerian economy can be found in Hugh Roberts, "The Algerian Bureaucracy," in *Sociology of "Developing Societies": The Middle East,* ed. Talal Asad and Roger Owen (New

York: Monthly Review Press, 1983); Peter R. Knauss, "Algeria under Boumedienne: the Mythical Revolution, 1965-1978," in *The Performance of Soldiers as Governors,* ed. I. J. Mowoe (Washington, DC: University Press of America, 1980); and "Algeria," in *Africa Contemporary Record: Annual Survey and Documents,* ed. Colin Legum (New York: Africana Publishing, 1982). Chapters 1, 2, and 5 of Karen Pfeifer, *Agrarian Reform under State Capitalism in Algeria* (Boulder, CO: Westview Press, 1985), also deal with some of these questions.

10. *Economist Intelligence Unit, Quarterly Economic Review of Algeria,* 1985, pp. 11-16, 22-23; 1984, pp.3-4, 10-11.
11. These are crude estimates calculated from data provided in International Monetary Fund, *International Financial Statistics,* 1983; 100-103, 1985 (May); 80-81, 95; and in *Economist Intelligence Unit* 1 (1985), 15. These data are nominal rates of growth in Algerian dinars corrected by the consumer price index; a GDP deflator was not included.
12. Development Committee, *Problems and Issues in Structural Adjustment,* issue papers of the joint ministerial committee of the World Bank and the IMF, no. 23 (Washington, DC: World Bank, 1990), pp. 63-67.
13. *World Development Report,* 1990, p. 168.
14. *World Development Report,* 1990, Table 25, p. 227. Algeria has been a donor of official development assistance (ODA), ranging from a high of $281 million in 1979 (0.9% of GNP) to $13 million in 1988 (0.02% of GNP), and has been a very small recipient of ODA, $171 million in 1988 ($7.20 per capita, or 0.3% of GNP), as compared to, say, Morocco, which received $482 million in 1988 ($20.10 per capita, 2.2% of GNP) or Tunisia, which received $316 million in 1988 ($40.50 per capita 3.2% of GNP). See *World Development Report,* 1990, Table 19, p. 215, and Table 20, p. 217.
15. *World Development Report,* 1988, Table 11, p. 243; Table 16, p. 253; Table 18, p. 257.
16. *World Development Report,* 1989, p. 193.
17. *World Development Report,* 1988, Table 7, p. 235.
18. This is described in World Bank/IMF literature, for example, see the *World Development Report,* 1985, pp. 65-69, 105-107; or Jose da Silva Lopes, "Policies of Economic Adjustment to Correct External Imbalances," pp. 21-33 (especially pp. 22-24) in Alan Roe, Jayanta Roy, and Jayshree Sengupta, *Economic Adjustment in Algeria, Egypt, Jordan, Morocco, Pakistan, Tunisia and Turkey,* Economic Development Institute of the World Bank, Policy Seminar Report no. 15, 1989.
19. See for example, National Bank of Egypt, "The International Monetary Fund and the Developing Countries," *Economic Bulletin,* 1988 (1 and 2), 5-17; and Roe, Roy and Sengupta, *Economic Adjustment in Algeria, Egypt, Jordan, Morocco, Pakistan, Tunisia, and Turkey,* 1989.
20. Manuel Pastor, Jr., "The Effects of IMF Programs in the Third World: Debate and Evidence from Latin America," *World Development,* vol. 15, no. 2 (1987), pp. 249-262; and Manuel Pastor, *The International Monetary*

Fund and Latin America: Economic Stabilization and Class Conflict (Boulder, CO: Westview Press, 1987).

21. The only Middle Eastern country which has been subject to a strict IMF stabilization program is Turkey after 1980. The economic crisis that led up to the implementation of the program and the details of the program itself are summarized succinctly from a world banker's point of view in the *World Development Report* of 1985, pp. 67-68, and by Christine Bogdanowicz-Bindert, "Portugal, Turkey, and Peru: Three Successful Stabilization Programmes under the Auspices of the IMF," *World Development*, vol. 11, 1983, pp. 65-70. A more in-depth and critical perspective is provided by Ronnie Margulies and Ergin Yildizoḡlu, "Austerity Packages and Beyond: Turkey since 1980," *Capital and Class*, vol. 36 (Winter 1988), pp. 143-147. The latter point out that it was only after a military coup and the imposition of martial law that the right conditions could be created for the IMF program to be imposed.
22. Andres Solimano, "Inflation and the Costs of Stabilization: Historical and Recent Experiences and Policy Lessons," *World Bank Research Observer* 5, no. 2 (July 1990), 171.
23. Solimano, "Inflation and the Costs of Stabilization," 174.
24. Solimano, "Inflation and the Costs of Stabilization," 179-183.
25. *World Development Report*, 1989, Table 7, pp. 176-177.
26. *Economist Intelligence Unit*, no. 3, 1990, pp. 3, 8.
27. US Department of State, *Country Reports on Economic Policy and Trade Practices*, Report submitted to the Committee on Foreign Relations, Committee on Finance of the US Senate, and the Committee on Foreign Affairs, Committee on Ways and Means of the US House of Representatives, February 1990, "Algeria," 1990, p. 585.
28. *Economist Intelligence Unit*, no. 1, 1990, p. 12. The second source is the World Bank, *Trends in Developing Economies* (Washington, DC: World Bank, 1990), p. 7.
29. *Economist Intelligence Unit*, no. 3, 1990, p. 7.
30. *Economist Intelligence Unit*, no. 2, 1990, p. 14.
31. *Economist Intelligence Unit*, no. 3, 1990, p. 3; U.S. Department of State, 1990, p. 585.
32. *World Development Report*, 1990, Table 9, p. 195.
33. *World Development Report*, 1990, Table 4, p. 185.
34. World Bank, *Trends in Developing Economies*, 1990, p. 6.
35. World Bank, *Trends in Developing Economies*, 1990, p. 6.
36. World Bank, *Trends in Developing Economies*, 1990, p. 5.
37. World Bank, *Trends in Developing Economies*, 1990, p. 5.
38. "Algeria," *Foreign Economic Trends* (Washington, DC: World Bank, 1989), 4-6.
39. World Bank, *Trends in Developing Economies*, 1990, p. 5.
40. *Economist Intelligence Unit*, no. 1, 1990, p. 5, and no. 2, p. 14.

41. *Economist Intelligence Unit,* no. 1, 1990, p. 16; U.S. Department of State, 1990, p. 591.
42. *Foreign Economic Trends,* "Algeria," pp. 4-6.
43. World Bank, *Trends in Developing Economies,* 1990, p. 5.
44. *World Development Report,* 1990, Table 4, p. 185.
45. World Bank, *Trends in Developing Economies,* 1990, p. 6.
46. World Bank, *Trends in Developing Economies,* 1990, p. 6.
47. *Economist Intelligence Unit,* no. 3, 1990, pp. 3, 8.
48. For more detail, see "An Interview with Mahfoud Bennoune: Algeria's Facade of Democracy," pp. 9-13, and "Chadli's Perestroika," by Rachid Tlemcani, pp. 14-18, both in *Middle East Report* no. 163, vol. 20 (March-April 1990).
49. *Economist Intelligence Unit, Country Report: Algeria,* p. 9; reiterated in no. 3, 1990, p. 7.
50. "Algeria," *Foreign Economic Trends,* pp. 3 and 5. *Economist Intelligence Unit, Country Report: Algeria,* pp. 11, 13-14.
51. *Economist Intelligence Unit,* no. 3, 1990, p. 8; US Department of State, 1990, pp. 588, 592.
52. *Economist Intelligence Unit, Country Report: Algeria,* pp. 9-10, quoting from the "latest report by the Washington-based Institute of International Finance (IIF), using data from both official sources and banks and multilateral agencies."
53. *Economist Intelligence Unit, Country Report: Algeria,* pp. 4-5. This reassurance is repeated in *Economist Intelligence Unit,* no. 3, 1990, p. 18.

8

Assessing the January 24, 1980 Economic Stabilization Program in Turkey

Birol A. Yeşilada and Mahir Fisunoğlu

INTRODUCTION

In late 1970s, the Turkish economy faced what was perhaps the worst crisis of its post-World War II history: it was saddled with foreign exchange problems, growing foreign debt, negative economic growth, high inflation and unemployment, series of shortages, and alarming trade and balance-of-payments deficits. With such difficulties, Turkey was the first major developing country to face debt-payment crisis after 1973.[1]

These economic problems were further intensified by growing social and political unrest in the country. During this time, political parties, state bureaucracy, student organizations, labor unions, and almost every possible interest association were completely politicized and ideologically factionalized.[2] In fact, the country faced conditions close to civil war; thousands of citizens lost their lives as result of terrorist activities between 1976 and 1980. Faced with growing economic and political problems, the last civilian government of the 1970s, headed by Süleyman Demirel, adopted a bold policy package on January 24, 1980, aimed at massive restructuring of the economy with an emphasis on export-oriented growth strategies. International finance organizations, like the IMF, hailed these measures. However, the government failed to implement these policy changes due to the political crisis that plagued Turkey. It was not until after the September 12, 1980 coup that the officials were able to put these policies into effect.

This article evaluates the nature of the January 24, 1980 stabilization program in Turkey and assesses its policy outcomes.

BACKGROUND CONDITIONS

As Miles Kahler notes, the 1980s is the decade in which the orthodox policies of the industrialized countries were also reflected, especially following the debt crisis, in the policies of the Less Developed Countries (LDCs).[3] However, the specific policies adopted among these countries for economic stabilization and balance-of-payments adjustments have varied greatly. While most stabilization policies in LDCs were characterized by a return to orthodoxy, a few other countries, namely Argentina, Brazil, and Israel, adopted heteredox programs.[4] The new orthodox (neoorthodox) policies were a reaction to the stagnation and crisis conditions that resulted from the difficulties associated with the completion of the first and second phases of import substituting industrialization and the subsequent transition to the much needed export-led growth strategies. During the ensuing crises, authoritarian regimes or conservative governments came to power determined to undo their predecessors' inward-looking policies.[5] The neoorthodox stabilization programs implemented in most LDCs shared a common feature in that they linked stabilization (the short-term goal), structural adjustment (the medium-term objective), and economic strategy (the long-term goal). Since in Turkey and elsewhere the structural adjustment policies were conditioned by the severity of the crisis that preceded their application, it is important to discuss the genesis of Turkey's 1980 economic crisis. The factors responsible for the near collapse of the Turkish economy in 1980 can be classified into two categories: (1) internal economic and political factors, and (2) external economic developments. Not surprisingly, each of these had a detrimental impact on the other further aggravating the overall condition.

High government spending, stagnant domestic savings, the inward-oriented development strategies, poor debt management, and political unrest were crucial internal factors. The result of the first three was serious balance-of-payments deficits that, in turn, led to heavy external borrowing. Balance-of-payment problems are not out of the ordinary for the Turkish economy. Since 1950, the country has experienced three growth cycles with important similarities: a period of rapid industrial growth followed by a major foreign-exchange crisis, a massive devaluation of the Turkish lira, and a slowdown in growth. The devaluations were remarkable: 100 percent in 1958, 66 percent in 1970, and 100 percent between March 1978 and January 1980. It is also important to note that at the end of each cycle Turkey experienced two developments that seemed to be related. First, at three junctures, in 1957-58, 1969-70, and 1978-80, the ruling governments adopted IMF-sponsored stabilization programs that included large devaluations. Shortly thereafter, growing social and political unrest resulted in the military interventions of 1960, 1971, and 1980. Among these military incursions, the ones in 1960 and 1980 were the most serious. Both times the military officers—having directly assumed control—remained in power for a short time and completely revised the existing constitutional framework in an attempt to restore law and order.[6] Yet, as historical facts demonstrate, each intervention was followed by a worsening of socioeconomic and political conditions in the country.

The significant external factors responsible for Turkey's economic problems were the sudden increases in oil prices in 1973 and 1979 and the country's deteriorating terms of trade. One can argue that recent economic problems began, in part, with the 1973 oil crisis that caused a drastic increase in the petroleum import bill. While the total oil import bill in 1973 was about 17 percent of export earnings, this figure reached 76 percent or a total of $1.4 billion in 1978.[7]

Despite the urgency of the problem, the ruling coalition governments were unwilling to alter their policies in the face of worsening economic crisis. They maintained high levels of investment to meet planned strategic targets and, in the process, ignored the danger signals in the economy. For example, the governments failed to increase domestic savings and the balance-of-payment policies remained inward-looking, favoring import substitution over export promotion despite the fact that Turkey's current account deficit increased steadily: 2.5 percent of GNP in 1974, 5.3 percent of GNP in 1975, 5.4 percent of GNP in 1976, and 7.1 percent of GNP in 1977. During this period, public investment increased from 7 percent of GNP in 1973 to 13.1 percent of GNP in 1977. At the same time, domestic savings stagnated for the private sector and actually declined from 8.8 percent of GNP in 1973 to 6.3 percent of GNP in 1977 for the public sector.[8] This is ironic because by 1975, Turkey had satisfied the first stage of import substituting industrialization—the completion of the domestic consumer market-oriented phase. The next stage ought to have been the expansion of industrial growth through export-oriented growth policies and intermediate and capital goods industries. Unfortunately, the various governments failed to make this needed transition.

This economic instability was accompanied by political instability.[9] In 1975 Prime Minister Demirel favored an IMF-type austerity program. However, his coalition partner, Necmettin Erbakan of the National Salvation Party, opposed the program and insisted on maintaining high levels of economic growth with emphasis on industrialization, social-welfare spending, and increased consumption. Also, as stated earlier, growing political unrest and ideological factionalization of the entire state apparatus made it almost impossible to reach a national consensus to solve these problems. Faced with such worsening conditions, the coalition government then resorted to financing the deficits by short-term commercial credits known as convertible Turkish lira deposits (CTLD)—or *Dövize Çevrilebilir Mevduat.* The scheme was simple. Foreign banks were granted government guarantees on the value of foreign currencies deposited for one or two years in Turkey. The Turkish banks then sold foreign currencies to the Central Bank, and the Central Bank in turn, sold them to importers. The scheme stimulated workers' remittances from Europe because the effective interest rate on these deposits was two points above the London Interbank Offered Rate (LIBOR). Thus, between 1974 and 1977, $2.2 billion in remittances entered Turkey under this scheme. The foreign banks also were favorably disposed toward the CTLDs. Foreign currencies could be lent at Turkish interest rates and then converted into foreign currencies at a government-guaranteed exchange rate.

This scheme temporarily solved the foreign-exchange problem until 1977 when the bottom fell out. By the end of 1977, half of Turkey's external debt was short-term (about $9-10 billion). The CTLD scheme caused serious outflow of foreign exchange when the deposits came due. This rapid growth in external indebtedness was an alarming development given that Turkey's foreign debt in 1973 was a mere $3 billion. The end result of the above scenario was the debt crisis of 1977. In fact, Turkey experienced its debt crisis well before Mexico, Brazil, and Argentina—all of which experienced debt problems after the second oil price shock of 1979. Under these circumstances a rescue operation was inevitable. Turkey could no longer service its debt, foreign lenders withdrew, foreign banks refused to roll over credits, and the government ran out of foreign-exchange reserves.

In their attempts to correct these problems, the weak coalition governments of Demirel (1978) and Bülent Ecevit (1979) adopted two IMF-based economic stabilization programs. They implemented several devaluations of the Turkish lira and tried to enforce monetary discipline. Yet both sets of measures failed miserably because of growing political instability in the country. The IMF survey of the Turkish economy in October 1979 found that the tight monetary policies had been substantially relaxed and stand-by agreements had been violated. In addition, as Dani Rodrik points out, problems with foreign exchange resulted in severe shortages and, when coupled with excess liquidity, resulted in inflation of almost 120 percent in the first quarter of 1980.[10] One "positive" aspect of the 1977-1980 period was the rescheduling of Turkey's short-term debt. Short-term debt, including the by now infamous CTLDs, in the amount of $9.8 billion was consolidated and converted into long-term debt. Finally in January 1980, the Demirel government approached the IMF for a major restructuring of the Turkish economy.

THE STABILIZATION PROGRAM

The stabilization program that the government adopted on January 24, 1980, emphasized the following points:

1. Institutional changes aimed at making policy formulation and implementation more effective;
2. A devaluation of the Turkish lira vis-à-vis the US dollar by 33 percent, followed by continuous mini-devaluations, and the limitation of multiple exchange-rate policies;
3. Greater liberalization of the trade and payment regulations;
4. Additional promotional measures for exports;
5. Substantial price increases for state traded goods and abolition of price controls;
6. Increased competition for State Economic Enterprises (SEEs) through elimination of state subsidies and abolition of price controls on their products;
7. Higher rates of interest;
8. Promotion of foreign investments;
9. Arrangements for consolidating Turkey's private commercial debt; and
10. Drafting of legislation for tax reform.[11]

Furthermore, the unwritten policy suggestion in this package, supported by the IMF, was the restoration of sociopolitical order to enable the government to carry out the economic measures. Through this austerity and stabilization package, Turkey embarked on a new policy designed not only as a comprehensive program of economic stabilization but also as a basic reorientation of economic programs away from detailed government regulation and control toward greater reliance on market forces, foreign competition, and foreign investments. All of these factors simply signaled the sharp acceleration of Turkey's economic integration with global capitalism. It is important to note that this policy closely resembles the neoorthodox adjustment programs discussed by Joan Nelson. The relative success of such programs depends on five sets of causal variables for decision-making and policy implementation: (1) the nature of the crisis; (2) the capacity of the state; (3) political structures; (4) political circumstances; and (5) the role of external agencies—such as the IMF.[12]

POLICY OUTCOMES

In discussing policy outcomes of the above austerity measures it is crucial to assess the political outcomes separately from macroeconomic ones. This would allow us to explain the structural changes in the Turkish political system that were deemed necessary by the post-1980 authoritarian government for success of the program.

Political Outcomes

As argued earlier, the Demirel government lacked the necessary power to carry out these policies. Despite the seriousness of the economic problems facing Turkey, even the parties supporting his government without directly participating in the cabinet were at odds with him over the nature of the austerity program. The Nationalist Movement Party of Alparslan Türkeş and the National Salvation Party of Erbakan opposed elimination of state subsidies and other populist measures. The opposition Republican Peoples Party viewed the economic package as total capitulation to IMF demands.[13] In essence, problems associated with the political circumstances, political structures, and state capacity prevented the government from carrying out these measures.

In terms of political circumstances, Prime Minister Demirel lacked the necessary political leadership to carry out his economic policies. As Henri J. Barkey explains, Demirel was "besieged on all sides by the centrifugal forces of the society."[14] The entire bureaucracy of the state and interest groups in all sectors of society were thoroughly factionalized and politicized. Thus, the increased factionalization within the political structures of the state that reflected the general societal polarization meant that the state had become vulnerable to outside influences and would also be deprived of its autonomy.[15] Under these circumstances the only interest group that clearly supported the stabilization program was the private sector, while all other societal groups showed clear signs of division on the matter. Faced with such chaos, Demirel's coalition government fell victim to a military coup on September 12, 1980.

Following the coup, the military regime moved very quickly to regain state's autonomy and to establish sociopolitical order, which was a prerequisite for carrying out the austerity program. Once in power, the ruling junta, known as the National Security Council (NSC), announced its adherence to the stabilization program of January 1980 as the only way out of Turkey's economic crisis.[16]

First, the NSC replaced the 1961 Constitution with an authoritarian document that greatly restricted individual civil and political rights and gave the state expanded powers to maintain social and political order.[17] Changes in university affairs is perhaps one of the best examples of these state controls and restrictions. According to the Higher Education Act of 1981 the newly created Higher Education Council (YÖK in the Turkish acronym) has powers to regulate all public universities in the country. YÖK has powers to: (1) hire and dismiss faculty and university administrators, (2) regulate curricula and research on campuses, (3) regulate the budgets of all campuses, (4) establish dress codes for students and faculty, and (5) appoint presidents of the universities.[18]

Second, the NSC suspended and, a year later, dissolved the pre-1980 political parties in the hope that former political figures would not come back to haunt the new rulers in the future. The new political system was to have totally new political parties with politicians who did not fall into the five- to ten-year prohibition category of the former politicians.[19] The NSC decided to settle the problem of the political parties by allowing only the three new political parties (the Motherland Party, the Populist Party, and the Nationalist Democracy Party) to enter the national elections of November 1983. All the leaders of these parties had ties to the military regime of 1980-83. It should be noted, however, that today only one of these parties is in existence—the ruling Motherland Party. Thirteen of today's 15 political parties represented in the National Assembly officially came into existence following transition to civilian rule.

Third, in order to ensure the continuity of the new political order following transition to a civilian rule, head of the NSC, General Kenan Evren, became the President of Turkey through a rather questionable election. In a November 1982 referendum, both the Constitution and Evren's unchallenged candidacy for the presidency were offered to the public on a single unified ticket.

Finally, the new political order provided the state with tight bureaucratic control over the affairs of the private-interest associations. The revision of various laws governing trade unionism, university affairs, and professional interest associations were in accordance with the letter and spirit of the new authoritarian constitution.[20] The new Associations Law (1983) prohibited soldiers, teachers, bureaucrats, and high school students from forming interest associations. Furthermore, professional organizations of artisans, craftsmen, physicians, lawyers, engineers, industrialists, or merchants were also banned from direct involvement in politics and association with political parties. In this regard trade unions suffered the most. As Birol Yeşilada explains:

> the NSC allowed only TÜRK-IŞ of the four precoup trade union confederations (TÜRK-IŞ, DISK, HAK-IŞ, and MISK) to continue functioning. Thus, TÜRK-IŞ had to restrict its activities to job unionism rather than political unionism, in keeping with the new laws. Furthermore, the new law on Trade Unions, Collective Bargaining, Strikes and Lockouts (No. 2821 and 2822) defined unions as organizations concerned only with the economic interests of workers and prohibited any form of political activity. It provided the right to strike, but banned political strikes, general strikes, and solidarity strikes as well as the occupation of work places.[21]

In effect, all of these changes were designed to depoliticize interest groups, universities, and the state bureaucracy. The type of political system that emerged from all of this was a bureaucratic-authoritarian state that exhibited the basic elements of exclusionary state corporatism. These characteristics of the authoritarian state remained in effect despite transfer of power to civilians after the 1983 national elections.

Despite the fact that Turkey has free elections for the national assembly, the government, through the structures of the state, enjoys authoritarian powers over interest groups and citizens at large. However, this control was not as tight as seen under military rule. The characteristics of the new political system of Turkey meet the basic criteria of a heterogeneous form of interest representation.[22] This model is a cross between state corporatism and pluralism because despite the extensive controls over interest-group activities by the state, daily political life in Turkey, since transition to civilian rule, has gradually moved toward some degree of pluralism.

While numerous semiautonomous and politically-active organizations have emerged since 1983, the degree of pluralism is still far less than that found in the previous 1961-80 political order. In reality, Turgut Özal has had a free hand in determining the nature of the stabilization program—first as the chief economic advisor under the NSC regime and then as the prime minister and president of post-1983 Turkey. This period has been termed by Rodrik as the "Özal decade" in Turkey. During this period, the Özal governments had complete autonomy in economic policymaking. However, in terms of foreign policy and security policies all post-1983 civilian governments were constrained by the military and hence lacked the requisite autonomy.

Macroeconomic Outcomes

In macroeconomic terms, the adjustment program basically concentrated on two main targets: monetary and fiscal policies, and external economic relations. It followed three stages of implementation. During the first stage, from 1980-81, the aim was to restore some degree of acceptable economic stability, by adopting fiscal and monetary discipline; to eliminate most of the shortages of essential commodities; and to emphasize export-oriented growth. In the second stage, 1982-83, the government tried to consolidate the climate of economic stability and to maintain the relative price realignment.[23] Finally, stage three started with transition to civilian rule in November 1983 and, under the direct leadership of Turgut Özal, continued until the 1991 parliamentary elections. During this last phase, the government emphasized deeper liberalization of trade and monetary regimes by adopting the 1984 liberalization program. The 1991 elections deprived Özal's party of its parliamentary majority and brought about the return of Demirel as the head of a coalition government obliged to cooperate with Özal as president.

The macroeconomic figures for policy outcomes of the stabilization program are presented in Table 8.1. Each issue area will be discussed in detail later with special attention given to stabilization policies pertaining to them. However, before going into an in-depth discussion a brief survey of the macroeconomic figures might prove helpful.

In the first half of the 1980s, the GNP growth rate increased steadily to 6.2 percent. However, the steady growth of these years were replaced with fluctuation in the second half of the decade ending with a sharp reduction by 1989. The highest growth rate in GNP occurred in 1987 at 7 percent. Yet the following years show a constant decline with 6.5 percent in 1987, 4.2 percent in 1988, and 0.8 percent in 1989. This decline in economic growth was coupled with an increase in the inflation rate, which reached 69.9 percent in 1989. This is a disturbing development because the stabilization program originally brought down the inflation rate from 107 percent in 1980 to 27 percent in 1982. Following a brief rise between 1983 and 1985, inflation

Table 8.1: Macroeconomic Indicators, 1978-1989

Year	GNP growth rate (%) in 1968 factor prices	inflation rate	imports	exports	trade deficit	debt service ratio	external debt as % of GNP	current deficit as % of GNP
1978	0.9	52.6	4599.0	2288.2	-2310.8	25.1	11.4	-2.6
1979	-0.1	63.9	5069.4	2261.7	-2808.2	87.7	18.2	-2.4
1980	-0.9	107.2	7909.4	2910.1	-4999.3	47.4	23.5	5.8
1981	3.4	36.8	8933.4	4702.9	-4230.5	31.9	24.7	-3.2
1982	4.0	27.0	8842.7	5746.0	-3096.7	31.2	32.5	-1.7
1983	3.5	30.5	9235.0	5727.8	-3507.2	38.2	35.7	-3.7
1984	6.2	50.3	10756.9	7133.6	-3623.3	31.0	41.0	-2.8
1985	4.2	43.2	11343.4	7958.0	-3385.4	30.7	47.5	-1.9
1986	7.0	29.6	11104.8	7456.7	-3648.1	35.8	54.7	-2.6
1987	6.5	32.0	14157.8	10190.0	-3967.8	32.3	59.0	-1.4
1988	4.2	68.3	14335.4	11662.1	-2672.7	36.2	57.8	2.0
1989	0.8	69.9	15763.0	11627.0	-4136.0	32.5	51.0	0.9

Source: State Planning Organization, *1980'den 1990'a Makroekonomik Politikalar, Tüfrkiye Ekonomisindeki Gelişmelerin Analizi ve Bazi Değerlendirmeler* (Ankara: SPO, 1990).

again declined to about 30 percent by 1987. Thus, it can be concluded that the short-term successes of the stabilization program were replaced with troubling results by the end of the decade.

A similar trend is also observed for Turkey's trade deficit. Despite efforts by officials that dramatically increased the country's exports from $4.5 billion in 1978 to $15.7 billion in 1989, the trade deficit did not fall below $2.6 billion. In fact, year after year, Turkey ran serious trade deficits that tainted its export performance. To make matters worse, all this occurred despite a continuous attempt at maintaining realistic exchange rates vis-à-vis the US dollar.

Another disturbing result pertains to Turkey's external debt. While this topic will be discussed in detail in a later section it is worth noting that before the adoption of the stabilization program in 1980, Turkey's external debt was around $16 billion. Ten years later, and after repeated attempts at monetary austerity, Turkey's foreign debt had more than doubled—to $42.8 billion or slightly over 50 percent of its GNP.[24] Furthermore, debt service continues to consume more than one-third of Turkey's export earnings.

One macroeconomic indicator that shows significant improvement is the current account deficit. In 1980, the current account deficit amounted to 5.8 percent of GNP. After the initial shock therapy of the stabilization program this figure improved to 1.7 percent of GNP in 1982. From this time until 1988, the deficit figures fluctuated between 3.7 and 1.4 percent of GNP. Finally in 1988, current account deficit as percentage of GNP showed a positive result (2.0 percent).

Monetary and Fiscal Policies

Monetary and fiscal policies comprised the first phase of the adjustment program. The primary objective was to increase exports and reduce inflation by lowering the national rate of absorption (broadly defined—the use of goods for the purposes of consumption and investment by the private and public sectors). The first two policy adjustments included the control of the money supply and the utilization of positive real interest rates to augment bank deposits. Along with these measures, the government announced a drastic devaluation of the lira by 70 percent to promote export earnings and to attract workers' remittances.

Another important aspect of the adjustment program was the control of nominal income growth in order to bring down inflation. In accordance with the program, the government eliminated the Price Control Committee, agricultural support prices were permitted to increase moderately while the

FIGURE 8.1: Real Deposits and Lending Rates (annual real return %)

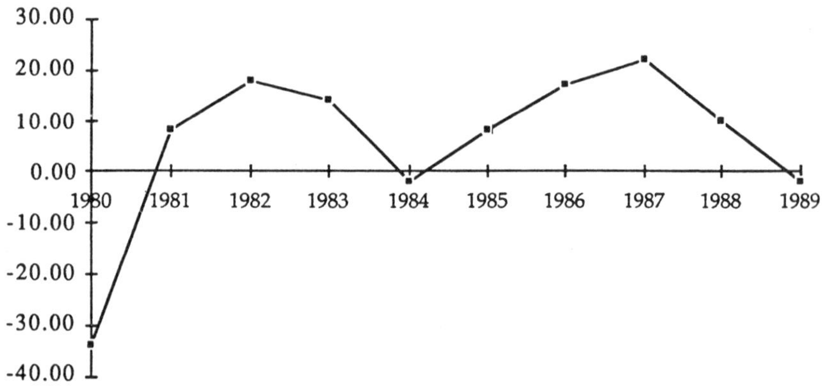

number of primary commodities covered by the program was reduced, and the export prices of agricultural commodities were determined in accordance with world-market prices. Prices of many cash crops are still fixed by the authorities and support payments are made in two installments, one in summer and another in fall. It is usually the case that these payments are late, so that large sums are paid over several months with serious consequences for the earnings of the producers. With regard to wages, the authoritarian government replaced collective bargaining with guidelines set by the Supreme Arbitration Board as the primary determinant of wage rates. The main goal behind this change was to keep real wages down in order to reduce domestic demand.[25]

In addition to these measures aimed at controlling inflation, subsidies for the SEEs were reduced and the prices of their products were allowed to increase sharply. Along with wage repression, reduced price supports for agriculture, and price increases for SEE products, Turkey's monetary restraint also emphasized increases in interest rates.

The government unpegged interest rates in July 1980. Following this decision, the banks raised their interest rates to a nominal level of 50 percent on time deposits and 60-65 percent on short- to medium-term loans. As a result, real interest rates became positive for the first time since the 1970s (see Figure 8.1). Similarly, Rodrik found that after taxes the effective earnings from deposits were somewhere around 40 percent.[26] Despite this development, concessionary loans were available for agriculture, small businessmen, and investors who obtained "investment-support certificates" from the State Planning Organization (SPO). Although these loans were in

FIGURE 8.2: Money-GNP Ratios, MB, M1, and M2 (% of GNP)

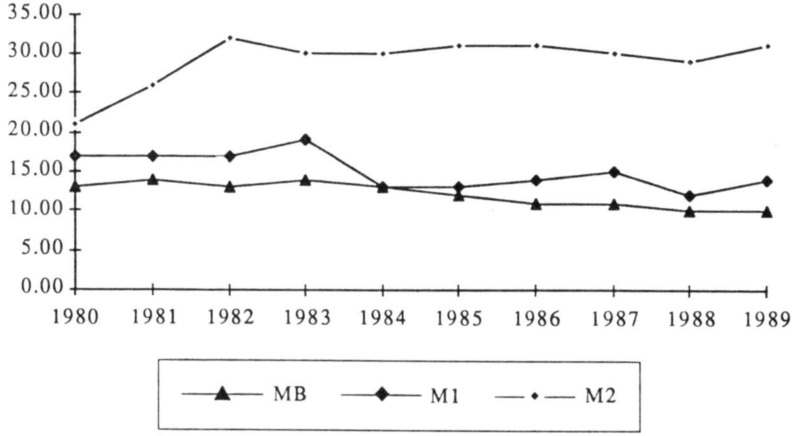

limited supply, demand increased significantly, adding to pressures for broad money as shown in Figure 8.2, with the M2/GNP ratio rising from 21 percent in 1980 to 30 percent in 1983. (The different money supply measures, M1, M2, and MB, refer to currency and demand deposits, currency and demand deposits (M1) plus time and savings deposits and commercial banks, and currency reserves at the Central Bank, respectively). It should be emphasized that although the rate of M2 growth was accelerating in 1981 it was the slowdown in the growth of M1 between 1980 and 1982 that was most directly associated with the fall in the inflation rate. The government resorted to rationing the funds for concessionary loans and directly contributed to the benefits of the influential borrowers. In contrast, firms without concessionary loans had to pay interest rates around 70-75 percent.

The situation considerably worsened by 1982 when liquidity problems of business firms reached critical dimensions. During this time, a new type of finance institution, the "brokers," entered the market. They collected large sums of money, mostly from small-scale savers, with offers of high interest rates on tradeable deposit certificates. Such deposits were transferred to illiquid firms by the brokers. During these days, it was not unusual to find depositors who actually sold their homes and trusted their entire savings to these brokers in the hope of making quick profits. This scheme collapsed during the summer of 1982, when many brokers, including the famous Banker Kastelli, became insolvent and many enterprises and banks faced liquidity shortages. Immediately the military government and the Central

Table 8.2: Money Supply (billions TL)

Year	M1	M2
1980	739.5	924.4
1981	1019.3	1709.7
1982	1407.0	2679.0
1983	2083.9	3477.0
1984	2447.6	5492.7
1985	3420.0	8539.7
1986	5357.4	12276.3
1987	8682.3	17702.0
1988	11311.5	27195.2
1989[a]	20358.3	49153.4

[a] estimates
Source: Central Bank of Turkey

Bank responded by extending official guarantees for the deposits of small savers and offered help to firms and banks in an attempt to prevent political unrest. At the same time, Turgut Özal, then the deputy prime minister in charge of economic affairs of the state, and Finance Minister Kaya Erdem were forced to resign.

The new finance minister, Adnan Kafaoğlu, was unable to solve the financial crisis. In the second half of 1982, the growth of money supply reached uncontrollable proportions. This shaky situation continued for almost a year when a new government, elected in November 1983, came to power under the leadership of Özal. Immediately, it requested that the existing IMF agreement be terminated so it could prepare a new one, with new monetary targets.

Nevertheless, the new monetary adjustment was again off the mark. Targets set by the IMF were observed only until mid-1984. Since then, money supply (see Table 8.2) increased more than expected, as indicated by M2 figures. There were three reasons for this development. First, foreign assets were inadequate, thus making it necessary in early 1985 to mobilize complementary domestic assets. Second, public spending by municipal and local administrations increased as they spent heavily for infrastructure, telecommunications, and energy. Finally, the SEEs continued to rely on the Central Bank for money supply. This situation had not changed since 1985, and one could argue that frequent elections (national in 1987 and local elections on three separate occasions) contributed to this problem as the ruling government party traded money for development projects for votes.

These trends in money supply prompted warnings from the IMF and World Bank in a series of reports. In September 1986, the World Bank warned Özal that he must reduce the budget deficit, increase exports, reform the banking sector, expand capital markets, freeze municipal and local administrations' spending, reduce government support for the SEEs, and finally bring inflation under control.[27] In order to assist the Özal government in carrying out the necessary policies, the World Bank provided $1.057 billion in credit during 1985. Despite the clarity of the World Bank warnings, the government continued to spend irresponsibly as it tried to appease voters during the local elections and the 1987 national elections. Finally, the World Bank issued an internal report that determined its policy strategy towards Turkey. In this report, the World Bank criticized the state of the Turkish economy and warned that unless crucial decisions were made economic crisis seemed inevitable. Specifically, the report argued that:

1. Tight monetary policy is necessary to prevent economic crisis.
2. Income distribution has worsened at alarming rate.
3. Real and nominal interest rates are abnormally high and the government's expansion of internal borrowing is dangerous.
4. One-third of bank credits are lost and another rescue operation by the Central Bank will result in higher inflation.
5. Public-sector investments are contributing to high inflation.
6. The profits of the SEEs are due to higher prices and not productivity.
7. State subsidies are the main reason behind increases in exports.[28]

The World Bank was worried about the worsening economic conditions in the country and favored a return to austerity by the Özal government. A similar worry was echoed by the IMF's Executive Committee. In an internal report the IMF listed almost the same observations as in the World Bank document and warned the Özal government of the negative economic consequences of its ongoing policies.[29] Based on these observations it can be concluded that the initial success of the stabilization program in monetary discipline quickly gave way to careless spending by the government and local administrations which, in turn, resulted in serious problems at the end of the 1980s.

Inflation, Real Wages, and Income Distribution

In a detailed analysis of inflation in post-1980 Turkey, Rodrik argues that the return of high inflation in the second half of the decade was due, in part, to financial liberalization of the Özal government.[30] As the data in Table 8.1 show, it seems that Turkey has returned to the dangerous levels of inflation that undermined its economic stability during the 1970s. An important issue that is not discussed widely in the works of scholars who analyze Turkey's economic development is the relationship between inflation and real wages. Fluctuations in real wages, with respect to inflation, is a crucial indicator of how the wage earners are faring in a country. Furthermore, this indicator gives some insight into the state of income distribution as well. As Rodrik explains, "income distribution is important in its own right, it also has implications for the likelihood of successful adjustment in the near future [because] fiscal retrenchment becomes more difficult when major popular sectors already feel that they have paid more then their due."[31] Table 8.3 provides the data in the index of real wages since 1980.

Figures in this table show that wage earners in Turkey did not fare well during the 1980s. With regard to public-sector workers, wages increased by five percentage points in 1981 and then declined dramatically to 61.0 in 1989. That is, at the end of the decade, these workers faced a 39 percent decline in their wages and benefits. The figures for the private-sector workers is better. These wages increased until 1982 and then declined to 87.5 by 1988. With the completion of a successful round of collective bargaining in 1988-89, the index figure for these workers' wages increased to 116.6. Hence, it can be concluded that workers in the private sector fared better than their counterparts in the public sector in the 1980s. The condition of the bureaucrats resemble those of the public-sector workers, with a slightly smaller decline in the index figures. Similar to the other figures for workers, the wages of the bureaucrats show a steady decline since Özal's Motherland Party came to power in 1983. By 1988, the bureaucrats had lost 27.1 percent of their wages in real terms. The improvement observed in 1989 was only 18.6 percent. The 1980 stabilization program stressed the need to reduce domestic demand. As the figures in Table 8.3 demonstrate, this reduction in domestic demand was achieved primarily by limiting wage increases to below the level of inflation which, in turn, restricted consumers' expenditures.

Additionally, a significant dimension of declining wages during the 1980s is revealed in the wage data from pre-1980 years. During 1963-1979, when Turkey subscribed to an economic development strategy based on import substitution, the real wages of workers in the public and private

Table 8.3: Index of Real Wages (1980 = 100)[a]

Year	Workers' wages and benefits: Public sector	Workers' wages and benefits: Private sector	Civil service salaries
1980	100.0	100.0	100.0
1981	105.2	107.6	107.2
1982	93.3	103.5	109.0
1983	90.0	95.0	106.8
1984	77.8	89.5	93.8
1985	65.2	83.3	88.7
1986	56.5	81.7	78.4
1987	57.3	92.0	79.7
1988	48.8	87.5	72.9
1989	61.0	116.6	86.5

[a] Based on weighted averages.

Source: Calculated from SPO and Social Security Administration wage data tables.

sectors and of bureaucrats had increased significantly. For example, wages of public-sector workers increased by 77 percent in real terms, or from 17.4 TL per day to 32.9 TL per day, between 1963 and 1976. By 1979, the average real wages of these workers declined 24.3 percent as a result of growing economic problems in the country. Yet, this figure was still almost 40 percent higher than the 1963 wage level. In the private sector a similar trend, though much smaller in scale, can be observed. Average daily wages of workers increased from 18.32 TL in 1963 to 24.5 TL in 1976 and declined to 18.32 TL in 1979. For the bureaucrats the average daily real wages increased from 29.9 TL in 1963 to 41.0 TL in 1977 and fell to 31.9 TL in 1979.[32] These increases in real wages were in accordance with the needs of the import-substituting industrialization model—basically the expansion of the domestic consumer market. Once economic growth strategies shifted from this model to export-oriented policies coupled with austerity, reduction in wages provided the vehicle for "belt tightening" among the consumers.

Another indicator of worsening income distribution in Turkey is the factor shares in national income (see Table 8.4). These are incomes derived from current production of goods and services. The figures display a worsening picture for income distribution in post-1980 Turkey. The net result has been a regression in income distribution from popular sectors (agriculture,

Table 8.4: Factor Shares in National Income (%)

Year	Agriculture	Wages and salaries	Rents, profits, and interest
1980	26.66	23.87	49.47
1981	24.57	23.06	52.36
1982	24.62	21.82	53.55
1983	24.78	20.52	54.69
1984	21.57	20.44	57.99
1985	18.84	19.08	62.08
1986	17.70	18.09	64.21
1987	15.60	16.30	69.10
1988	13.20	15.80	71.00

Source: Central Bank of Turkey

wages, and salaries) to profits, rents, and interest income. Factor shares as percent of national income for agriculture (farmers' income) declined from 26.7 in 1980 to 13.2 in 1988. During the same period, the share of wages and salaries fell from 23.9 to 15.8 percent. On the other hand, the share of rents, profits, and interest income increased from 49.5 percent in 1980 to 71 percent in 1988. These figures clearly show that a shift benefitting the bourgeoisie at the expense of the workers and farmers has occurred. This seems to be the legacy of the "Özal decade" in Turkey. As a result, we can expect opposition from the "losers" to possible future stabilization programs in the 1990s. Already suspicious of the government's intentions with the earlier stabilization programs, the popular sectors feel that they have paid much more than their share in the adjustment policies of the last decade—a fact endorsed by Rodrik's earlier observation on income distribution.

Foreign Debt Management

The growth of Turkey's foreign debt over the last two decades has followed an unusual trajectory. Because of its military and strategic assets, Turkey has become one of the largest recipients of foreign loans in the world. As shown in Table 8.1, the debt/GNP ratio increased significantly to surpass the 50 percent mark by the end of 1980s. During the same period, the debt-service ratio remained above 30 percent, thus putting pressure on export earnings. A detailed description of Turkey's external debt is provided in Table 8.5.

Table 8.5: Scale and Structure of Turkey's Debt,[a] 1978-1988 (US $ millions)

	1978	1979	1980	1981	1982	1983	1984	1985	1986	1987	1988[c]
Total outstanding (by maturity)	14,416	14,234	16,222	16,823	17,619	18,385	21,288	25,017	31,228	38,304	37,694
Medium-and long-term	7,230	10,638	13,722	14,667	15,455	15,346	16,702	18,395	24,317	29,612	29,990
Short-term	7,186	3,556	2,500	2,156	2,164	3,039	4,506	6,617	6,911	8,692	7,704
Medium- and long-term (by debtors)											
Public sector (incl. SEEs)	6,704	7,047	10,197	11,199	11,497	11,439	12,791	14,330	18,091	22,196	23,031
Central Bank	170	3,232	3,307	3,227	3,053	3,067	3,093	3,175	5,269	6,176	5,656
Private sector	356	359	218	241	905	840	898	890	957	1,240	1,303
Short-term											
Public sector (incl. SEEs)	10	40	640	504	73	194	215	230	597	491	242
Central Bank	1,894	1,104	828	695	1,031	2,190	2,509	3,543	2,329	3,651	3,146
Private sector	5,282	2,452	1,032	957	1,060	655	1,782	2,844	3,985	4,570	4,316
Medium- and long-term (by creditors)											
Multilateral institutions	2,175	2,445	3,242	3,857	4,531	4,916	5,434	6,103	6,588	7,780	7,750
IMF	622	630	1,054	1,322	1,455	1,572	1,426	1,326	1,085	770	299
IBRD, IDA, IFC	945	1,180	1,438	1,783	2,115	2,488	3,028	3,470	3,643	4,452	5,005
European Resettlement Fund	145	148	253	287	383	399	554	801	1,197	1,757	1,819
Islamic Development Bank	16	16	35	23	117	22	12	35	53	91	21
OPEC Fund	—	—	15	15	40	40	40	35	29	25	20
IFAD	—	—	—	—	—	2	4	7	8	9	11
Bilateral donors	4,212	4,370	6,026	6,712	7,115	6,566	7,305	8,013	10,187	12,316	11,066
OECD countries	3,871	3,976	5,253	5,901	6,146	5,613	6,168	6,776	8,270	10,324	9,714
OPEC countries	26	55	392	449	587	535	602	637	1,027	1,118	896
Other countries	315	339	381	362	382	418	535	600	890	874	456
Commercial banks	487	3,464	3,436	3,257	3,229	3,262	3,693	4,014	4,833	5,702	7,224
Private creditors	356	359	1,018	841	580	608	350	265	229	163	117
Short-term											
Islamic Development Bank	10	40	20	45	73	94	65	30	33	36	17
Bilateral donors	570	308	620	459	68	—	—	—	—	—	—
Commercial banks	1,302	575	608	407	146	392	941	1,465	2,624	3,663	2,903
Private creditors	5,304	2,673	1,252	1,245	1,877	2,553	3,500	5,122	4,254	4,993	4,783
Dresdner Bank	363	344	365	473	817	1,251	1,778	2,678	3,788	5,617	5,897
Total deposits of Turkish nationals	(3,223)[b]	(961)	(908)	(946)	(1,402)	(1,898)	(2,322)	(3,402)	(5,038)	(7,362)	(7,582)

Source: Central Bank of Turkey [a] Disbursed loans at year end. [b] Including CTLDs of foreign commercial banks. [c] Estimates.

As described in the earlier section "Background Conditions," Turkey faced serious balance-of-payments and debt-service problems by 1977. Turkish officials devalued the lira and applied to the IMF to revise the performance criteria on Turkey's foreign debt. However, there was a serious difference of opinion between the two sides. Turkish officials claimed that there were no structural problems in the economy—only temporary difficulties caused by imported energy costs. The IMF, on the other hand, insisted that the devaluation was inadequate and a larger devaluation was needed to improve Turkey's export performance. Finally in 1978, the IMF sponsored a limited rescheduling of Turkey's short-term debt. Yet, this effort proved insufficient. The share of short-term debt in Turkey's total debt continued to remain high. The debt service ratio increased from 8 percent in 1974 to 30 percent in 1977 and 87 percent in 1979. It became clear that the IMF, OECD, and commercial banks had underestimated the magnitude of Turkey's debt problem. Therefore, the IMF sponsored a series of debt reschedulings for Turkey, in the amount of $8.2 billion, that covered the period between June 1979 and March 1982. If the 1978 figures are also included then the grand total of short-term debt scheduling in this period becomes $9.8 billion.[33]

The stabilization program and the military takeover in September 1980 created an optimistic environment for the creditors because these developments indicated return to stability and order. Also, Turkey's exports increased significantly, as shown by data in Table 8.1. The IMF and World Bank provided a medium-term adjustment program with multinational stand-by arrangements and structural adjustment loans (SALs). The purpose of the SALs was to support programs of policy and institutional changes that were necessary to modify the structure of the economy so that it could maintain both its growth rate and the viability of its balance-of-payments in the medium-term. This financing program, the medium-term rescheduling arrangements with commercial banks, and the additional loans provided Turkey with a breathing space in the early 1980s.

Nevertheless, despite these efforts, the external debt continued to increase due to persistent current-account deficits. The high level of the debt-service ratio further aggravated the problem. As officials looked for external sources of finance, the level of foreign debt as percentage of the GNP increased from 23.5 in 1980 to 51 percent in 1989. In monetary value this translates to an increase from $16.2 billion in 1980 to $37.7 billion in 1988, and to $41 billion in 1989.[34] One striking feature of this jump in foreign debt is short-term borrowing. This type of debt, which was reduced from about $9.8 billion in 1978 to $2.1 billion in 1981, again increased to $8.7 billion in 1987. The trend is alarming because it implies that long-term debt is retired by transferring it to short-term debt. Furthermore, almost all of Turkey's short-term debt is from private sources—commercial banks and private creditors.

An important development with regard to Turkey's short-term debt is the growing importance of the Dresdner Bank accounts. According to Rodrik, the Dresdner Bank serves as the intermediary between the Turkish guest workers and the Central Bank of Turkey. Deposits made in Germany are transferred to Turkey.[35] This scheme was developed to facilitate the flow of the Turkish workers' savings from Europe to Turkey. In recent years, these transfers increased significantly to reach $5.9 billion ($2.1 billion in short-term deposits) in 1988. When this scheme proved successful, the government also decided to allow Turkish citizens and foreigners residing in Turkey to hold foreign-exchange accounts in Turkish banks. Earlier, foreigners were permitted to have foreign exchange accounts but interest rates on these deposits were much lower than in the case of the Dresdner scheme. By offering interest rates as high as 4-7 percentage points above LIBOR, the government was able to attract large deposits into these accounts. Total deposits in these accounts increased from $1.9 billion in 1983 to $7.6 billion in 1988. Despite the appeal of these accounts for the officials, such schemes have a serious danger for the economy. Even a modest run on these accounts could prove disastrous for Turkey's foreign debt problem.

Liberalization of Trade and Investment

Following the liberalization of trade and investment regimes, export earnings of Turkey and foreign investments improved significantly. With regard to exports, figures in Table 8.1 show an improvement from $2.9 billion in 1980 to $11.6 billion in 1989. The share of industrial exports in these figures were $1 billion and $9.1 billion respectively. In other terms, the share of industry in Turkey's exports jumped from 36 to 73.8 percent of total in this period. Table 8.6 provides data on these developments.

Export-oriented growth strategies also increased Turkey's exposure to international trade as a percentage of GNP. Total trade as a percentage of GNP increased from 18.6 percent in 1980 to 35.4 percent in 1989. However, these improvements did not result in the reduction of imports. The share of imports in GNP increased from 13.6 percent in 1980 to about 20 percent in 1989. At the same time, the share of export earnings in GNP jumped from 5 percent to 14.4 percent respectively. Yet these improvements failed to reduce Turkey's trade deficit, as shown in Figure 8.3.

Table 8.6: Trade Statistics, 1980-1989 (%)

Year	Exports/ Imports	Exports/ GNP	Imports/ GNP	Total trade/ GNP	Industry exports/ total exports
1982	65.0	10.6	16.3	26.9	59.7
1983	62.0	11.1	17.9	29.0	63.9
1984	66.3	14.2	21.4	35.5	72.1
1985	70.2	14.8	21.1	36.5	75.3
1986	67.1	12.7	18.9	31.8	71.4
1987	72.0	14.9	20.1	35.9	79.1
1988	81.4	16.5	20.2	36.9	76.7
1989	73.8	14.4	19.6	35.4	78.2

Source: SPO, *1980'den 1990'a*, Table 32.

The stabilization program of the 1980s clearly succeeded in increasing export earnings significantly. What were the crucial determinants of this improvement in exports? Rodrik identifies five causes for this improvement: (1) the Iran-Iraq War provided important markets for Turkish products; (2) the government's active exchange-rate policy; (3) the relatively restrained monetary and fiscal policies of the early 1980s reoriented businesses toward foreign markets; (4) the liberalization of trade might have caused a general-equilibrium effect of promoting exports; and (5) the overinvoicing of exports by Turkish exporters who received subsidized credits tax rebates from the government for their activities.[36]

With regard to Turkey's exports to the Middle East, the Iran-Iraq War is of crucial importance. During the war, Turkey's exports to Iran averaged around $1.1 billion, and exports to Iraq averaged $1.2 billion.[37] In total, during the first half of the 1980s, trade with these two countries accounted for almost 40 percent of Turkey's total trade. However, during the latter part of the decade, Turkey's trade with the OECD countries and, since most of these are members of the European Community (EC), with EC members improved significantly, rising from $4.1 billion in 1984 to $7.2 billion in 1989.

There has been a great deal of discussion in the Turkish press regarding the overinvoicing of exports (*hayali ihracat*), or the exaggeration of export claims with fictional earnings. To what extent is the apparent success of

FIGURE 8.3: Ratio of Imports and Exports to the GNP, 1979-1989 (%)

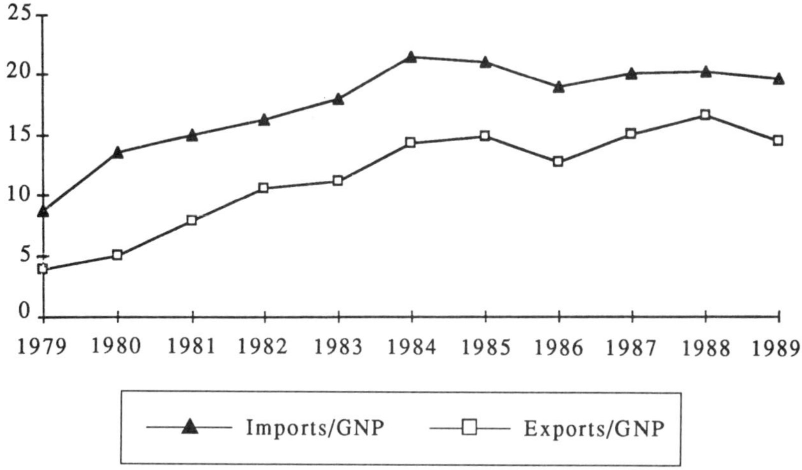

Turkey's export performance, as indicated by significant improvements in export earnings, a product of overinvoicing? Rodrik's analysis of these fictional exports shows that the extent of overinvoicing was around 16 percent during 1981-85 compared to 0 percent in the previous five-year period.[38] However, the latest figures reported by Rodrik indicates that this practice might be on the rise.

A close examination of Turkey's comparative export performance (CEP) in comparison to other countries exporting to the European Community reveals a rather mixed picture for the period from 1980 to 1988. The analysis, which focuses on the EC markets since they represent the most important outlets for Turkey's exports,[39] indicates that Turkey's competitiveness in agricultural products has declined since 1980. However, among industrial products, Turkey displays increasing CEP in textiles and leather. In other areas performance is not very successful. The findings, therefore, suggest that textiles are the main reason for Turkey's overall improvement in its competitive posture. The declining competitiveness of Turkey's agricultural exports in EC markets was compensated by the start of the Iran-Iraq War, which provided these commodities with additional markets and thus contributed to the overall expansion of export earnings during most of the 1980s.

Another key feature of the economic stabilization program was foreign investment. The National Security Council liberalized the investment regime in 1980 and the Özal government liberalized it further in February 1986. The new policy gave foreign capital the same rights and obligations as domestic capital, with guarantees of transferring back profits, fees, and royalties. It also recognized the Foreign Investment Directorate as the single authority in Turkey that would guide, receive, review, and negotiate all foreign-investment applications. Furthermore, during the 1980s, the growing number of agreements for bilateral reciprocal protection, promotion of investment, and avoidance of double taxation provided increased confidence in the stability of the investment environment in Turkey.[40] The results of these efforts have been rather dramatic. Whereas the cumulative foreign capital inflow into Turkey during 1954-80 amounted to $228 million, the corresponding figure for the 1980-89 period is $4.4 billion. The number of foreign firms involved in these transactions also increased from 100 in 1980 to 1,484 in 1989.[41] Thus, it appears that policies aimed at economic integration with global capitalism have been relatively successful in terms of attracting foreign capital to Turkey. Through liberalization of trade and investment regimes in this context, a previously unfamiliar type of foreign investment also entered the country—Saudi Arabian and other "Islamic" finance houses, which brought with them an alternative form of "banking." The impact of these types of finance institutions on the Turkish economy and politics has a been a topic of great controversy.[42]

The flow of foreign investment also benefitted from the establishment of "free-trade zones" in Mersin, Antalya, Adana/Yumurtalik, and Izmir/Nemut in 1985. The last site was rezoned in 1987 as the Izmir/Gaziemir free zone. According to statistics obtained from the SPO, there are 567 firms operating in these areas with a total investment of $299.3 million. Some 18,556 workers are employed by these firms and their value-added operations is $943.6 million.[43]

CONCLUSIONS

To what extent can the Turkish stabilization experience serve as a model for adjustment programs in other countries? There is no clear and simple answer to this question. Turkey's internal political and economic situation and its geopolitical importance for Western security interests set it apart from most other developing countries. During the period between 1978 and 1983, Turkey benefitted from its strategic position as its Western allies rushed to bail her out of her economic predicament. In general, the overall outcome of the stabilization program of the 1980s is mixed. On the positive side, Turkey reoriented its economic-growth model from import substitution to an export-led strategy. As a result of more realistic exchange rates and the government's export-promotion policies, export earnings increased significantly and, by the end of the decade, the current account balance finally emerged out of its perennial deficit. Within trade figures the share of industrial products increased from 36 percent to 78 percent of total exports. Also, the share of total trade in GNP doubled between 1980 and 1989. Finally, liberalization of the investment regime attracted a sizable stock of foreign investment into the Turkish economy.

As to the negative results of the stabilization program the following important observations can be made: (1) The export-oriented model failed to eliminate trade deficits. Turkey continues to run an annual trade deficit of about $2.6-4 billion per year; (2) The money supply (M2) has shown a steady increase since 1980; (3) The high inflation rate has almost returned to its previous levels; (4) Real wages of workers and bureaucrats have declined significantly; (5) The income-distribution pattern worsened as relative factor shares in national income shifted away from popular sectors to profits, interest, and rents income; and (6) Özal's government's reliance on excessive borrowing from abroad resulted in a very large external debt whose servicing needs consumes more than one-third of the country's annual export earnings. These results raise some crucial concerns about the success of economic stabilization in Turkey. Our analysis suggests that neoorthodoxy in Turkey has brought about a significant redistribution of national income and wealth in favor of the rich at the expense of the poor (laborers, peasants, most of the bureaucrats, and countless others who do not appear on national labor figures).

Finally, it is especially important to keep these economic outcomes in a broader policy perspective. One significant result of the stabilization program is the rise of an authoritarian-bureaucratic state in Turkey. In an attempt to restore peace and order to the country, the military authorities of the September 1980 coup completely revised the constitutional and legal order of the state. The outcome of their efforts can be seen in the restrictions placed on individual civil and political rights, and on other measures of democracy. This raises the important question of whether such an authoritarian state is a prerequisite for the implementation of the stabilization program in developing countries like Turkey.

NOTES

1. Merih Celasun and Dani Rodrik, "Turkish Experience with Debt: Macroeconomic Policy and Performance," in *Developing Country Debt and the World Economy,* ed. Jeffrey D. Sachs (Chicago: University of Chicago Press, 1989), 193.
2. For detailed analysis of these crises see Cüneyt Arcayürek, *Demokrasinin Sonbahari: 1971-1978* (Istanbul: Bilgi Yayinevi, 1985) and *Müdahalenin Ayaksesleri* (Istanbul: Bilgi Yayinevi, 1985); Frank Tachau, *Turkey: Authority, Democracy, and Development* (New York: Praeger, 1984); C. H. Dodd, *The Crisis of Turkish Democracy* (North Humberside: Eothen Press, 1983); Türk Silahli Kuvvetleri, Genel Kurmay Başkanliği, *Türkiye'deki Anarşi ve Terörün Gelimeşi, Sonuçlari, ve Güvenlik Kuvvetlerince Önlenmesi* (Ankara: Genel Kurmay, 1982); and Birol A. Yeşilada, "Problems of Political Development in the Third Turkish Republic," *Polity,* vol. 21, no. 2 (Winter 1988), 345-72.
3. Miles Kahler, "Orthodoxy and Its Alternatives: Explaining Approaches to Stabilization and Adjustment," in *Economic Crisis and Policy Choice: The Politics of Adjustment in the Third World,* ed. Joan M. Nelson (Princeton: Princeton University Press, 1990), 33.
4. For a detailed discussion see Joan M. Nelson, ed., *Economic Crisis and Policy Choice.*
5. For example see Joan M. Nelson, ed., *Economic Crisis and Policy Choice; Guillermo O'Donnell, Modernization and Bureaucratic Authoritarianism* (Berkeley: University of California Press, 1979); David Collier, ed., *The New Authoritarianism in Latin America* (Princeton: Princeton University Press, 1979); and Henri J. Barkey, *The State and the Industrialization Crisis in Turkey* (Boulder, CO: Westview Press, 1990).
6. Yeşilada, "Problems of Political Development," 345-50. In 1971 the military did not close parliament, but exercised power behind the scenes through civilian governments it appointed.
7. State Statistics Institute, *Foreign Trade Statistics, 1983* (Ankara: SSI Publications, 1984).
8. TOBB, *Planli Dönemde Rakamlarla Türkiye Ekonomisi* (Ankara: TOBB, 1990), Tables 8 and 75; and World Bank, *World Tables* (Baltimore: Johns Hopkins University Press, 1985).
9. For detailed discussion of these issues see Henri J. Barkey, *The State and the Industrialization Crisis in Turkey,* and Birol A. Yeşilada, *Breakdown of Democracy in Turkey,* unpublished Ph.D. dissertation, University of Michigan, 1984, chapters 2-3.
10. Dani Rodrik, "Premature Liberalization, Incomplete Stabilization: The Özal Decade in Turkey," paper presented at the conference "Lessons of Economic Stabilization and Its Aftermath," Jerusalem, January 31-February 1, 1990, 3.

11. OECD, *Economic Surveys: Turkey* (Paris: OECD Publications, 1980), 25. It should be noted that a complete text of the new policy package is described in detail in the annex of this publication.
12. Joan M. Nelson, "Conclusions," *Economic Crisis and Policy Choice,* 321-61.
13. Birol A. Yeşilada, *Breakdown of Democracy in Turkey.*
14. Henri J. Barkey, *The State and the Industrialization Crisis in Turkey,* 173.
15. It is crucial to note that by September 1980, the country faced conditions resembling civil war. Between 1975 and 1980, deaths from political violence grew steadily: 35 in 1975, 90 in 1976, 260 in 1977, 800-1,000 in 1978, 1,500 in 1979, and about 3,500 during the first eight and a half months of 1980. For details of political problems and anarchy see Birol A. Yeşilada, "Problems of Political Development," 351. For a detailed discussion of loss of state autonomy see Henri J. Barkey, *The State and the Industrialization Crisis in Turkey,* especially chapters 6 and 7.
16. For a detailed discussion see Yeşilada, "Problems of Political Development," 351-52.
17. Republic of Turkey, *The Constitution of the Republic of Turkey* (Ankara, 1982), Articles 13, 33, 34, and 52.
18. Yeşilada, "Problems of Political Development," 353.
19. Yeşilada, "Problems of Political Development," 352. In all, 723 persons were barred from politics.
20. Yeşilada, "Problems of Political Development," 352.
21. Yeşilada, "Problems of Political Development," 353-54.
22. Yeşilada, "Problems of Political Development," 351-65, and Robert Bianchi, "Interest Group Politics in the Third World," *Third World Quarterly,* vol. 8, no. 2 (April 1986), 508-12.
23. Celasun and Rodrik, "Turkish Experience with Debt," 203.
24. *Cumhuriyet* (Turkish daily), September 22, 1990.
25. OECD, *Economic Surveys, 1983-1984: Turkey* (Paris: OECD Publications, 1984), 11-13.
26. Rodrik, "Premature Liberalization," 7.
27. *Hürriyet* (Turkish daily), September 22, 1986, from an interview with the World Bank's vice-president, Willy Hans Wapenhaus, by Tuna Köprülü.
28. *Cumhuriyet,* March 24, 1988.
29. *Cumhuriyet,* March 24, 1988.
30. Rodrik, "Premature Liberalization," 10-20.
31. Rodrik, "Premature Liberalization," 24.
32. These figures are estimated from the statistics obtained from the State Planning Organization, Social Security Association, and the Yüksek Denetleme Kurulu. For a detailed discussion of this topic see Birol A. Yeşilada, *Breakdown of Democracy in Turkey.*
33. World Bank, *Turkey: Country Economic Memorandum-Recent Economic Development and Medium-Term Prospects,* vol. 2, June 3, 1983, Table A 2.7 as cited in Rodrik, "Premature Liberalization," 30-31.

34. Figures for 1989 are from *Cumhuriyet,* September 22, 1990. Other figures can be found in Table 8.5.
35. Dani Rodrik, "External Debt and Economic Performance in Turkey," in *Liberalization and the Turkish Economy,* ed. Tevfik F. Nas and Mehmet Odekon (New York: Greenwood Press, 1988), 173.
36. Rodrik, "External Debt," 176.
37. SPO, *1980'den 1990'a Makroekonomik Politikalar, Türkiye Ekonomisindeki Gelişmelerin Analizi ve Bazi Değerlendirmeler* (Ankara: SPO, 1990), Table 39. See also Henri J. Barkey, "The Silent Victor: Turkey's Role in the Iran-Iraq War," in *The Iran-Iraq War: Impact and Implications,* ed. Efraim Karsh (London: Macmillan, 1989).
38. Rodrik, "External Debt," 177 and "Türkiye'nin Ihracat Patlamasinin Ne Kadari Hayali," *Bilim ve Sanat,* no. 42 (Summer 1988), 133-36.
39. CEP estimates for the product categories (Nimexe two-digit) are based on the following method:

    $$CEP = [\ (X_i / X) / (X_iw / X^w)\ ]$$

    where: *X* refers to exports; *i* denotes an economic sector at the two-digit Nimexe categories; and *w* refers to the world. For a detailed discussion of this method see Birol A. Yeşilada, "Impact of the European Community's Second Enlargement and Project 1992 on Relations with the Mediterranean Basin," paper presented at the 1990 Annual Midwest Political Science Association Conference, Chicago, April 5-7, 1990.
40. Birol A. Yeşilada, "Turkey's Foreign Policy Towards the Middle East," in *Socioeconomic and Political Transformation of Turkey During the 1980s,* ed. Atila Eralp, Muharrem Tunay, and Birol A. Yeşilada (New York: Praeger, forthcoming).
41. SPO, *1980'den 1990'a,* Table 41.
42. See Clement Henry Moore, "Islamic Banks and Competitive Politics in the Arab World and Turkey," *Middle East Journal* 44, no. 2 (Spring 1990), 234-55; Uğur Mumcu, *Rabita* (Istanbul: Tekin Yayinevi, 1987); and Birol A. Yeşilada, "Islam, Dollars, and Politics: The Political Economy of Saudi Capital in Turkey," paper presented at the 23rd Annual Meeting of the Middle East Studies Association in Toronto, Canada, November 15-18, 1989.
43. SPO, *1980'den 1990'a,* 49-50.

Part IV

Conclusion

9

What's So Good About Stability?

Patrick Clawson

The 1980s were a difficult decade for the non-oil-producing nations of the Middle East. Faced with deteriorating economic performance and encouraged (or pressured) by international institutions and Western governments, many Middle Eastern nations launched programs to restore macroeconomic stability: to curtail inflation, to contain budget deficits, and to cut foreign borrowing. The aim of this essay is to evaluate whether these policies have been worth the effort invested in them, both by the region's governments and by the foreign aid community: By what criteria should the stabilization efforts be judged? Has stabilization set the stage for future growth? Has stabilization impeded progress towards democracy? Has outside pressure for reform made much difference? Has foreign aid helped promote reforms? Before turning to these questions, however, the essay reviews the stylized facts about Middle Eastern economic performance, especially to ask what proportion of Middle Eastern economic problems have been due to an unfavorable international economic environment rather than to the actions of the Middle Eastern states.

THE STYLIZED FACTS

The experience of each country is unique and the product of many local circumstances. Nevertheless, it can be useful to look for some broad trends—what economists like to call stylized facts—among the individual histories.

This section puts forward the thesis that there was a general deterioration in economic performance in the Middle East in the 1980s. It goes on to weigh the influence of several regionwide factors, specifically, the military burden, the Third World debt crisis, the general international economic environment, and the end of the oil boom.

Poorer Economic Performance in the Middle East

The basic picture that emerges from the World Bank data base is that the Middle Eastern nations had solid economic growth in the 1970s but serious problems in the 1980s. The attached graphs and the tables present data from the World Bank for the seven countries under consideration: Algeria, Egypt, Israel, Jordan, Syria, Tunisia, and Turkey.

The most basic indicator of well-being is per capita GNP. Figure 9.1 shows per capita GNP in 1989 US dollars for six nations (data for Jordan is missing); note that, in order to fit on the graph, Israel's per capita GNP is shown as only one third its actual level. Per capita GNP rose nicely in the 1970s in five nations, while Egypt had only slight growth in production. In the 1980s, per capita income fell in five nations; the exception was Israel, which continued to grow.[1] In Egypt, Syria, and Turkey, the per capita income in 1989 was little if anything above the 1970 level, while in Algeria and Tunisia the problems of the 1980s did not erase all of the gains made in the 1970s.

Not only did per capita production drop off in the 1980s, but so did the income from remittances.[2] The most dramatic effect of this drop among the countries considered here was in Egypt. Adding workers' remittances to GNP, the national income per capita went from $687 in 1970 to $826 in 1980 and then fell to $713 in 1989.[3] While Egypt's GNP per capita was quite flat from 1970 to 1989, Egypt fits the same pattern as Algeria, Syria, Tunisia, and Turkey: a rise from 1970 through 1980 followed by a drop from 1980 to 1989. The crisis of the 1980s hit hardest at the availability of foreign goods (Figure 9.2). Per capita imports of goods and services (in 1989 US $) fell in six of the seven nations during the 1980s (Turkey being the exception). Per capita imports plummeted 57 percent in Algeria and 68 percent in Syria. Israel, despite its growing income, curtailed its consumption of foreign goods, with per capita imports dropping 11 percent. The lower availability of foreign goods in the 1980s is only in comparison to the import boom of the 1970s. If the comparison is made between 1970 and 1989, then each country had a solid growth in per capita imports: the oddball number is that for 1980, a time when imports had gone through the roof. In other words, the 1970s were years when the economies became accustomed to importing at a level that the country could not keep up, and the 1980s were a return to more sustainable levels.

Not surprisingly, the adjustment to lower imports was not a smooth process. In most countries, the high import bill had been sustained by incurring large amounts of debt. The foreign debt per capita rose sharply in the 1970s in each of the six countries for which there are data. The debt levels became unsustainable, and governments were generally unable—usually due to the unwillingness of the world community to provide more finance—to increase their per capita debt in the 1980s. This pattern had more variation than the other trends discussed here: Algerian debt fell sharply, while Turkish debt grew some and Jordanian debt soared. But the overall pattern was to lessen the use of debt, and what debt was incurred (as in Jordan's case) was politically motivated rather than commercially inspired.

As income fell and less debt was available to supplement that income, most countries responded by cutting into their savings. National savings fell as a percent of GNP in four of the six countries for which there are data.[4] With lower savings, nations had fewer resources to finance investment, and the result—not very surprising—was lower income. The two countries that were able to sustain their national savings during the 1980s—Israel and Turkey—were the two countries that were able to increase their per capita income and per capita imports, respectively.

Military Expenditures — How Much of a Burden?

It is tempting to conclude that if the Middle East nations had not had such heavy military burdens, their growth would have been higher. Unfortunately, there is little reason to believe that this is the case. The simple fact is that much of the military spending was financed by foreigners who would not have provided the same level of aid had it not been for the military spending. For instance, there is good evidence that the Syrian military buildup after the 1977 Camp David accords was financed entirely by foreign aid; the effect of the military spending was to boost the local economy by providing more employment, by training Syrians in skills useful in the civilian economy, and by increasing demand for goods and services.[5]

It would be nice to think that successful resolution of the Arab-Israeli conflict would bring an important peace dividend to the region, but there is little reason to expect such a happy outcome. Not only is the area rife with other conflicts that may motivate governments to maintain large military machines, but in addition the reduction in military spending is likely to be paralleled by a falloff in foreign aid. It is all too optimistic to calculate the Middle East military spending and then to proclaim that these resources could be devoted to other purposes, because aid donors may be providing high aid precisely to allow their allies to sustain their military position.[6] It is depressing to realize that Middle Eastern nations imported $165 billion of armaments from 1977 through 1987, including $56 billion from the USSR, $34 billion from the United States, and $41 billion from Western Europe.[7] Surely Plato's philosopher-kings could have found a better use for much of that money. But that is not a relevant consideration for two fundamental reasons: first, it is not clear how much of those resources would have been available to Middle East countries had they not been spent on arms (that is, some of the weapons imports were financed by aid tied to weapons); and second, it is not clear that additional money would have been spent in a way that promoted growth instead of financing artificial consumption. Furthermore, there is a vigorous debate in the economic literature about whether military spending hurts economic growth; it is certainly striking that some of the most rapidly growing nations (such as South Korea and Taiwan) maintain large military forces.[8] After all, the military may take youths who would otherwise being do little and provides them with good work habits and with training in use and maintenance of advanced equipment.

Debt

The argument could be made that the Middle East's worse economic performance in the 1980s was the product of a cutoff in capital flows to the region, after the Third World debt crisis broke in 1982. The concept would be that with sufficient capital, the Middle East could have continued to grow, but the capital flows fell because of the world debt crisis. That thesis is implausible, however, because the evidence shows that Middle Eastern nations used capital poorly: they were not able to grow enough, using the borrowed funds, to repay the loans. The best measure of how well a country uses its resources is how much capital is required to produce each additional unit of output—what economists call the ICOR (incremental capital output ratio). Middle East ICORs have averaged around 5.0 in the 1980s, which means that each additional unit of output requires twice as much investment as in the newly industrialized nations, which require only 2.5 units of new capital.

Algeria is almost a prototype of a country that incurred heavy debt primarily to fund investment of low efficiency. Karen Pfeiffer in this volume demonstrates how the borrowing was associated with a large investment program and with the imported materials necessary to make the new industries function. The result was that the borrowed funds were used up without increasing productive capacity sufficiently to service the debts. Algeria faced a particularly acute problem because its per capita foreign debt burden (in 1989 US $) rose 650 percent between 1970 and 1980—see Figure 9.4. Furthermore, Algeria's debt problem was compounded by its insistence on servicing its debt on the original terms, rather than rescheduling. The more customary course in the 1980s would have been not to repay the debt, or, more euphemistically, to reschedule repeatedly with each round being on more favorable terms than the last while emphasizing (with little reason for the statement) that the debt will eventually be serviced in full. With the benefit of hindsight, it is hard to see any advantages in the pay-in-full strategy Algeria adopted compared to the Latin American promise-to-repay-someday approach.

While we are discussing the efficiency with which capital is used in the Middle East, it is necessary to point out that the 1980s have seen a spectacular increase in the amount of capital needed to produce an extra unit of output. Of the five countries for which the World Bank provides data, the amount of capital needed rose in four (Turkey being the exception), and in each case the rise was not small. In theory, adjustment programs should remove the barriers to using capital efficiently and should concentrate investments on those areas with the most promise. In practice, stabilization seems to imply vastly more capital is needed to increase output. Perhaps the new investments are in fact productive, and the figure for the economywide ratio of capital to output is distorted by the shutdown of inefficient factories, which reduces output (making the denominator smaller and therefore raising the ratio). Perhaps.

Worse International Environment

The debt crisis was one manifestation of a more general problem in the 1980s, namely, the decline in world economic performance. The industrial nations experienced a profound recession early in the decade and ended the decade on a weak note, with the result that growth over the period (despite the strong burst in mid-decade) was mediocre. The high-income OECD nations saw their per capita GNP (in 1989 US $) rise 64 percent during the 1970s but only 24 percent from 1980 through 1989.[9]

The poorer economic performance of the advanced industrial nations affected the developing countries in manifold ways, only one of which was the debt crisis. More important was the slower growth in world trade, combined with the increasing restrictions on exports from developing

Table 9.1: Incremental Capital/Output Ratios

	1973-1980	1980-1987
Algeria	5.8	15.2
Egypt[a]	3.2	5.6
Jordan	3.0	5.6
Tunisia	5.1	10.2
Turkey	7.3	4.8

[a] Egypt: 1974-1981 and 1982-1987.
Source: World Bank, Trends 1990.

nations. Because of this more difficult international environment, per capita incomes fell throughout the Third World in the 1980s, despite the adoption of sounder economic policy in country after country. The drop in income was sharpest in Latin America and Africa, as Figure 9.3 shows. Even East Asia saw a drop in per capita income, as the growth in the newly industrialized countries was swamped by the problems in the People's Republic of China and Indonesia. In this context, the performance of the Middle East nations was normal: not as good as East or South Asia, not as bad as Latin America or Sub-Saharan Africa.

Any conclusion about the effect of the international environment on the Mideast has to remain tentative until the exact transmission mechanisms are identified. It seems appropriate, nevertheless, to advance as a distinct possibility that the major reason for the problems of the Middle East was that the world environment turned negative. In other words, the world climate was a major factor in the problems in each individual country, however much inappropriate policies may have contributed. In a better world climate, the effects of those bad policies would have been less pernicious, because the rising tide would have lifted the boat despite a few leaks.

The End of the Oil Boom

The most obvious and most correct explanation for the economic problems that beset the Middle East in the 1980s was the end of the oil boom. Every state in the region other than Israel was profoundly affected by the increase in exports from the big four—Kuwait, Libya, Saudi Arabia, and the United Arab Emirates—from $22 billion in 1970 to $224 billion in 1980, followed by the decline to $78 billion in 1989 (in 1989 US $).[10] Export receipts from the big four went to other Middle East nations through various channels: labor migration, aid, purchase of goods and services, investment, et cetera. While the combined direct and indirect receipts of the other nations of the Middle East from the big four were only a small portion of their export earnings, the sums involved were immense relative to the region's economies.

The situation of Algeria, Israel, and Turkey are somewhat different from that of the other four nations under consideration: Algeria because it is itself a producer of oil and gas, Israel because it was almost entirely isolated from the oil boom, and Turkey because the effects of the oil boom were nearly canceled by the negative impact of the higher oil import bill.

The four other states under consideration were, however, buffeted by the winds of the oil market and should have set their sails accordingly. Of course, they were bystanders to the developments in the oil market; they could not have affected the outcome no matter what they did. The issue for these states is to what extent they had cushioned themselves against fluctuations in oil income. The answer is depressingly simple: when income was high, governments assumed that income would not only stay high but continue to grow at something close to the phenomenal rates of the preceding years. The result was that no cushion was built up to soften the blow. The obvious advice would have been to at least accumulate foreign-exchange reserves.

In their defense, the four governments could claim that their policy was to develop the national economies with the aim of reducing the importance of the oil-related income. Such a claim would ring hollow indeed. Consider the case of Egypt. The oil boom of the 1970s transformed Egypt into a labor-exporting society, with the extra income (in foreign exchange, no less) going to the masses, given that many of the migrants came from villages. Unfortunately, that income growth was frittered away by government policies that encouraged consumption, for example, by holding energy prices so low that it was artificially attractive to buy a car or use electrical appliances. The opportunity offered by the remittances was wasted when little was done to attract the funds into entrepreneurial investment; indeed, the government adopted a whole set of policies to protect the vested interests of government-owned firms.

RESPONSES TO THE IMBALANCES

In response to the imbalances that arose in the economy, the government in each of the countries under consideration had to implement far-reaching

Figure 9.1: Per Capita GNP (1989 US $)

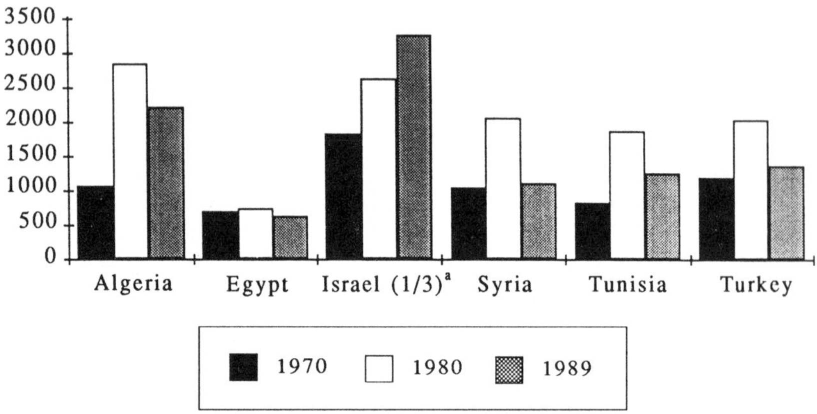

[a] Note that the figures for Israel were divided by 3 for purposes of this figure

Figure 9.2: Imports Per Capita (1989 US $)

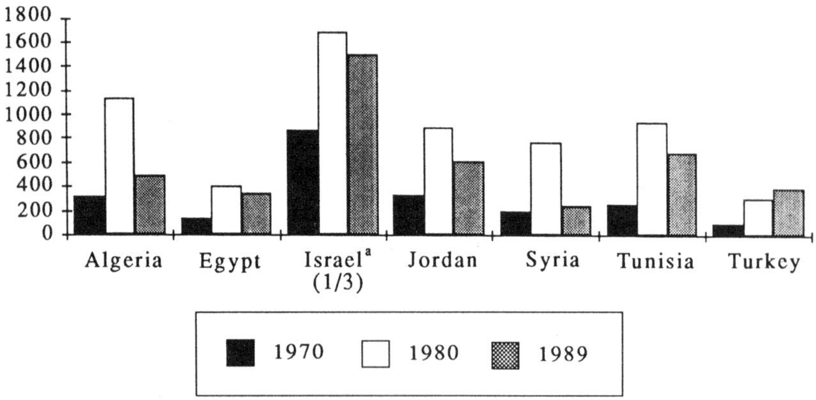

[a] Note that the figures for Israel were divided by 3 for purposes of this figure

programs of economic adjustment. This is not the place to enter into the heated and multisided debates about the appropriate design for adjustment programs, for example, about the phasing and timing of foreign trade reform relative to liberalization of capital flows and of domestic trade, or about the appropriate fiscal, monetary, and income policies for lowering inflation. This chapter looks instead at issues that are of more immediate interest to Western politicians.

Figure 9.3: Third World Nations Per Capita GNP (1989 US $)

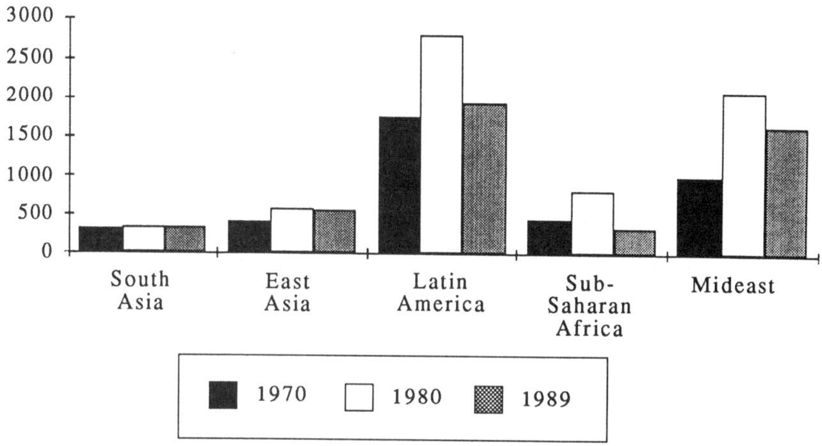

Figure 9.4: External Debt Per Capita GNP (1989 US $)

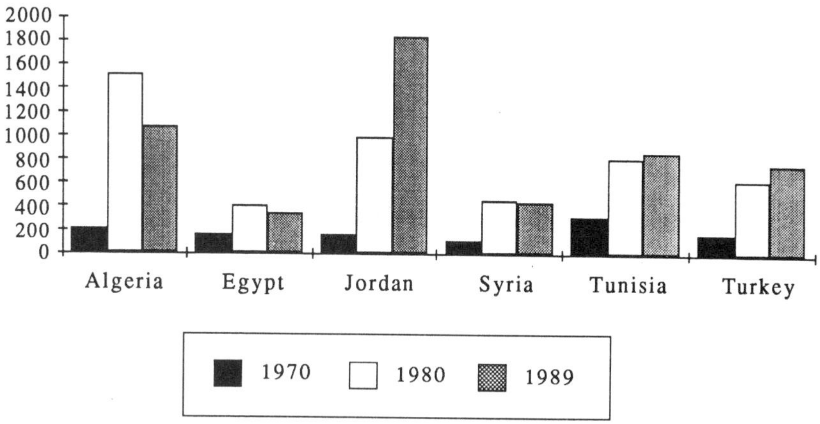

What is the Aim of Stabilization?

In order to judge the success of stabilization programs, it is necessary to ask what their goals are. The immediate goal proclaimed by the International Monetary Fund (IMF), the World Bank, and the industrial countries is the reestablishment of macroeconomic equilibrium: a budget deficit that can be financed without provoking high inflation, a current account deficit in the balance of payments that can be financed without exhausting foreign-exchange reserves, an exchange rate realistic enough to keep the black market at a trivial size, money supply growth tight enough to keep inflation flow, and interest rates high enough to be an effective limit on the demand for credit.

A macroeconomist or a banker may find these goals soul-stirring, but it is not clear that ordinary citizens would care much about them. One could make arguments that the average person wants stable prices and imported goods in the stores, which are the by-products of macroeconomic equilibrium. On the other hand, price stability and import availability come at the expense of other goals that many ordinary people may be loath to make sacrifices for in order to reach. For instance, containing inflation may require raising taxes, reducing government services, and ending the easy credits that keep publicly owned factories open. There is no clear reason to believe that we can formulate a general rule that citizens would prefer to make these sacrifices for the sake of price stability. Similarly, import availability may require sky-high prices in local currency terms. It is hard to see an a priori reason why public sentiment would always favor stores full of imports at high prices instead of rationing at low prices plus black markets.

The essential argument in favor of the restoration of macroeconomic equilibria is, as the World Bank puts it, "macroeconomic stability is necessary for sustainable growth."[11] The Bank summarizes the lessons of the 1970s and 1980s about development in its 1991 *World Development Report,* which includes an evaluation of the role of macroeconomics:

> Sound fiscal and monetary policy create a hospitable climate for private investment and thus promote productivity . . . Macroeconomic stability certainly does not by itself lead to development—but without it all other efforts are likely to be in vain.

It is worth reminding ourselves that growth in national income is desirable because it is the necessary (but not sufficient) condition for "a sustainable increase in living standards that encompasses material consump-

Table 9.2: Private Consumption (per capita in 1989 US $)

	1970	1980	1989
Algeria	1,190	1,190	1,480
Egypt[a]	390	570	620
Jordan	n.a.	n.a.	1,630
Syria[b]	490	1,050	900
Tunisia	410	790	870
Turkey	620	760	950

[a] Egypt: figure is for 1970 instead of 1974.
[b] Syria: figure is for 1988 instead of 1989.
Source: World Bank, World Tables, 1991.

tion, education, health, and environmental protection"—the World Bank's definition of economic development.[12] To be sure, national income may be inequitably distributed—nowhere so obviously so as in the oil-rich states of the Middle East, in which much of the national income accrues to hereditary rulers or dictators, who have done little to earn that income. Nevertheless, the best measure of economic development remains the per capita GNP figures cited earlier, and the best index of the success of stabilization programs is the extent to which they raise per capita GNP above where they would otherwise have been.

One alternative measure of national welfare that bears monitoring is per capita private consumption. Private, because government consumption provides few benefits to most citizens, especially given that the GNP accounts measure government consumption simply by taking what the government spends on goods and services—so the more bureaucrats earn, the more GNP goes up. Consumption is measured rather than income because it can be argued that people care about what they have to consume, not what they earn. The gap between income and consumption is defined as savings. In societies where savings are used efficiently, the income/consumption gap can be kept small, whereas in societies with inefficient use of savings, the gap must be larger. In the Middle East, the gap can be small in a society that gets enough grants from abroad to cover the national savings needs—in which case consumption can be high even though income is rather low, because citizens need not save much.

Private consumption per capita in the Middle East shows less variation among countries than does GNP. Part of the reason is that the proportion of private consumption in GNP in the countries under consideration in 1989 ranged from 88 percent to 56 percent.[13] But another reason is that the economic data are only rough indicators, not precise measures. The problems are both inaccuracies (or deliberate errors) and weak concepts. Statisticians are acutely aware of the many conceptual problems in measuring something as slippery as income or consumption in a way that permits meaningful comparison among countries and through time. The World Bank data below on private consumption were calculated by the Bank on a somewhat different basis than the income data reported earlier,[14] and there are some glaring inconsistencies (Turkey's private consumption per capita in 1980 is but a third of its income, which is silly). Rather than recalculating the consumption data on the same basis as the income data, I would rather report the two series to show just how approximate are many of the statistics we use.

Let's return to the question of why growth is an important goal. The prospects for growth are of vital importance both to the region and to the West. For the region, economic growth at a level which is quite high by world standards is needed just to maintain living standards because of the high population growth rate. The Middle East faces a little-noted but extraordinary demographic challenge, with population growth rates that will cause the region's population to double every 20 years. The high birth rates in the Middle East are partly due to the fact that women in poorer countries have more children because they can not be sure that all the children will live, and furthermore farmers can profit from the labor of children at an early age. Middle Eastern women are having more children than women in other regions at the same income level and the same level of urbanization. The average number of children born to a woman (technically, the total fertility rate) is as high in the Gulf and the Levant as in any African nation: 7 in Saudi Arabia, 6.6 in Syria, 6.3 in Jordan, 6.9 in Kenya, and 6.5 in Nigeria.[15] The North African states are more moderate, but still well in excess of Asia or Latin America: 5.3 in Algeria, 4.5 in Egypt, 4.1 in India, and 3.4 in Mexico (the latter two are high for their regions). In this regard, Turkey, with its total fertility rate of 3.7, is more like the Balkans than the Middle East.[16]

The West has an interest in Middle Eastern economic growth beyond simple humanitarianism. There are two main groups of possibilities. The first is that growth remains as low as it has been in the 1980s, in which case the West must anticipate accelerated social tension. While such tension might take the form of unrest (more Lebanon-like wars), the manifestation most troubling to the West would be emigration. No matter what controls are implemented, the links of history, of economics, and of easy access across the Mediterranean make unrealistic any scheme to block emigration from increasingly poor Middle East countries. Acutely aware of its front-line status, Italy has been promoting a variety of Europe-wide initiatives to concentrate on restarting Middle Eastern growth. If the low-growth scenario is troubling, the second scenario—good growth—is not necessarily reassuring. Iraq is not the only state in the region that could decide to devote its increasing wealth to military ends. For reasons of culture, of history, of domestic political constraints, and of recent international political events, Middle Eastern rulers have been more tempted than their counterparts elsewhere to acquire world-class military machines. With greater wealth, these militaries could become more self-sufficient, possibly acquiring more weapons of mass destruction. The West has therefore a strong interest in promoting Middle Eastern growth but ensuring that the additional resources are ploughed back into the economy, not siphoned off into a military machine.

Does Stabilization Lead to Growth?

Having said that the basic criteria by which the success of stabilization should be judged is growth, the obvious question is: does stabilization lead to growth? In theory, as the IMF and World Bank proclaim, stabilization should lead to the restoration of macroeconomic equilibria and that stability should promote growth through myriad ways such as the following:

- A realistic exchange rate—roughly, a rate at which anyone who wants foreign exchange can buy it easily without facing government restrictions—boosts local production in two ways. It makes imports expensive, which encourages the substitution of local products for imports, and it makes exports worth more in local currency, which makes exports more profitable.
- A realistic interest rate—roughly, a rate at which credit is made available to any borrower with good security prepared to pay the going interest rate—makes credit available to those who can use it most productively rather than to state enterprises or other borrowers with good political connections, who absorbed the available credit when interest rates were kept artificially low.
- A low inflation rate, thanks to limits on the growth in credit and on the budget deficit, permits more rational long-term planning and an environment that encourages long-term investment. Under high inflation, by contrast, production may be less profitable than speculation, for example, buying a commodity whose price has lagged behind the

general inflation in the hopes of selling it when its price catches up to the overall level.

- A sustainable government budget deficit keeps inflation low (no need to resort to the printing press to finance the government) and offers the prospect that taxes will be kept low in the future (no fear that today's deficit will lead to next year's tax increases).
- A sustainable deficit of the current account in the balance of payments offers assurance that foreign exchange will continue to be available at the present exchange rate, whereas a deficit that exhausts much of the nation's foreign exchange reserves can create anxiety that foreign exchange will soon be rationed and/or that the exchange rate will be devalued.

The World Bank and the IMF admit that the initial impact of stabilization on growth is often negative. They argue that businesses have to adjust to the new circumstances, for example, to shift into producing goods which can no longer be profitably imported. This period of adjustment is shorter in economies with more diverse industrial structures and is longer in economies dominated by a narrow range of products, often primary products. Similarly, the adjustment period is shorter the more credible the government program, that is, the more confidence the business community has that the new policies will be sustained long enough to make new investments worthwhile.

The evidence from around the world on whether stabilization policies do actually lay the groundwork for future growth is mixed, as the World Bank admits.[17] For one thing, the point of comparison is hard to determine. It is not appropriate to compare growth prestabilization with growth post-stabilization. Proponents of stabilization policy can plausibly argue that countries that have to adopt such measures are likely to be in trouble: because they had been spending more than they could afford, the excessive spending probably fueled a burst of growth which was unsustainable and temporary. In other words, the growth rate was inevitably headed down, whether or not stabilization policies were adopted. The true test of the effects of stabilization policy on growth is whether growth would fall less with or without stabilization policies. Still, it is not very satisfying to economists—much less to the general public or to politicians—to proclaim that stabilization was a success because it limited the extent to which the economy fell. Stabilization policies can be seen as unqualified successes if they restore sick economies to positive per capita growth.

The evidence from the Middle East is mixed. Part of the problem is that some Middle Eastern nations have a long history of adopting some reform measures while eschewing others. The proponents of stabilization can therefore seize on any subsequent improvement as signs of what even limited measures can provide, while explaining any problems as the product of inadequate implementation of the stabilization measures. Naturally, the opponents of stabilization can reverse the reasoning. There are two relatively pure cases of sustained implementation of a sizable number of stabilization measures: Israel since 1985 and Turkey since the early 1980s. In Israel's case, there can be no mistaking the results. In the four years before the stabilization measures (1981-85), Israel's per capita GNP (in 1989 US $) fell 11 percent; in the four years afterwards (1985-89), per capita GNP rose 39 percent. That is quite a turnaround.

For Turkey, the evidence is less clear, perhaps in part because the record of reforms is less clear. As Birol Yeşilada and Mahir Fisunoğlu explain in this volume, the 1980 stabilization program encompassed a wide range of measures including devaluation, tighter credit to state enterprises, higher interest rates, reduction of subsidies, and price decontrol. The program was not and has not been systematically implemented. In particular, throughout the 1980s, Turkey has had continuing problems with inflation, because of an unwillingness to curtail fiscal deficits, to cut credit for state enterprises with poor commercial prospects, and to end "back door" foreign borrowing (promising to repay depositors in foreign exchange when their money was being lent for local currency).

Yeşilada and Fisunoğlu present data on GNP growth, which rose after 1982 more than the 2.3 percent population growth rate when GNP is measured in constant price Turkish lira. However, measurement in local currency can be misleading, especially when comparing countries. The problem is that while export earnings rose, so too did foreign debt. Servicing that debt increased the demand for foreign exchange, which drove the exchange rate lower. As economic theory suggests, the equilibrium exchange rate falls as net factor service payments increase. Because the exchange rate fell so quickly, per capita GNP in US dollars fell steadily from 1980 through 1985. The situation stabilized after 1986, with steady growth in US dollar terms, totaling 27 percent in the five years 1986-90. Unfortunately, that still leaves Turkey at only 76 percent of the 1980 level.

The most optimistic claim that can be made for stabilization policy in Turkey is that it has laid the basis for future growth, which can return the country to the levels it artificially achieved in the days when foreign borrowing temporarily propped up inefficient industries, before the bill came due for the borrowing. Furthermore, Yeşilada and Fisunoğlu suggest that the more rapid decline in wages than in rents, profits, and interest has created resentment among many Turks that the costs of stabilization have been borne disproportionately by poorer groups, which may undermine efforts to sustain the adjustment process.

Does Stabilization Imperil Good Government?

Stabilization programs have to be judged by the degree to which they address vital social problems. If one such problem is low income, then surely a secondary problem is bad government, especially the lack of human rights and of democracy. The Middle East badly needs better government. It is, sadly, the part of the world least touched by the recent wave of enthusiasm for democracy and liberty. No one particularly expects stabilization to promote good government, but some critics argue that it undermines democracy and human rights—the Pinochet theory of economic stabilization.

The common view that economic adjustment programs imperil governments would seem to have been corroborated by the coup that overthrew the Turkish government nine months after the dramatic January 1980 stabilization program, the "IMF riots" that shook Sudan, Egypt, and Tunisia in the mid-1980s and those in Jordan in the late 1980s. The poor seem to riot when governments, at IMF urging, eliminate subsidies, especially those on bread. In the Sudanese case, the riots led directly to the overthrow of the Numeiri government; in other cases, they have weakened governments, leading to replacement of prime ministers (Jordan) or contributing to later overthrows of heads of state (Tunisia). The author can testify from experience in IMF and World Bank negotiating teams that government officials cite the danger of such riots as an important reason to postpone reforms. Middle East governments have persuaded OECD governments and the Bretton Woods institutions that one reason governments persist in inappropriate policies is because they fear the riots that will follow the adoption of better policies. In response, donor governments and the World Bank have constructed elaborate programs to reduce the effects of adjustment programs on the poor, most recently in Egypt.

In fact, the theory that adjustment imperils good government is narrow in two ways. First, the reason for riots is fundamentally that the people do not trust the government. That is hardly surprising, given that the governments in question are authoritarian. Western governments often jettison their theoretical support for democracy when a friendly tyrant is in danger. Besides being a morally objectionable stance, support for authoritarian rulers against the people is short-sighted. There are clear problems with supporting these rulers however accommodating they may be in the short term. First, every authoritarian ruler is mortal, so the only question is when he will be replaced. Second, a popular uprising is certainly messy and may bring to power a group not as pliant to Western concerns as the previous authoritarian ruler—the most obvious case being Jordan, whose king has ingratiated himself to the West for decades and which has a popular political movement prone to extreme anti-Western sentiments. However many problems democracy may cause in the short term, it is the only system that will ensure stability over the long term and is the best guarantee against aggressive wars—democracies rarely make war on each other. Furthermore, those who fear Arab democracy betray a lack of confidence in the lessons of recent history, namely, that the most disparate peoples—from Burma to Albania—want democracy and liberty.

Second, stabilization policies strengthen the governments that adopt them, after the initial disorders, if any. To persist in the old path would have been to run into more massive problems for the poor than those caused by a stabilization program. It was not Algeria's stabilization program that stripped the goods off the store shelves; it was not Jordan's stabilization program that led the dinar to lose nearly half of its value. Both these governments knew that they lacked the resources to sustain their policies, and therefore the choice they faced was not adjustment versus no adjustment: it was more-or-less planned adjustment versus brutal, abrupt, and unplanned adjustment when the country ran out of cash. This argument—that a World Bank/IMF program allows the government to control what would otherwise be a chaotic adjustment and therefore reduces the prospects for social unrest—is a favorite thesis of World Bank/IMF officials, both with Third World governments and with their backers among the industrial countries. A corollary is to argue that the stabilization program will attract foreign capital and reduce debt service, allowing the governments to muddle through.

There is more than an element of truth to the argument that stabilization strengthens governments. Governments that enter into stabilization programs become eligible for Paris Club reschedulings of their official debt (the Paris Club will not act unless a country has a program with the IMF)[18] and typically receive balance-of-payment support from various governments to complement that coming from the Bretton Woods twins—for example, from France for Algeria and Tunisia. The geopolitical reality is that the industrial country governments use the IMF and the World Bank as the whipping boy to enforce whatever reforms they want to extract from the country in question, so that criticism goes to the Bretton Woods institutions while the industrial country governments can receive praise for their support. The stabilization programs are not designed by economic theoreticians—quite the contrary, as anyone can find by discussing economic theory with World Bank loan officers—but at the direction of the industrial countries, passed down in both general and country-specific terms through the boards and management of the Bretton Woods institutions. The industrial countries are interested in propping up their allies, and they use the IMF and World Bank as part of a strategy to accomplish that aim while minimizing the antagonism directed at themselves. In recent years, another part of that strategy has been to encourage slow democratization.

The general lesson of the Middle East in the 1980s has been that economic stabilization leads to more democracy, as seen in the rising power of the Jordanian parliament, the partially free elections in Algeria, the greater opening in post-Bourguiba Tunisia, and the slow opening up of Egyptian politics. The reasons are not hard to find. Tyrants want to monopolize power when the rewards of power are greatest, that is, during periods of prosperity. When all there is to be shared is the pain, then the tyrant is more willing to see others share in the responsibilities for the unpopular decisions. If our sole aim were to promote democracy, then the best economic policy would be to force Middle Eastern (and all Third World) nations into such tough economic situations that the tyrants cede power to the elected politicians.

How Much Does Outside Pressure for Reform Matter?

The IMF and the World Bank in particular are often said to more or less control economic policy in countries with adjustment programs that they support. As an ex-staff member of both institutions, I have never found that a convincing argument. The more accurate formulation is that the Bretton Woods institutions provide a blessing and a credibility for a program that the government has decided to adopt. At most, the Bretton Woods twins provide supporting arguments for one side in the internal policy debates. The typical pattern is the Central Bank and the IMF agree almost entirely on what needs to be done; the real struggle is selling the reforms to the rest of the government.

A particularly clear case study of the limited roles of the international institutions is provided in this volume. The history of the Tunisian reforms is recounted by Dirk Vandewalle with barely a reference to the Bretton Woods twins, and that is an entirely appropriate reading of the situation. While the 1986 stabilization program (the *plan de redressement économique*) was launched after negotiations with the IMF, the key "negotiations" over national economic policy have been the internal disputes. The replacement of President Bourguiba with Zine el-Abidine Ben Ali in 1987, the process of arriving at a social consensus around the National Pact of 1988, and the response to the Islamist opposition were the main events in the defining of the scope and character of economic reform. Vandewalle provides a wonderful example of what happens when the IMF insists on a step that the government does not agree with: restrictions on interest rates were lifted in January 1987, but within a few days, the *Societé Tunisienne de Banque* "informally" proposed new rates that all banks adopted.

Consider two cases in which the IMF and World Bank did not get involved, in order to see if their intervention results in any substantive change. The first is Israel, which did not turn to the Bretton Woods institutions when it got into serious economic difficulties in the mid-1980s. Instead, it adopted a program that was essentially exactly what the IMF would have recommended. There are two stories about how this program came to be. The Washington version is that the United States, under the leadership of Secretary of State George Shultz, who had a personal interest in the issue, pushed Israel into adopting the program. Henri Barkey's chapter in this volume presents the second story, namely, that the reform package of 1985 was adopted because of Israeli decisions and for domestic political reasons, not because of outside pressure. Under either version, the absence of the IMF was inconsequential: Israel was compelled by its situation and/or by its most important ally to adopt a stabilization program essentially identical to what an IMF stand-by agreement would have entailed.

The second case is Syria. As explained in detail in Steven Heydemann's chapter in this volume, Syria was unable to pay for its imports in 1985-86. External arrears accumulated, both on debt and on bills for current imports. Syria was not about to turn to the IMF, both because of Syrian ideological objections and because the IMF would have been remarkably uncooperative given the severing of ties by the major Western powers in wake of the Syrian effort to bomb an El Al plane from London to Tel Aviv. Syria had to act on its own to respond to a situation that had deteriorated badly. The stabilization program it put in place has certainly differed in important respects from what the Bretton Woods institutions would have recommended: the exchange-rate reforms have been small, the interest-rate policy has remained poor, and the state enterprises have had even fewer reforms than the handful in the typical World Bank program. Nevertheless, Heydemann may exaggerate the differences with the typical World Bank/IMF program when he describes the Syrian process as "selective stabilization," in that the typical World Bank/IMF program proceeds in fits and starts and with so many holes that it quite resembles the selective stabilization process he describes.

As Heydemann argues, the Syrian stabilization program has shared in common with IMF programs the one characteristic that most worries politicians: austerity. Syrian government data are certainly suspect, but the trend is probably right. Government consumption in real terms is reported to have fallen 25 percent from 1984 to 1988. Private consumption per capita in real terms is reported to have fallen 13 percent during the same period (26 percent from the 1983 peak to the 1987 trough). This is a level of austerity that fully matches what the IMF would have insisted on. Indeed, it is quite possible that an IMF program would have entailed more foreign aid which would been used to sustain consumption at a higher level. In other words, austerity was adopted because it was inevitable in such difficult circumstances, not because of the power of the IMF.

Does Aid Help?

The Middle East has had its full share of aid. The World Bank publishes data on "official development assistance," which excludes military aid. In 1989, per capita aid averaged $8.70 worldwide, while the average for the countries considered here was $24.30 (excluding Syria for which no data are available).[19] Israel received $264 per capita; Egypt, $31; Jordan, $72; and Tunisia, $31—although Algeria got $6 and Turkey $2. By contrast to the $24.30 for these six Middle Eastern nations, the much poorer nations of South Asia received $5.40 per person. The only part of the world that did better than these Middle Eastern nations was Sub-Saharan Africa, which received $27.70 in aid per capita. Again, recall that these data refer only to official development assistance, which excludes military aid. If military aid were included, these Middle Eastern nations would have the world's highest levels of per capita by far, exceeding Africa.

There is remarkably little evidence that aid has helped the Middle East. Victor Lavy and Eliezer Sheffer have argued, "An abundance of aid in the decade of prosperity did not build a more prosperous future and is responsible for the countries' current economic misery," a phenomenon they explain by arguing that "when foreign resources are abundant, governments tend to want to spend a lot fast—often overinvesting in large-scale, low-return projects that are difficult to abandon when economic conditions change."[20] Khaled Sherif has made a parallel argument, namely, that foreign aid to Egypt provided additional resources for public enterprises that proceeded to rack up large losses, a process which in addition undermined private-sector producers who could have made a profit providing the goods that the public-sector companies made at a loss.[21] Even the 1985 Israeli case—which the United States regards as buying economic reform with more aid—is a dubious argument for more aid, in that the record can just as easily be read to say that the reason the Israeli economy got into such a mess to begin with was that the flow of U.S. aid permitted successive Israeli governments to postpone difficult decisions in the expectation—rewarded, in the end—that manna from Washington would save Israel from starving in the desert.

Hope springs eternal, and economists typically argue that foreign aid could promote development if it were used in support of sound economic policies.[22] The flaw in the argument is that foreign aid can provide the resources that permit governments to avoid making the hard decisions about changing past profligate practices—or as the World Bank admitted in its 1991 *World Development Report,* "sometimes aid can permit countries to postpone improving macroeconomic management and mobilizing domestic resources."[23] When interviewing government officials in Jordan in July 1990, this author asked what they would recommend be done with an additional $500 million in aid were it to become available. The typical response was that extra aid of that magnitude would hurt Jordan's economy because it would create irresistible pressure for government wage increases that would require correspondingly higher private sector-wages, thereby undermining the competitiveness of Jordanian industry. Moshe Syrquin of Bar-Ilan University has argued with respect to Israel that aid "permitted inefficiencies to go on, reforms to be postponed, and eventually generated additional aid 'requirements.' "[24]

Whether aid has contributed to growth is unclear, but it is quite apparent that additional aid flows in the 1980s were not a viable alternative to the adjustment policies adopted by Middle East nations. The Middle East countries could not have mobilized the additional aid they would have needed to continue to run the large current account deficits to which they had become habituated by the early 1980s. The Middle East was already receiving more than its share of the world's aid if shares are based on per capita need; nor could the Middle East argue that aid sent its direction was particularly effective and therefore a better investment than aid to other regions. Most important of all, the political environment was not ripe for additional aid, during a period of little progress in the Arab-Israeli peace process.

If the industrial countries wish to promote more rapid growth in the Middle East, then the most effective step they could take would be to open up their own economies to more trade. Trade would reward those who take steps to help themselves, while aid often goes to those who devote their efforts to political manipulation rather than to economic activity. Trade would benefit the peoples of the Middle East, while the best that can be said for aid is that billions spent seem to have little negative effect and may help some groups. Trade would bring benefits to consumers in the industrial nations, who would have access to lower-cost goods. The greatest advantage to the Middle East would come from increased access to the European market, but that does not let the United States off the hook. The United States, the Middle East, and Europe would all benefit if the United States offered to make some concession on U.S. protectionism against Europe in return for European concessions to the Middle East.

CONCLUSION

Has economic stabilization been worth the price? The basic answer is, "Yes." There were few alternatives for Middle Eastern governments: they could not have mobilized additional foreign funds to maintain their high level of spending on imports, they could have gained relatively little from cutting military spending (because aid would have fallen at much the same pace), and they could not count on a rapid recovery of export earnings given the weaknesses in the international economy. Furthermore, the political price of economic stabilization has been rather low: it has if anything helped rather than hurt progress towards democracy, and it has not entailed any substantial erosion of national sovereignty. To be sure, there is no convincing evidence yet that stabilization creates the conditions for future growth, though the experience of Israel is encouraging.

NOTES

1. For Syria, data refer to 1988 instead of 1989.
2. The treatment of workers' remittances in GNP data varies from source to source. GNP includes net factor income from abroad, and some sources classify remittances in net factor income. GNP excludes transfers (such as grants from one government to another), and other sources classify remittances with transfers. Just to complicate things further, some sources split remittances between the two categories.
3. Workers' remittances per capita (in 1989 US $) went from $3 in 1970 to $96 in 1980 and $83 in 1989, according to data in the World Bank, *World Tables 1991*.
4. National savings equals GNP less consumption plus net current transfers—i.e., grant aid and workers' remittances. National savings and GNP are used throughout this chapter rather than domestic savings and GDP, because the

latter two concepts exclude the cost of servicing the foreign debt. For heavily indebted countries, it is important to recognize the price they have to pay for their debt.

5. Cf. Patrick Clawson, *Unaffordable Ambitions: Syria's Military Build-up and Economic Crisis* (Washington, DC: Washington Institute for Near East Policy, 1989).
6. A point quite overlooked in the chapter "Defense's Drain on Growth and Development," in Victor Lavy and Eliezer Sheffer, *Foreign Aid and Economic Development in the Middle East* (New York: Praeger, 1991).
7. U.S. Arms Control and Disarmament Agency, *World Military Expenditures and Arms Transfers 1988* (Washington, DC: Government Printing Office, 1990), 118.
8. The basic case that military spending helps development is made in Emil Benoit, "Growth and Defense Spending in Developing Countries," *Economic Development and Cultural Change* 26 (1978). The basic response is in Sadet Deger, *Military Expenditure in Third World Countries* (London: Routledge, Kegan and Paul, 1986).
9. World Bank, *World Tables 1991*. High-income OECD is the World Bank term which excludes Turkey, Portugal, and Greece from the OECD total.
10. World Bank, *World Tables 1991*. For Libya and United Arab Emirates, the figures are for 1988 instead of 1989. For UAE, excludes factor services.
11. World Bank, *World Development Report 1991*, p. 94. The following quote is from the same page.
12. World Bank, *World Development Report 1991*, p. 31.
13. Private consumption as a percent of GNP in 1989 was: Algeria, 55.7; Egypt, 87.6; Israel, 60.1; Jordan, 84; Syria (1988), 68.2; Tunisia, 67.7; Turkey, 69.4.
14. The earlier data use the Bank's calculation of GNP per capita in US dollars, using its "Atlas methodology" (a method to smooth exchange rates explained in its publications), which I converted to constant 1989 dollars by dividing by the U.S. GNP deflator. The private consumption data are from the Bank's calculation of 1987 dollar consumption—using what method I do not know—which I converted to 1989 dollars with the U.S. GNP deflator.
15. All data are from the World Bank, *World Tables 1991*.
16. The total fertility rate in Israel is only 2.9; however, Israel faces a demographic challenge if it is to continue to absorb immigrants at a rate equal to 1.0% to 0.5% of the population per annum.
17. *World Development Report 1991*, 114.
18. The exception being nonmembers of the IMF, such as Cuba.
19. World Bank, *World Development Report 1991*. To be fair however, the world total is low because China and India receive aid equal to $2.00 and $2.30 per capita respectively. The world average without China and India is $14.40 per capita.
20. Lavy and Sheffer, *Foreign Aid*, 5, 145.

21. Khaled Sherif (of the American University in Cairo and the World Bank), presentation at the Carter Center conference, "Economic Development in the Middle East," November 29, 1990.
22. A case made strongly by Lavy and Sheffer, *Foreign Aid.*
23. *World Development Report 1991*, 48. That page is devoted to a debate about whether aid has a positive or negative effect on growth. Interestingly, the main arguments for aid refer to financing of specific projects, not of policy reforms.
24. Comment made at a seminar held by the Israel International Institute, quoted in *The Financial Times*, June 27, 1989.

REFERENCES

Abdalla, A. *The Student Movement and National Politics in Egypt.* London: Al Saqi Books, 1985.

Abdallah, I. S. "The Current Call for Conversion from the Public Sector to the Private Sector." In *The Public Sector and the Private Sector in the Arab World,* edited collection in Arabic, 173-93. Beirut: Markaz Dirasat al-Wihda al-'Arabiya, 1990.

Abdel-Khalek, G. "Looking Outside, Or Turning Northwest? The Meaning and External Dimension of Egypt's Infitah 1971-1980." *Social Problems* 28, no. 4 (April 1981), 394-409.

Abdel-Rahman I. H., and M. S. Abu Ali. "Role of the Public and Private Sectors with Special Reference to Privatization: The Case of Egypt." In *Privatization and Structural Adjustment in the Arab Countries,* edited by S. El-Naggar, 141-81. Washington, DC: IMF, 1989.

Adda, S. "Enjeux: Le possible et le probable . . ." In *Tunisie au présent: une modernité au-dessus de tout soupçon?* edited by M. Camau. Paris: Editions du C.N.R.S., 1987.

Alavi, H. "The State in Post-Colonial Societies: Pakistan and Bangladesh." *New Left Review* 74 (July-August 1972).

"Algeria." In *Africa Contemporary Record: Annual Survey and Documents,* edited by Colin Legum, 3-17. New York: Africana Publishing, 1982.

Amnesty International. "Egypt: Ten Years of Torture." (October 1991).

Anderson, L. "Democracy Frustrated: The Mzali Years in Tunisia." In *The Middle East and North Africa,* edited by R. Simon. New York: Columbia University Press, 1990.

———. *The State and Social Transformation in Tunisia and Libya, 1830-1980.* Princeton: Princeton University Press, 1986.

Ansari, H. Egypt: *The Stalled Society.* Albany: State University of New York Press, 1986.

Antoun, R. T. "Ethnicity, Clientship and Class: Their Changing Meaning." In *Syria: Society, Culture, Polity,* edited by R. T. Antoun and D. Quataert. Albany: University of New York Press, 1991.

Arcayürek, C. *Demokrasinin Sonbahari, 1971-1978.* Istanbul: Bilgi Yayinevi, 1985.

———. *Müdahalenin Ayaksesleri.* Istanbul: Bilgi Yayinevi, 1985.

Arian, A. *Politics in Israel: The Second Generation.* Chatham, NJ: Chatham House Publishers, 1989.

Aronoff, M. J. "Israel under Labor and the Likud: The Role of Dominance Considered." In *Democratic Oddities: One Party Dominance in Comparative Perspective,* edited by T. J. Pempel. Ithaca: Cornell University Press, 1988.

Ayalon, A. "The Arab Republic of Egypt." *Middle East Contemporary Survey.* Tel Aviv: Tel Aviv University, 1982-1983.

Ayari, C. "L'application des Programmes d'Ajustement Structurel (PAS) en Tunisie (1986-1989): Un bilan critique." *Le Maghreb.* February 16, 23, 1990; March 2, 9 and 16, 1990.

Balassa, B., and D. F. McCarthy. *Adjustment Policies in Developing Countries, 1979-83, An Update.* World Bank Staff Working Papers, no. 675, Washington, DC, 1984.

Bank of Israel. *Annual Report.* Jerusalem: Bank of Israel, selected years.

Barkai, H. "Israel's Attempt at Economic Stabilization." *Jerusalem Quarterly* 43 (Summer 1987), 3-20.

———. "Reflections on the Economic Cost of the Lebanon War." *Jerusalem Quarterly* 37 (Winter 1986), 95-106.

Barkey, H. J. *The State and the Industrialization Crisis in Turkey.* Boulder, CO: Westview Press, 1990.

———. "State Autonomy and the Crisis of Import Substitution." *Comparative Political Studies* 22, no. 3 (October 1989).

———. "The Silent Victor: The Role of Turkey in the Iran-Iraq War." In *The Iran-Iraq War: Impact and Implications,* edited by Efraim Karsh. London: Macmillan, 1989.

Bates, R., ed. *Towards a Political Economy of Development: A Rational Choice Perspective.* Berkeley: University of California Press, 1988.

Beblawi, H., and G. Luciani, eds. *The Rentier State.* New York: Croom Helm, 1987.

Benachenhou, A. *L'expérience algérienne de planification et de développement, 1962-1982.* 2nd ed. Algiers: Office des Publications Universitaires, 1982.

Bennamane, A. *The Algerian Development Strategy and Employment Policy*, monograph no. 9. Swansea, Wales: Center for Development Studies, 1980.

Benoit, E. "Growth and Defense Spending in Developing Countries." *Economic Development and Cultural Change* 26 (1978).

Berglas, E. "Defense and the Economy." In *The Israeli Economy: Maturing through Crises*, edited by Y. Ben Porath. Cambridge, MA: Harvard University Press, 1986.

Bianchi, R. *Unruly Corporatism: Associational Life in Twentieth Century Egypt*. New York: Oxford University Press, 1989.

———. "Interest Group Politics in the Third World." *Third World Quarterly* 8, no. 2 (1986).

Blejer, M., and N. Liviatan. "Fighting Hyperinflation: Stabilization Strategies in Argentina and Israel, 1985-86." *IMF Staff Papers* 34, (September 1987) 409-438.

Block, F. L. *The Origins of the International Economic Disorder*. Berkeley: University of California Press, 1977.

Bogdanowicz-Bindert, C. "Portugal, Turkey, and Peru: Three Successful Stabilization Programmes under the Auspices of the IMF." *World Development* 11, (1983), 65-70.

Bouaouaja, M. "Privatization in Tunisia: Objectives and Limits." In *Privatization and Structural Adjustment in the Arab Countries*, edited by S. El-Naggar. Washington: International Monetary Fund, 1989.

Brett, E. A. *International Money and Capitalist Crisis: The Anatomy of Global Disintegration*. Boulder, CO: Westview Press, 1983.

Brown, C. L. *The Tunisia of Ahmad Bey, 1837-1855*. Princeton: Princeton University Press, 1974.

Brumberg, D. "The University Intelligentsia and the Struggle for Democracy in Contemporary Egypt." Doctoral dissertation, University of Chicago, 1991.

Bruno, M. "Economic Analysis and the Political Economy of Policy Formation." *European Economic Review* 34 (1990), 273-301.

———. "External Shocks and Domestic Response: Macroeconomic Performance, 1965-1982." In *The Israeli Economy: Maturing through Crises*, edited by Y. Ben Porath. Cambridge, MA: Harvard University Press, 1986.

———. "Sharp Disinflation Strategy: Israel 1985." *Economic Policy* 2 (April 1986), 379-402.

Bruno, M., and S. Fischer. "The Inflationary Process: Shocks and Accommodation." In *The Israeli Economy: Maturing through Crises,* edited by Y. Ben Porath. Cambridge, MA: Harvard University Press, 1986.

Bruno, M., and S. Piterman. "Israel's Stabilization: A Two Year Review." In *Inflation Stabilization: The Experience of Israel, Argentina, Brazil, Bolivia and Mexico,* edited by M. Bruno, G. Di Tella, R. Dornbusch, and S. Fischer. Cambridge, MA: MIT Press, 1988.

Callaghy, T. *The State-Society Struggle: Zaire in Comparative Perspective.* New York: Columbia University Press, 1984.

———. "Lost Between State and Market: The Politics of Economic Adjustment in Ghana, Zambia and Nigeria." In *Economic Crisis and Policy Choice: The Politics of Adjustment in the Third World,* edited by J. M. Nelson, 257-319. Princeton: Princeton University Press, 1990.

Camau, M. ed. *La Tunisie au présent: Une modernité au-dessus de tout soupçon?* Paris: Editions du C.N.R.S., 1987.

Casonava, P. G. *Democracy in Mexico.* New York: Oxford University Press, 1970.

Celasun, M., and D. Rodrik. "Turkish Experience with Debt: Macroeconomic Policy and Performance." In *Developing Country Debt and the World Economy,* edited by J. D. Sachs. Chicago: University of Chicago Press, 1989.

Chaudhry, K. A. "The Price of Wealth: Business and State in Labor Remittance and Oil Economies." *International Organization* 43, no. 1 (Winter 1989), 101-45.

Clawson, P. *Unaffordable Ambitions: Syria's Military Build-up and Economic Crisis.* Washington, DC: Washington Institute for Near East Policy, 1989.

Cohen, Y. "Democracy from Above: The Political Origins of Military Dictatorship in Brazil." *World Politics* 40 (October 1987).

Collier, D., ed. *The New Authoritarianism in Latin America.* Princeton: Princeton University Press, 1979.

Cukierman, A. "The End of High Israeli Inflation: An Experience in Heterodox Stabilization." In *Inflation Stabilization: The Experience of Israel, Argentina, Brazil, Bolivia and Mexico,* edited by M. Bruno, G. Di Tella, R. Dornbusch, and S. Fischer. Cambridge, MA: MIT Press, 1988.

Dann, U. *King Hussein and the Challenge of Arab Radicalism, Jordan 1955-1967.* New York: Oxford University Press, 1989.

Deger, S. *Military Expenditure in Third World Countries.* London: Routledge, Kegan and Paul, 1986.

Dessouki, A. H., ed. *Intikhabat Majles Al-Sh'ab 1984*. Cairo: Al-Ahram Center for Political and Strategic Studies, 1986.

Development Committee. *Problems and Issues in Structural Adjustment*. Papers of the Joint Ministerial Committee of the Boards of Governors of the World Bank and the International Monetary Fund on the Transfer of Real Resources to Developing Countries, no. 23, Washington, DC, 1990.

Diamond, L., S. M. Lipset, and J. Linz. "Building and Sustaining Democratic Government in Developing Countries: Some Tentative Findings." *World Affairs* (Summer 1987).

Dodd, C. H. *The Crisis of Turkish Democracy*. North Humberside: Eothen Press, 1983.

Dornbusch, R., and S. Fischer. "Stopping Hyperinflations: Past and Present." *Weltwirtschaftliches Archiv* (January 1986), 1-47.

El-Naggar, S., ed. *Adjustment Policies and Development Strategies in the Arab World*. Washington, DC: International Monetary Fund, 1987.

———, ed. *Privatization and Structural Adjustment in the Arab Countries*. Washington, DC: International Monetary Fund, 1989.

el-Sadat, A. *Waraqat Uktubar*. Cairo: Hay'at al-Isti'malat, Jumhouriya Misr al-'Arabiya, 1974.

Falk, P., ed. *Inflation: Are We Next? Hyperinflation and Solutions in Argentina, Brazil and Israel*. Boulder, CO: Lynne Rienner, 1990.

Federation of Syrian Chambers of Commerce. *Al-taqrir al-sanawi, 1990* (Annual Report, 1990).

Firro, K. "The Syrian Economy Under the Assad Regime." In *Syria Under Assad*, edited by M. Maoz and A. Yaniv. New York: St. Martin's Press, 1986.

Fischer, S. "Inflation and Indexation: Israel." In *Inflation and Indexation: Argentina, Brazil, and Israel*, edited by J. Williamson. Washington, DC: Institute for International Economics, 1985.

———. "The Israeli Stabilization Program, 1985-86" *AEA Papers and Proceedings* (May 1986), 275-278.

Frieden, J. "International Finance and the Third World." *MERIP Reports*, no. 117, volume 13 (September 1983), 3-11.

Geertz, C. "Comment." *Daedalus* (Winter 1989).

George, A. "An Economy Saved by Circumstances." *The Middle East* (December 1988).

Gilbar, G. "The Economics of Interdependence: The United States and the Arab World 1973-1977." In *The Middle East and the United States,* edited by H. Shaked and I. Rabinovich. New Brunswick, NJ: Transaction Books, 1990.

Grissa, A. "The Tunisian State Enterprises and Privatization Policy." In *Tunisia: The Political Economy of Reform,* edited by I. W. Zartman. Boulder, CO: Lynne Rienner, 1991.

Haggard, S. "The Politics of Adjustment: Lessons from the IMF's Extended Fund Facility." In *The Politics of International Debt,* edited by Miles Kahler, 157-86. Ithaca: Cornell University Press, 1986.

Haggard, S., and R. Kaufman. "Economic Adjustment in New Democracies." In *Fragile Coalitions: The Politics of Economic Adjustment,* edited by J. M. Nelson. Washington, DC: Overseas Development Council, 1990.

Halevi, N., and J. Baruh. "Israel." In *Liberalizing Foreign Trade: The Experience of Israel and Yugoslavia,* edited by D. Papageorgiou, M. Michely, and A. Choksi. Cambridge, MA: Basil Blackwell, 1991.

Hamdi, A. "Regard sur le mouvement Youssefiste." *Realités* (February 21, 1988).

Hannoyer, J., and M. Seurat. *Etat et secteur public industriel en Syrie.* Beirut: CERMOC, 1979.

Hermassi, E., and D. Vandewalle. "The Second Stage of State-Building in the Maghreb." In *State and Society in Contemporary North Africa,* edited by I. W. Zartman. Boulder, CO: Westview Press, forthcoming.

Heymann, D. "The Austral Plan." *AEA Papers and Proceedings* (May 1987), 284-287.

Hinnebush, R. A. *Egyptian Politics Under Nasser: The Post-Populist Development of An Authoritarian-Modernizing State.* Boulder, CO: Lynne Rienner, 1988.

Hopfinger, H. "Capitalist Agro-Business in a Socialist Country? Syria's New Shareholding Corporations as an Example." Unpublished paper, 1990.

Huntington, S. *Political Order in Changing Societies.* New Haven: Yale University Press, 1968.

Ihonvbere, J. O. "Structural Adjustment, the April 1990 Coup, and Democratization in Nigeria." Paper presented at the African Studies Association Annual Conference, Baltimore, MD, November 1990.

International Monetary Fund. *Syrian Arab Republic: Recent Economic Developments* (March 9, 1988).

Kanovsky, E. "Jordan's Economy: From Prosperity to Crisis." Dayan Center for Middle Eastern and African Studies, Occasional Papers, no. 106, May 1989.

———. "What's Behind Syria's Current Economic Problems?" Dayan Center for Middle Eastern and African Studies, Occasional Papers. Tel Aviv: Tel Aviv University, 1985.

Kaufman, R. R. "Democratic and Authoritarian Responses to the Debt Issue: Argentina, Brazil, Mexico." In *The Politics of International Debt,* edited by Miles Kahler, 187-217. Ithaca: Cornell University Press, 1986.

———. "Stabilization and Adjustment in Argentina, Brazil and Mexico." In *Economic Crisis and Policy Choice: The Politics of Adjustment in the Third World,* edited by J. M. Nelson. Princeton: Princeton University Press, 1990.

Khelil, I. "Lettre de Ismail Khelil au Président de la Rėpublique." *Realités,* September 16, 1988.

Knauss, P. R. "Algeria under Boumedienne: the Mythical Revolution, 1965-1978." In *The Performance of Soldiers as Governors,* edited by I. J. Mowoe, 27-100. Washington, DC: University Press of America, 1980.

Lavy, V., and E. Sheffer. *Foreign Aid and Economic Development in the Middle East.* New York: Praeger, 1991.

Lawson, F. H. "Liberalisation économique en Syrie et en Irak." *Maghreb-Machrek,* no. 128 (April-May-June 1990), 27-52.

———. "Political-Economic Trends in Ba'thi Syria: A Reinterpretation." *Orient* 29, no. 4 (December 1988), 579-94.

Lawyers Committee for Human Rights. "Freedom of Opinion and Expression in Egypt, A Report by the Egyptian Organization for Human Rights." August 1990.

Le Pacte Nationale. Tunis: Ministry of Information. 1988. Mimeographed.

Leca, J. "Social Structure and Political Stability: Comparative Evidence from the Algerian, Syrian, and Iraqi Cases." In *Beyond Coercion: The Durability of the Arab State,* edited by A. Dawisha and I. W. Zartman, 164-202. New York: Croom Helm, 1988.

Leys, C. "The 'Overdeveloped' Post Colonial State: A Re-evaluation." *Review of African Political Economy* 5 (Jan-April 1976).

Liviatan, N., and S. Piterman. "Accelerating Inflation and Balance of Payments Crises, 1973-1984." In *The Israeli Economy: Maturing through Crises,* edited by Y. Ben Porath. Cambridge, MA: Harvard University Press, 1986.

Longueness, E. "Syrie, secteur public industriel: les enjeux d'une crise." *Maghreb-Machrek,* no. 109 (July-August-September 1985), 5-22.

Ludlam, J. "Reform and the Redefinition of the Social Contract Under Gorbachev." *World Politics* 43 (January 1991), 284-312.

Mahjoub, A. "Etat, secteur publique et privatisation en Tunisie." *Annuaire de l'Afrique du Nord 1987.* Paris: Editions du C.N.R.S., 1989.

Margulies, R., and E. Yildizoğlu. "Austerity Packages and Beyond: Turkey since 1980." *Capital and Class* 36 (Winter 1988), 141-162.

Marquand, D. *The Unprincipled Society: New Demands and Old Policies.* London: Jonathan Cape, 1988.

Meyer, G. "Economic Development in Syria Since 1970." In *Politics and the Economy in Syria,* edited by J. A. Allen, 39-62. London: Centre of Near and Middle Eastern Studies, SOAS; 1987.

Middle East Watch. "Egyptian Government Moves to Dissolve Prominent Arab Women's Organization" (September 1991).

Middlebrook, K. "The Sounds of Silence: Organized Labor's Response to Economic Crisis in Mexico." Paper delivered at the annual meeting of the American Political Science Association, Washington, DC, September 1-4, 1988.

Midoun, M. "Entreprises publiques et développement économique." In *Administration et Développement en Tunisie.* Tunis: Institut Internationale des Sciences Administratives, 1985.

Migdal, J. S. "The Crystallization of the State and the Struggles over Rulemaking: Israel in a Comparative Perspective." In *The Israeli State and Society: Boundaries and Frontiers,* edited by B. Kimmerling. Albany: State University of New York Press, 1989.

———. *Strong State and Weak Societies: State-Society Relations and State Capabilities in the Third World.* Princeton: Princeton University Press, 1988.

Ministry of National Economy. *Commission d'Etude, chargée de l'examen du fonctionnement des Entreprises publiques et de leurs relations avec l'Etat.* Tunis: Ministry of National Economy, 1973.

Moore, C. H. *Tunisia since Independence: The Dynamics of One-Party Government.* Berkeley: University of California Press, 1965.

———. "Islamic Banks and Competitive Politics in the Arab World and Turkey." *Middle East Journal* 44, no. 2 (Spring 1990), 234-255.

———."Money and Power: The Dilemma of the Egyptian Infitah." *Middle East Journal* 40, no. 4 (Autumn 1986), 634-57.

Mumcu, U. *Rabita*. Istanbul: Tekin Yayinevi, 1987.

National Bank of Egypt. "The International Monetary Fund and the Developing Countries." *Economic Bulletin,* nos. 1-2 (1988), 5-17.

J. M. Nelson, "Introduction: The Politics of Economic Adjustment in Developing Nations." In *Economic Crisis and Policy Choice: The Politics of Adjustment in the Third World,* edited by J. M. Nelson. Princeton: Princeton University Press, 1990.

———. "The Political Economy of Stabilization: Commitment, Capacity and Public Response." *World Development* 12, no. 10, (1984), 983-1006.

———. "The Politics of Long-Haul Economic Reform." In *Fragile Coalitions: The Politics of Economic Adjustment,* edited by J. M. Nelson, 3-26. Washington, DC: Overseas Development Council, 1990.

O'Donnell, G. *Modernization and Bureaucratic Authoritarianism*. Berkeley: University of California Press, 1979.

———. "Tensions in the Bureaucratic-Authoritarian State and the Question of Democracy." In *The New Authoritarianism in Latin America,* edited by D. Collier, 285-318. Princeton: Princeton University Press, 1979.

Organization for Economic Cooperation and Development (OECD), *External Debt of Developing Countries, 1983 Survey*. Paris: OECD, 1984.

Pastor, M. *The International Monetary Fund and Latin America: Economic Stabilization and Class Conflict*. Boulder, CO: Westview Press, 1987.

———. "The Effects of IMF Programs in the Third World: Debate and Evidence from Latin America." *World Development* 15, no. 2 (1987), 249-262.

Perthes, V. "Syria's Parliamentary Elections of 1990: A Renewed Base for the Old Regime." *Middle East Report,* no. 174 (January-February 1992).

———. "The Bourgeoisie and the Ba'th: A Look at Syria's Upper Class." *Middle East Report,* no. 170 (May-June 1991).

Pfeifer, K. *Agrarian Reform under State Capitalism in Algeria*. Boulder, CO: Westview Press, 1985.

———. "State Capitalism and Development." *MERIP Reports,* no. 78, volume 9 (June 1979), 3-11.

Portes, A., M. Castells, and L. Benton, eds. *The Informal Economy: Studies in Advanced and Less Developed Countries*. Baltimore: Johns Hopkins University Press, 1989.

Posusney, M. P. "Labor as an Obstacle to Privatization: The Case of Egypt 1974-1987." Paper delivered at the annual meeting of the Middle East Studies Association, Toronto, Canada, November 15-18, 1989, 7-8.

Przeworski, A. "Some Problems in the Transition from Authoritarianism." In *Transitions from Authoritarian Rule,* Vol. 3, edited by G. O'Donnell, P. Schmitter, and L. Whitehead. Baltimore: Johns Hopkins Press, 1986.

Quandt, W. *The United States and Egypt.* Washington, DC: Brookings Institute, 1990.

Raffinot, M. and P. Jacquemot. *Le capitalisme d'état algerien.* Paris: Maspero, 1977.

Rejwan, N. *Charter of National Action in Nasserist Ideology: Its Exponents and Its Critics*. New York: John Wiley, 1974.

Remmer, K. L. "New Wine or Old Bottlenecks? The Study of Latin American Democracy." *Comparative Politics* 23, no. 4 (July 1991), 479-95.

———. "The Politics of Economic Stabilization: IMF Standby Programs in Latin America, 1954-1984." *Comparative Politics* 19, no. 1 (October 1986).

Republic of Turkey. The Constitution of the Republic of Turkey. Ankara, 1982.

Reshef, Y. "Political Exchange in Israel: Histradut-State Relations." *Industrial Relations* 25, no. 3 (1986).

Roberts, H. "The Algerian Bureaucracy." In *Sociology of 'Developing Societies': The Middle East,* edited by T. Asad and R. Owen, 95-114. New York: Monthly Review Press, 1983.

Rodrik, D. "Premature, Incomplete Stabilization: The Özal Decade in Turkey." Paper presented at the conference "Lessons of Economic Stabilization and Its Aftermath," Jerusalem, January 31-February 1, 1990.

———. "Türkiye'nin Ihracat Patlamasinin Ne Kadari Hayali?" *Bilim ve Sanat,* no. 42 (Summer 1988), 133-136.

———. "External Debt and Economic Performance in Turkey." In *Liberalization and the Turkish Economy,* edited by T. F. Nas and M. Odekon. New York: Greenwood Press, 1988.

Roe, A., R. Jayantra, and S. Jayshree. *Economic Adjustment in Algeria, Egypt, Jordan, Morocco, Pakistan, Tunisia, and Turkey*. Economic Development Institute of the World Bank, Policy Seminar Report, no. 15, 1989.

Sachs, J., ed. *Developing Country Debt and the World Economy*. Chicago: University of Chicago Press, 1989.

Sadowski, Y. "Ba'thist Ethics and the Spirit of State Capitalism: Patronage and the Party in Contemporary Syria." In *Power and Ideology in the Middle East,* edited by R. Pranger and P. J. Chelkowski, 160-84. Durham, NC: Duke University Press, 1988.

———. "Cadres, Guns, and Money: The Eighth Regional Congress of the Syrian Ba'ath." *MERIP Reports,* no. 134 (July-August 1985).

Saket, B. K. *Foreign Aid to Jordan, 1924/25-1972/73: Its Magnitude, Composition and Effect*. Doctoral dissertation, University of Keele, 1976.

Sargent, T. J. *Rational Expectations and Inflation*. New York: Harper and Row, 1986.

Satloff, R. *Troubles on the East Bank: Challenges to the Domestic Stability of Jordan*. Washington, DC: Washington Institute for Near East Policy, 1986.

———. "Jordan Looks Inward." *Current History* (February 1990).

Schelling, T. *Micromotives and Macrobehavior*. New York: Norton, 1978.

Shalev, M. "The Political Economy of Labor-Party Dominance and Decline in Israel." In *Democratic Oddities: One Party Dominance in Comparative Perspective,* edited by T. J. Pempel. Ithaca: Cornell University Press, 1988.

Sharon, E. "Israel and the Success of the Shekel: The Key Years, 1984-1987." In *Inflation: Are We Next? Hyperinflation and Solutions in Argentina, Brazil and Israel,* edited by P. Falk. Boulder, CO: Lynne Rienner, 1990.

———. "Israel's Stabilization Program: Lessons in Political Economy." Paper presented at a conference on hyperinflation at Instituto Fernand Braudel de Economia Mundial, Sao Paolo, Brazil, August 28-31, 1989.

Sheahan, J. "Market-Oriented Economic Policies and Political Repression in Latin America." *Economic Development and Cultural Change* 28 (January 1980).

Sherif, K. "Economic Development in the Middle East." Paper presented at Carter Center conference, November 29, 1990.

Skidmore, T. "The Politics of Stabilization in Postwar Latin America." In *Authoritarianism and Corporatism in Latin America,* edited by J. Malloy, 149-90. Pittsburgh: University of Pittsburgh Press, 1977.

Smith, W. C. *Authoritarianism and the Crisis of the Argentine Political Economy*. Stanford: Stanford University Press, 1989.

Solimano, A. "Inflation and the Costs of Stabilization: Historical and Recent Experiences and Policy Lessons." *World Bank Research Observer* 5, no. 2 (July 1990), 167-185.

State Planning Organization (SPO). *1980'den 1990'a Makroekonomik Politikalar, Türkiye Ekonomisindeki Gelişmelerin Analizi ve Bazi Değerlendirmeler*. Ankara: SPO, 1990.

———. *Main Economic Indicators*. Ankara: SPO Publications, 1986-1990.

State Statistics Institute. *Foreign Trade Statistics, 1983*. Ankara: SSI Publications, 1984.

Tachau, F. *Turkey: Authority, Democracy, and Development*. New York: Praeger, 1984.

Tlemcani, R. "An Interview with Mahfoud Bennoune: Algeria's Facade of Democracy." *Middle East Report* 20, no. 163 (March-April 1990), 9-13.

———. "Chadli's Perestroika." *Middle East Report* 20, no. 163 (March-April 1990), 9-13.

Türkiye Odalar ve Borsalar Birliği (TOBB). *Planli Dönemde Rakamlarla Türkiye Ekonomisi*. Ankara: TOBB, 1990.

Türk Silahli Kuvvetleri, Genel Kurmay Baskanligi. *Türkiye'deki Terörün Gelişmesi Sonuçlari, ve Güvenlik Kuvvetlerince Önlenmesi*. Ankara: Genel Kurmay, 1982.

U.S. Department of Commerce. *Foreign Economic Trends, Algeria*. Washington, DC: Government Printing Office, December 1983, March 1989.

U.S. Department of State. *Country Reports on Economic Policy and Trade Practices, Algeria*. Report submitted to the Committee on Foreign Relations and Committee on Finance of the U.S. Senate, and the Committee on Foreign Affairs and Committee on Ways and Means of the U.S. House of Representatives. Washington, DC: Department of State, 1990.

U.S. General Accounting Office. *Report on Security Assistance: Foreign Military Sales Debt Refinancing*. Washington, DC: Government Printing Office, 1989.

Vandewalle, D. "Bourguiba, Charismatic Leadership and the Tunisian One-Party System." *Middle East Journal* 34, no. 2 (Spring 1980).

———. "From the New State to the New Era: Toward a Second Republic in Tunisia." *Middle East Journal* 42, no. 4 (Autumn 1988).

Waterbury, J. *The Egypt of Nasser and Sadat: The Political Economy of Two Regimes*. Princeton: Princeton University Press, 1988.

———. "The Political Management of Economic Adjustment and Reform." In *Economic Adjustment in Algeria, Egypt, Jordan, Morocco, Pakistan, Tunisia and Turkey*. Economic Development Institute of the World Bank Seminar Report No. 15, pp. 55-65. Washington DC: World Bank, 1989.

———. "The Political Management of Economic Adjustment and Reform." In *Fragile Coalitions: The Politics of Economic Adjustment*, edited by J. M. Nelson, 39-56. Washington, DC: Overseas Development Council, 1990.

———. "The 'Soft State' and the Open Door: Egypt's Experience with Economic Liberalization, 1974-1984." *Comparative Politics* 12, no. 1 (October 1985), 65-84.

Weisskoff, R. "The Political Economy of the Israeli Inflation." In *Inflation: Are We Next? Hyperinflation and Solutions in Argentina, Brazil and Israel*, edited by P. Falk. Boulder, CO: Lynne Rienner, 1990.

Whitehead, L. "Democratization and Disinflation: A Comparative Approach." In *Fragile Coalitions: The Politics of Economic Adjustment*, edited by J. M. Nelson, 79-93. Washington, DC: Overseas Development Council, 1990.

Wintrobe, R. "The Tinpot and the Totalitarian: An Economic Theory of Dictatorship." *American Political Science Review* 84, no. 3, (September 1990), 849-72.

World Bank. "Liberalizing Trade: Bank Research on the Hows and Whats." *Research Report* 7, no. 2 (Fall 1986).

———. *Turkey: Country Economic Memorandum—Recent Economic Developments and Medium-Term Prospects*, Vol. 2. Washington, DC: World Bank, 1983.

Yeşilda, B. A. *Breakdown of Democracy in Turkey*. Doctoral dissertation, University of Michigan, Ann Arbor, 1984.

———. "Islam, Dollars, and Politics: The Political Economy of Saudi Capital in Turkey." Paper presented at the 23rd Annual Meeting of the Middle East Studies Association, Toronto, Canada, November 15-18, 1989.

———. "Problem of Political Development in the Third Turkish Republic." *Polity* 21, no. 2 (Winter 1988), 345-372.

———. "Turkey's Foreign Policy Towards the Middle East." In *Socioeconomic and Political Transformation of Turkey during the 1980s*, edited by A. Eralp, M. Tunay and B. A. Yeşilada. New York: Praeger, forthcoming.

INDEX